QuickBooks® 6 For Dummies®

Cheat Sheet

Iconbar Shortcuts for Busy People

The QuickBooks iconbar is a handy row of buttons you click to do things really fast. To display the iconbar, click the Company tab of the QuickBooks Navigator and click the Preferences icon. Then click the Iconbar icon from the list at the left and choose one of the first three options for showing the iconbar. (You may need to first click the My Preferences tab, if it isn't already displayed.) You can also use this dialog box to customize the icons on your iconbar. You can add new icons, edit the names or pictures of existing icons, remove icons, and change the order and spacing of icons on the iconbar.

Click This Icon	To Do This
Estimate	Create a project estimate.
Invoice	Prepare a customer invoice.
PO	Create a purchase order.
Time	Track the time you and your employees spend working on various projects over the course of a week.
Check	Simultaneously record a bill and write a check to pay the bill.
Bill	Record bills that you want to pay later.
Reg	Display the register of the account you're currently using. If no account is in use, clicking this icon displays the Chart of Accounts window so that you can select an account.
Accnt	Display your Chart of Accounts. Use it to add new accounts or edit existing accounts.
Cust	Work with your list of customers and jobs.
Vend	Work with your list of vendors.
Item	Work with your list of items.
MemTx	Work with your list of memorized transactions.
Rmnd	Review your reminders.
Find	Conduct a search based on the filters you choose.
Backup	Tell QuickBooks that you want to back up the company file.
Qcards	Show or hide QuickBooks' Qcards.
Help	Display help about the active window.

D1573045

...For Dummies: #1 Computer Book Series for Beginners

QuickBooks® 6 For Dummies®

Cheat Sheet

Speedy Keyboard Shortcuts

PC Shortcut	QuickBooks Does This
Ctrl+A	Displays the Chart of Accounts window
Ctrl+J	Displays the Customer:Job List window
Ctrl+I	Displays the Create Invoice window
Ctrl+W	Displays the Write Checks window
Ctrl+Ins	Inserts a line into a list of items or expenses
Ctrl+Del	Deletes the selected line from a list of items or expenses
Ctrl+M	Memorizes a transaction
Crtl+T	Displays the memorized transaction

Some Cool Date-Editing Tricks

If the selection cursor is on a date field, you can use these tricks to edit the date:

Press	What Happens
+	Adds one day to the date shown
t	Replaces the date shown with today's date
–	Subtracts one day from the date shown
y	Changes the date to the first day in the year
r	Changes the date to the last day in the year
m	Changes the date to the first day in the month
h	Changes the date to the last day in the month

Some Windows Tricks

- ✔ To get help related to the task at hand, click the How Do I? button in the upper-right corner of the dialog box. Then choose a help topic from the drop-down menu.

- ✔ To move quickly to list box entries that begin with a specific letter, press the letter.

- ✔ To select a list box entry and choose a dialog box's suggested command button, double-click the entry.

- ✔ To move the insertion point to the beginning of a field, press Home.

- ✔ To move the insertion point to the end of a field, press End.

- ✔ To close a window or dialog box, click the close button: ☒

- ✔ To minimize a window so that only a teensy part of the title bar is showing, click the minimize button: ▬

  This works both for the application window — the window for the program — and the individual windows shown within each program.

- ✔ To show a window without covering the entire monitor screen, click this middle button: ⧉

- ✔ When the same middle button shows one box in it, clicking it maximizes the QuickBooks desktop so that it fills the monitor screen: ▢

Keeping Your Debits and Credits Straight

Account Type	Debits	Credits
Assets	Increase asset accounts	Decrease asset accounts
Liabilities	Decrease liability accounts	Increase liability accounts
Owner's equity	Decrease owner's equity accounts	Increase owner's equity accounts
Income	Decrease income accounts	Increase income accounts
Expenses	Increase expense accounts	Decrease expense accounts

QUICKBOOKS® 6
FOR
DUMMIES®

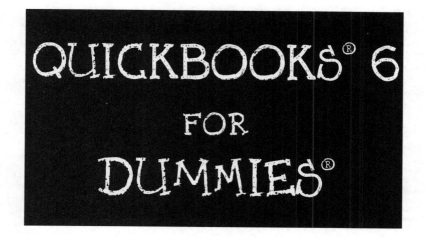

QUICKBOOKS® 6 FOR DUMMIES®

by Stephen L. Nelson

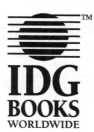

IDG BOOKS WORLDWIDE

IDG Books Worldwide, Inc.
An International Data Group Company

Foster City, CA ♦ Chicago, IL ♦ Indianapolis, IN ♦ New York, NY

QuickBooks® 6 For Dummies®

Published by
IDG Books Worldwide, Inc.
An International Data Group Company
919 E. Hillsdale Blvd.
Suite 400
Foster City, CA 94404
www.idgbooks.com (IDG Books Worldwide Web site)
www.dummies.com (Dummies Press Web site)

Library of Congress Catalog Card No.: 98-85842

ISBN: 0-7645-0330-8

Printed in the United States of America

10 9 8 7 6 5

1B/SZ/QW/ZY/IN

Distributed in the United States by IDG Books Worldwide, Inc.

Distributed by Macmillan Canada for Canada; by Transworld Publishers Limited in the United Kingdom; by IDG Norge Books for Norway; by IDG Sweden Books for Sweden; by Woodslane Pty. Ltd. for Australia; by Woodslane (NZ) Ltd. for New Zealand; by Addison Wesley Longman Singapore Pte Ltd. for Singapore, Malaysia, Thailand, and Indonesia; by Norma Comunicaciones S.A. for Colombia; by Intersoft for South Africa; by International Thomson Publishing for Germany, Austria and Switzerland; by Distribuidora Cuspide for Argentina; by Livraria Cultura for Brazil; by Ediciencia S.A. for Ecuador; by Ediciones ZETA S.C.R. Ltda. for Peru; by WS Computer Publishing Corporation, Inc., for the Philippines; by Contemporanea de Ediciones for Venezuela; by Express Computer Distributors for the Caribbean and West Indies; by Micronesia Media Distributor, Inc. for Micronesia; by Grupo Editorial Norma S.A. for Guatemala; by Chips Computadoras S.A. de C.V. for Mexico; by Editorial Norma de Panama S.A. for Panama; by Wouters Import for Belgium; by American Bookshops for Finland. Authorized Sales Agent: Anthony Rudkin Associates for the Middle East and North Africa.

For general information on IDG Books Worldwide's books in the U.S., please call our Consumer Customer Service department at 800-762-2974. For reseller information, including discounts and premium sales, please call our Reseller Customer Service department at 800-434-3422.

For information on where to purchase IDG Books Worldwide's books outside the U.S., please contact our International Sales department at 317-596-5530 or fax 317-596-5692.

For information on foreign language translations, please contact our Foreign & Subsidiary Rights department at 650-655-3021 or fax 650-655-3281.

For sales inquiries and special prices for bulk quantities, please contact our Sales department at 650-655-3200 or write to the address above.

For information on using IDG Books Worldwide's books in the classroom or for ordering examination copies, please contact our Educational Sales department at 800-434-2086 or fax 317-596-5499.

For press review copies, author interviews, or other publicity information, please contact our Public Relations department at 650-655-3000 or fax 650-655-3299.

For authorization to photocopy items for corporate, personal, or educational use, please contact Copyright Clearance Center, 222 Rosewood Drive, Danvers, MA 01923, or fax 978-750-4470.

is a trademark under exclusive license to IDG Books Worldwide, Inc., from International Data Group, Inc.

About the Author

Steve Nelson has a simple purpose in life. He wants to help you (and people like you) manage your business finances by using computers. Oh, sure. This personal mandate won't win him a Nobel prize or anything, but it's his own little contribution to the world.

Steve's education and experiences mesh nicely with his special purpose. He has a B.S. in accounting and an M.B.A. in finance. He's a CPA. He used to work as a senior consultant with Arthur Andersen & Co., the world's largest public accounting firm. He also has been the controller and treasurer of a 50-person manufacturing firm. Nelson, whose books have sold more than 2,000,000 copies in English and have been translated into 11 other languages, is also the bestselling author of *Quicken 98 For Windows For Dummies* and *Small Business Windows 98 For Dummies* (IDG Books Worldwide, Inc.).

ABOUT IDG BOOKS WORLDWIDE

Welcome to the world of IDG Books Worldwide.

IDG Books Worldwide, Inc., is a subsidiary of International Data Group, the world's largest publisher of computer-related information and the leading global provider of information services on information technology. IDG was founded more than 25 years ago and now employs more than 8,500 people worldwide. IDG publishes more than 275 computer publications in over 75 countries (see listing below). More than 90 million people read one or more IDG publications each month.

Launched in 1990, IDG Books Worldwide is today the #1 publisher of best-selling computer books in the United States. We are proud to have received eight awards from the Computer Press Association in recognition of editorial excellence and three from *Computer Currents'* First Annual Readers' Choice Awards. Our best-selling *...For Dummies®* series has more than 50 million copies in print with translations in 38 languages. IDG Books Worldwide, through a joint venture with IDG's Hi-Tech Beijing, became the first U.S. publisher to publish a computer book in the People's Republic of China. In record time, IDG Books Worldwide has become the first choice for millions of readers around the world who want to learn how to better manage their businesses.

Our mission is simple: Every one of our books is designed to bring extra value and skill-building instructions to the reader. Our books are written by experts who understand and care about our readers. The knowledge base of our editorial staff comes from years of experience in publishing, education, and journalism — experience we use to produce books for the '90s. In short, we care about books, so we attract the best people. We devote special attention to details such as audience, interior design, use of icons, and illustrations. And because we use an efficient process of authoring, editing, and desktop publishing our books electronically, we can spend more time ensuring superior content and spend less time on the technicalities of making books.

You can count on our commitment to deliver high-quality books at competitive prices on topics you want to read about. At IDG Books Worldwide, we continue in the IDG tradition of delivering quality for more than 25 years. You'll find no better book on a subject than one from IDG Books Worldwide.

IDG BOOKS WORLDWIDE

John J. Kilcullen
John Kilcullen
CEO
IDG Books Worldwide, Inc.

Steven Berkowitz
Steven Berkowitz
President and Publisher
IDG Books Worldwide, Inc.

VIII WINNER
Eighth Annual Computer Press Awards ≥ 1992

IX WINNER
Ninth Annual Computer Press Awards ≥ 1993

Tenth Annual Computer Press Awards ≥ 1994

X WINNER

XI WINNER
Eleventh Annual Computer Press Awards ≥ 1995

IDG Books Worldwide, Inc., is a subsidiary of International Data Group, the world's largest publisher of computer-related information and the leading global provider of information services on information technology. International Data Group publishes over 275 computer publications in over 75 countries. More than 90 million people read one or more International Data Group publications each month. International Data Group's publications include: **ARGENTINA:** Buyer's Guide, Computerworld Argentina, PC World Argentina; **AUSTRALIA:** Australian Macworld, Australian PC World, Australian Reseller News, Computerworld, IT Casebook, Network World, Publish, Webmaster; **AUSTRIA:** Computerwelt Osterreich, Networks Austria, PC Tip Austria; **BANGLADESH:** PC World Bangladesh; **BELARUS:** PC World Belarus; **BELGIUM:** Data News; **BRAZIL:** Annuário de Informática, Computerworld, Connections, Macworld, PC Player, PC World, Publish, Reseller News, Supergamepower; **BULGARIA:** Computerworld Bulgaria, Network World Bulgaria, PC & MacWorld Bulgaria; **CANADA:** CIO Canada, Client/Server World, ComputerWorld Canada, InfoWorld Canada, NetworkWorld Canada, WebWorld; **CHILE:** Computerworld Chile, PC World Chile; **COLOMBIA:** Computerworld Colombia, PC World Colombia; **COSTA RICA:** PC World Centro America; **THE CZECH AND SLOVAK REPUBLICS:** Computerworld Czechoslovakia, Macworld Czech Republic, PC World Czechoslovakia; **DENMARK:** Communications World Danmark, Computerworld Danmark, Macworld Danmark, PC World Danmark, Techworld Denmark; **DOMINICAN REPUBLIC:** PC World Republica Dominicana; **ECUADOR:** PC World Ecuador; **EGYPT:** Computerworld Middle East, PC World Middle East; **EL SALVADOR:** PC World Centro America; **FINLAND:** MikroPC, Tietoverkko, Tietoviikko; **FRANCE:** Distributique, Hebdo, Info PC, Le Monde Informatique, Macworld, Reseaux & Telecoms, WebMaster France; **GERMANY:** Computer Partner, Computerwoche, Computerwoche Extra, Computerwoche FOCUS, Global Online, Macwelt, PC Welt; **GREECE:** Amiga Computing, GamePro Greece, Multimedia World; **GUATEMALA:** PC World Centro America; **HONDURAS:** PC World Centro America; **HONG KONG:** Computerworld Hong Kong, PC World Hong Kong, Publish in Asia; **HUNGARY:** ABCD CD-ROM, Computerworld Szamitastechnika, Internetto online Magazine, PC World Hungary, PC-X Magazin Hungary; **ICELAND:** Tolvuheimur PC World Island; **INDIA:** Information Communications World, Information Systems Computerworld, PC World India, Publish in Asia; **INDONESIA:** InfoKomputer PC World, Komputek Computerworld, Publish in Asia; **IRELAND:** ComputerScope, PC Live!; **ISRAEL:** Macworld Israel, People & Computers/Computerworld; **ITALY:** Computerworld Italia, Macworld Italia, Networking Italia, PC World Italia; **JAPAN:** DTP World, Macworld Japan, Nikkei Personal Computing, OS/2 World Japan, SunWorld Japan, Windows NT World, Windows World Japan; **KENYA:** PC World East African; **KOREA:** Hi-Tech Information, Macworld Korea, PC World Korea; **MACEDONIA:** PC World Macedonia; **MALAYSIA:** Computerworld Malaysia, PC World Malaysia, Publish in Asia; **MALTA:** PC World Malta; **MEXICO:** Computerworld Mexico, PC World Mexico; **MYANMAR:** PC World Myanmar; **NETHERLANDS:** Computer! Totaal, LAN Internetworking Magazine, LAN World Buyers Guide, Macworld Netherlands, Net, WebWereld; **NEW ZEALAND:** Absolute Beginners Guide and Plain & Simple Series, Computer Buyer, Computer Industry Directory, Computerworld New Zealand, MTB, Network World, PC World New Zealand; **NICARAGUA:** PC World Centro America; **NORWAY:** Computerworld Norge, CW Rapport, Datamagasinet, Financial Rapport, Kursguide Norge, Macworld Norge, Multimediaworld Norge, PC World Ekspress Norge, PC World Nettverk, PC World Norge, PC World ProduktGuide Norge; **PAKISTAN:** Computerworld Pakistan; **PANAMA:** PC World Panama; **PEOPLE'S REPUBLIC OF CHINA:** China Computer Users, China Computerworld, China InfoWorld, China Telecom World Weekly, Computer & Communication, Electronic Design China, Electronics Today, Electronics Weekly, Game Software, PC World China, Popular Computer Week, Software Weekly, Software World, Telecom World; **PERU:** Computerworld Peru, PC World Profesional Peru, PC World SoHo Peru; **PHILIPPINES:** Click!, Computerworld Philippines, PC World Philippines, Publish in Asia; **POLAND:** Computerworld Poland, Computerworld Special Report Poland, Cyber, Macworld Poland, Networld Poland, PC World Komputer; **PORTUGAL:** Cerebro/PC World, Computerworld/Correio Informático, Dealer World Portugal, Mac*In/PC*In Portugal, Multimedia World; **PUERTO RICO:** PC World Puerto Rico; **ROMANIA:** Computerworld Romania, PC World Romania, Telecom Romania; **RUSSIA:** Computerworld Russia, Mir PK, Publish, Seti; **SINGAPORE:** Computerworld Singapore, PC World Singapore, Publish in Asia; **SLOVENIA:** Monitor; **SOUTH AFRICA:** Computing SA, Network World SA, Software World SA; **SPAIN:** Communicaciones World España, Computerworld España, Dealer World España, Macworld España, PC World España; **SRI LANKA:** Infolink PC World; **SWEDEN:** CAP&Design, Computer Sweden, Corporate Computing Sweden, Internetworld Sweden, it branschen, Macworld Sweden, MaxiData Sweden, MikroDatorn, Natverk & Kommunikation, PC World Sweden, PCaktiv, Windows World Sweden; **SWITZERLAND:** Computerworld Schweiz, Macworld Schweiz, PCtip; **TAIWAN:** Computerworld Taiwan, Macworld Taiwan, NEW ViSiON/Publish, PC World Taiwan, Windows World Taiwan; **THAILAND:** Publish in Asia, Thai Computerworld; **TURKEY:** Computerworld Turkiye, Macworld Turkiye, Network World Turkiye, PC World Turkiye; **UKRAINE:** Computerworld Kiev, Multimedia World Ukraine, PC World Ukraine; **UNITED KINGDOM:** Acorn User UK, Amiga Action UK, Amiga Computing UK, Apple Talk UK, Computing, Macworld, Parents and Computers UK, PC Advisor, PC Home, PSX Pro, The WEB; **UNITED STATES:** Cable in the Classroom, CIO Magazine, Computerworld, DOS World, Federal Computer Week, GamePro Magazine, InfoWorld, I-Way, Macworld, Network World, PC Games, PC World, Publish, Video Event, THE WEB Magazine, and WebMaster; online webzines: JavaWorld, NetscapeWorld, and SunWorld Online; **URUGUAY:** InfoWorld Uruguay; **VENEZUELA:** Computerworld Venezuela, PC World Venezuela; and **VIETNAM:** PC World Vietnam.
5/7/98

Dedication

To the entrepreneurs and small-business people of the world. You folks create most of the new jobs.

Author's Acknowledgments

Hey, reader, lots of folks spent lots of time working on this book to make QuickBooks easier for you. You should know who these people are. You may just possibly meet them some day at a produce shop, squeezing cantaloupe, eating grapes, and looking for the perfect peach.

Those folks are Diane Steele, Mary Bednarek, Mike Kelly, Andrea C. Boucher, Bill Helling, Wendy Hatch, Michael Lerch, and Kaarin Dolliver.

Publisher's Acknowledgments

We're proud of this book; please register your comments through our IDG Books Worldwide Online Registration Form located at http://my2cents.dummies.com.

Some of the people who helped bring this book to market include the following:

Acquisitions, Editorial, and Media Development

Project Editors: Andrea C. Boucher, Bill Helling

Acquisitions Editor: Michael Kelly

Copy Editor: Wendy Hatch

Technical Editor: Michael Lerch

Editorial Manager: Elaine Brush

Editorial Assistant: Paul E. Kuzmic

Production

Project Coordinator: E. Shawn Aylsworth

Layout and Graphics: Lou Boudreau, Maridee V. Ennis, Angela F. Hunckler, Drew R. Moore, Heather Pearson, Anna Rohrer, Brent Savage, Janet Seib, M. Anne Sipahimalani, Michael A. Sullivan

Proofreaders: Christine Berman, Kelli Botta, Rachel Garvey, Nancy Price, Rebecca Senninger, Ethel M. Winslow, Janet M. Withers

Indexer: Becky Hornyak

General and Administrative

IDG Books Worldwide, Inc.: John Kilcullen, CEO; Steven Berkowitz, President and Publisher

IDG Books Technology Publishing: Brenda McLaughlin, Senior Vice President and Group Publisher

Dummies Technology Press and Dummies Editorial: Diane Graves Steele, Vice President and Associate Publisher; Mary Bednarek, Director of Acquisitions and Product Development; Kristin A. Cocks, Editorial Director

Dummies Trade Press: Kathleen A. Welton, Vice President and Publisher; Kevin Thornton, Acquisitions Manager

IDG Books Production for Dummies Press: Michael R. Britton, Vice President of Production and Creative Services; Cindy L. Phipps, Manager of Project Coordination, Production Proofreading, and Indexing; Kathie S. Schutte, Supervisor of Page Layout; Shelley Lea, Supervisor of Graphics and Design; Debbie J. Gates, Production Systems Specialist; Robert Springer, Supervisor of Proofreading; Debbie Stailey, Special Projects Coordinator; Tony Augsburger, Supervisor of Reprints and Bluelines

Dummies Packaging and Book Design: Robin Seaman, Creative Director; Jocelyn Kelaita, Product Packaging Coordinator; Kavish + Kavish, Cover Design

◆

The publisher would like to give special thanks to Patrick J. McGovern, without whom this book would not have been possible.

◆

Contents at a Glance

Cartoons at a Glance

By Rich Tennant

page 7

page 259

page 299

page 69

page 173

Fax: 978-546-7747 • E-mail: the5wave@tiac.net

Table of Contents

Introduction

I think that running or working in a small business is one of the coolest things a person can do. Really. I mean it. Sure, sometimes it's a dangerous environment. Kind of like the Old West. But it's also an environment in which you have the opportunity to make tons of money. And it's an environment in which you can build a company or a job that fits you. In comparison, many brothers and sisters working in big-company corporate America are furiously trying to fit their round pegs into painfully square holes. Yuck.

You're wondering, of course, what any of this has to do with this book or with QuickBooks. Quite a lot, actually. The whole purpose of this book is to make it easier for you to run or work in a small business by using QuickBooks.

About This Book

This book isn't meant to be read from cover to cover like some John Grisham page-turner. Instead, it's organized into tiny, no-sweat descriptions of how you do the things you need to do. If you're the sort of person who just doesn't feel right not reading a book from cover to cover, you can, of course, go ahead and read this thing from front to back. You can start reading Chapter 1 and continue all the way to the end (which means through Chapter 21 and the appendixes). I actually don't think this from-start-to-finish approach is bad. You can find out a bunch of stuff.

But you also can use this book like an encyclopedia. If you want to know about a subject, you can look it up in the table of contents or the index. Then you can flip to the correct chapter or page and read as much as you need or enjoy. No muss. No fuss.

I should, however, mention one thing: Accounting software programs require you to do a certain amount of preparation before you can use them to get real work done. If you haven't started to use QuickBooks yet, I recommend that you read through the first few chapters of this book to find out what you need to do first.

What You Can Safely Ignore

Sometimes I provide step-by-step descriptions of tasks. I feel very bad about having to do this. So to make things easier for you, I describe the tasks by using bold text. That way, you know exactly what you're supposed to do. I also provide a more detailed explanation in regular text. You can skip the regular text that accompanies the step-by-step descriptions if you already understand the process.

Here's an example that shows what I mean:

1. **Press Enter.**

    Find the key that's labeled Enter or Return. Extend your index finger so that it rests ever so gently on the Enter key. In one sure, fluid motion, press the Enter key by using your index finger. Then release your finger.

Okay, that example is kind of extreme. I never actually go into that much detail. But you get the idea. If you know how to press Enter, you can just do that and not read further. If you need help — maybe with the finger part or something — just read the nitty-gritty details.

Is there anything else you can skip? Let me see now . . . You can skip the Technical Stuff sidebars, too. The information in these sidebars is really there only for those of you who like that kind of stuff.

For that matter, I guess that you can safely ignore the stuff in the Tip sidebars, too — even if the accumulated wisdom, gleaned from long hours slaving over a hot keyboard, could save you much weeping and gnashing of teeth. If you're someone who enjoys trying to do something another way, go ahead and read the tips.

(By the way, this program is Year 2000 compliant, so you don't have to worry about this, either.)

What You Should Not Ignore (Unless You're a Masochist)

Don't skip the Warning sidebars. They're the ones flagged with the picture of the 19th century bomb. They describe some things that you really shouldn't do.

Out of respect for you, I'm not going to put stuff such as "don't smoke" in these sidebars. I figure that you're an adult. You can make your own lifestyle decisions.

So I'm reserving the Warning sidebars for more urgent and immediate dangers — things akin to "Don't smoke while you're filling your car with gasoline."

Three Foolish Assumptions

I'm making three assumptions:

- ✔ **You have a PC with Microsoft Windows 95 or later, or Windows NT 4.0 or higher.**
- ✔ **You know a little bit about how to work with your computer.**
- ✔ **You have or will buy a copy of QuickBooks or QuickBooks Pro for each computer on which you want to run the program.**

Note: This book applies to both the standard version of QuickBooks as well as QuickBooks Pro. Personally, I use QuickBooks Pro, so this book includes some features unique to the Pro version. If you're trying to decide which version to buy, I should tell you that QuickBooks Pro includes networking capabilities (described in Chapter 3), the ability to create estimates and bids (described in Appendix C), and the Timer program for tracking the time you spend on jobs (described in Appendix D). The standard version of QuickBooks doesn't include these features.

By the way, if you haven't already installed QuickBooks and need help, refer to Appendix A, which tells you how to install QuickBooks in eleven easy steps. And if you're just starting out with Microsoft Windows, peruse Chapter 1 of the *Windows User's Guide* or one of IDG's books on your flavor of Windows, such as *Small Business Windows 95 For Dummies, Small Business Windows 98 For Dummies, Windows 98 For Dummies,* or *Windows NT For Dummies.*

How This Book Is Organized

This book is divided into five mostly coherent parts.

Part I: You Gotta Start Someplace

Part I covers some up-front stuff that you need to take care of before you can start using QuickBooks. This part also introduces the networking capabilities of QuickBooks Pro. I promise I won't waste your time here. I just want to make sure that you get off on the right foot.

Part II: Daily Chores

The second part of this book explains how you use QuickBooks for your daily financial record keeping: preparing customer invoices, recording sales, paying bills. That kind of stuff.

I guess you could say that these chores are just data entry stuff. And you'd be correct. But you'll be amazed at how much easier QuickBooks will make your life. QuickBooks is a really cool program.

Part III: Stuff You Do Every So Often

Part III talks about the kinds of things you should do at the end of the week, the end of the month, or the end of the year. This part explains, for example, how you print checks, explore QuickBooks online resources, do payroll, balance your bank account, create reports, take care of some housekeeping tasks, and create a business budget.

While I'm on the subject, I also want to categorically deny that Part III contains any secret messages that you can decipher by reading it backward. Yllaer.

Part IV: The Part of Tens

Gravity isn't just a good idea; it's also a law.

By tradition, the same is true for this part of a ...*For Dummies* book. The Part of Tens provides a collection of lists: ten things you should do if you get audited, ten things you should do if you own a business, ten things to do when you next visit Acapulco — oops, sorry about that last one. Wrong book.

By the way, also by tradition, these ten-item lists don't need to have exactly ten items. You know the concept of a baker's dozen, right? You order a dozen doughnuts but get 13 for the same price. Well, ...*For Dummies* ten-item lists have roughly ten items. (If Dummies Man — the bug-eyed, paleface guy suffering from triangle-shaped-head syndrome who appears on the cover of this book and on icons throughout these pages — were running the bakery, a ten-doughnut order might mean that you get anywhere from 8 to 13 doughnuts.)

Part V: Appendixes

It's an unwritten rule that computer books have appendixes, so I've included four. Appendix A tells you how to install QuickBooks in eleven easy steps. Appendix B explains small business accounting, provides a short biography of an Italian monk, and explains double-entry bookkeeping. Appendix C describes project estimating. And Appendix D describes how you use the Timer program included with the Pro version of QuickBooks to keep track of the time you spend on projects.

Conventions Used in This Book

To make the best use of your time and energy, you should know about the conventions used in this book.

When I want you to type something such as **the hydraulics screamed as the pilot lowered his landing gear**, it's in bold letters. When I want you to type something that's short and uncomplicated, such as **Jennifer**, it still appears in boldface type.

By the way, except for passwords, you don't have to worry about the case of the stuff you type in QuickBooks. If I tell you to type **Jennifer**, you can type JENNIFER. Or you can follow poet e. e. cummings' lead and type jennifer.

Usually, I'll use the QuickBooks Navigator as my starting point when I give instructions on how to get somewhere in QuickBooks. Each time I do this, I'll tell you which tab and which icon to click. (Tabs are the little boxes along the left side of the Navigator, and icons are the cute little pictures in the Navigator that often light up when you run the mouse over them.) For example, if I want to tell you how to write a check, I'll say that you need to display the Write Checks window by clicking the Checking and Credit Cards tab of the QuickBooks Navigator and then clicking the Write Checks icon.

Whenever I tell you to choose a command from a menu, I say something like, "Choose Lists⇨Items," which simply means to first choose the Lists menu and then choose Items. The ⇨ separates one part of the command from the next part.

You can choose menus and commands and select dialog box elements with the mouse or with the keyboard. To select them with the mouse, you just click the menu or command. To select them with the keyboard, you press

Alt and the underlined letter in the menu, command, or dialog box. For example, the letter F in File and the letter O in Open are underlined in the command File⇨Open, so if you don't want to use the mouse to choose the command, you can press Alt and F at the same time and then press O to get the same results. (I also identify keyboard selection keys like this in the numbered steps in this book.) You can select many commands by clicking icons on the iconbar as well.

One thing I don't always do, I should confess, is give the Alt+key combinations for selecting window and dialog box elements: text boxes, option buttons, list boxes, and so on. I have an excuse. Sort of. QuickBooks isn't very consistent about its use of this interface convention. So because you can't use it much of the time, I figured, "Why bother?"

Special Icons

Like many computer books, this book uses icons, or little pictures, to flag things that don't quite fit into the flow of things. The *...For Dummies* books use a standard set of icons that flag little digressions, such as the following:

This icon points out nerdy technical material that you may want to skip (or read, if you're feeling particularly bright).

Whee, here's a shortcut to make your life easier!

This icon is just a friendly reminder to do something.

This icon lets you know that this is a feature or way of doing things that's new to QuickBooks 6.

And this icon is a friendly reminder not to do something . . . or else.

Part I
You Gotta Start Someplace

The 5th Wave   By Rich Tennant

"It's a football/accounting program. We're tackling customer invoices, going long for inventory, and punting employee payroll."

In this part . . .

All accounting programs — including QuickBooks —
make you do a bunch of preliminary stuff. Sure, this
is sort of a bummer. But getting depressed about it won't
make things go any faster. So if you want to get up and
going with QuickBooks — and if you want to find out
about the cool network features QuickBooks offers —
peruse the chapters in this first part. I promise that I'll get
you through this stuff as quickly as possible.

Chapter 1

The Big Interview

In This Chapter

▶ Getting ready to do the big interview

▶ Not getting discouraged about the big interview

▶ Surviving the big interview

▶ Telling your friends all sorts of war stories about the big interview

▶ Making the accrual-accounting adjustment

▶ Supplying the missing numbers

I know that you're eager to get started. You've got a business to run. But before you can start using QuickBooks, you need to do some up-front work. Specifically, you need to prepare for the QuickBooks EasyStep Interview, and then you need to walk through the EasyStep Interview. (The EasyStep Interview is just a thorough question-and-answer session that QuickBooks uses to set itself up for you.) After you finish with the EasyStep Interview, you also probably need to fiddle with QuickBooks to get everything working just right. This chapter describes how you do all this stuff.

Note: I assume that you know how Windows works. If you don't, take the time to read Chapter 1 of your *Windows User's Guide.* Or try *Small Business Windows 95 For Dummies* and *Small Business Windows 98 For Dummies* (both from IDG Books Worldwide, Inc.).

Getting Ready for the Big Interview

You need to complete three tasks to get ready for the EasyStep Interview. You need to make an important decision about your conversion date (the date you convert from your old accounting system to QuickBooks). You need to prepare a trial balance as of the conversion date. And you need to go on a scavenger hunt to collect a bunch of stuff that you'll need or find handy for the interview.

The big decision

Before you even start fiddling with your computer or the QuickBooks software, you need to choose the date — the so-called *conversion date* — on which you want to begin using QuickBooks for your financial record keeping.

This decision is hugely important because the conversion date you choose dramatically affects both the work you have to do in order to get QuickBooks running smoothly and the initial usefulness of the financial information that you collect and record by using QuickBooks.

You've got three basic choices you can make:

- ✔ **The right way:** You can convert at the beginning of your accounting year (which is almost certainly the same as the beginning of the calendar year). This way is the right way for two reasons. First, converting at the beginning of the year requires the least amount of work from you. Second, it means that you have all the current year's financial information in one system.

- ✔ **The slightly awkward way:** You can convert at the beginning of some interim accounting period (probably the beginning of some month or quarter). This approach works, but it's slightly awkward because you have to plug your year-to-date income and expenses numbers from the old system into the new system. (If you don't know what an *interim accounting period* is, read Appendix B.)

- ✔ **The my-way-or-the-highway way:** You can convert at some time other than what I call the right way and the slightly awkward way. Specifically, you can choose to convert whenever you jolly well feel like it. You create a bunch of unnecessary work for yourself if you take this approach, and you pull out a bunch of your hair in the process. But you also have the satisfaction of knowing that through it all, you did it your way — and without any help from me.

I recommend the right way. What this choice means is that if it's late in the year — say, October — I suggest that you just wait until January 1 of the next year to convert. If it's still early in the year, you can also retroactively "convert" as of the beginning of the year. (If you do this, you need to go back and do your financial record-keeping for the first part of the current year by using QuickBooks: entering sales, recording purchases, and so on.)

If it's sometime in the middle of the year — say, Memorial Day or later — then you probably want to use the slightly awkward way. (I'm actually going to use the slightly awkward way in this chapter because if you see how to convert to QuickBooks by using the slightly awkward way, you know how to use both the right way *and* the slightly awkward way.)

The trial balance of the century

After you decide when you want to convert, you need a *trial balance*.

"Yikes," you say. "What's a trial balance?" Well, a trial balance simply lists all your assets, liabilities, and owner's equity account balances as well as the year-to-date income and expense numbers on a specified date (which, not coincidentally, happens to be the conversion date). You need this data for the EasyStep Interview and for some fiddling around that you need to do after you complete the EasyStep Interview.

Creating a trial balance doesn't have to be as hard as it sounds. If you've been using another small-business accounting system, such as Microsoft Profit, you may be able to have your old system produce a trial balance on the conversion date. In that case, you can get the balances from your old system. (You can consider yourself lucky if this is the case.)

If your old system is rather informal (perhaps it's a shoe box full of receipts) or if it tracks only cash (perhaps you've been using Quicken), you need to do a bit more work.

To get your cash balance, you need to reconcile your bank account or bank accounts (if you've got more than one bank account) as of the conversion date.

To get your accounts receivable balance, you need to tally up the total of all your unpaid customer invoices.

To get your other asset account balances, you need to know what each asset originally cost. For depreciable fixed assets, you also need to provide any accumulated depreciation that you've charged. (*Accumulated depreciation* is just the total depreciation that you've charged on an asset.) By the way, refer to Appendix B if you have questions about accounting or accounting terminology such as depreciation.

To get your liability account balances, you need to know how much you owe on each liability. If you trust your *creditors* — the people you owe the money to — you may also be able to get this information from their statements.

You don't need to worry about the owner's equity accounts. QuickBooks can calculate your owner's equity account balances for you, based on the difference between your total assets and your total liabilities. This method is a bit sloppy, and accountants may not like it, but it's a pretty good compromise. (By the way, if you do have detailed account balances for your owner's equity accounts, you should use these figures. You also should know that you're one in a million.)

If you're using the slightly awkward way to convert to QuickBooks — in other words, if your conversion date is some date other than at the beginning of the accounting year — then you also need to provide year-to-date income and expense balances. To get your income, cost of goods sold, expense, other income, and other expense account balances, you need to calculate the year-to-date amount of each account. If you can get this information from your old system, that's super. If not, you need to get it manually. (If you suddenly have images of yourself sitting at your desk, late at night, tapping away on a ten-key, you're probably right. What's more, you probably also need to allocate another half-Saturday to getting up and running with QuickBooks.)

Just for fun, I created the sample trial balance shown in Table 1-1. This table shows you what a trial balance might look like if you convert at some time other than the beginning of the accounting year.

Table 1-1	A "Slightly Awkward Way" Sample Trial Balance	
Trial Balance Information	**Debit**	**Credit**
Assets		
Checking	$5,000	
Fixed Assets	$60,000	
Accumulated Depreciation (fixed assets)		$2,000
Liabilities information		
Loan Payable		$10,000
Owner's equity and income statement information		
Opening Bal Equity		$20,000
Sales		$60,000
Cost of Goods Sold	$20,000	
Supplies Expense	$2,100	
Rent Expense	$4,900	
Totals	$92,000	$92,000

By the way, if you were converting at the very beginning of the accounting year, your trial balance would look like the one shown in Table 1-2. Notice that this trial balance doesn't have any year-to-date income or expense balances.

About those debits and credits

Don't get freaked out about those debits and credits. You just need to keep them straight for a few minutes. Here's the scoop: For assets and expenses, a debit balance is the same thing as a positive balance. So a cash debit balance of $5,000 means that you have $5,000 in your account. And $20,000 of cost of goods sold means that you incurred $20,000 of costs of goods expense. For assets and expenses, a credit balance is the same thing as a negative balance. So, if you have a cash balance of −$5,000, your account is overdrawn by $5,000. In the example trial balance shown in Table 1-1, the accumulated depreciation shows a credit balance of $2,000, which is, in effect, a negative account balance.

For liabilities, owner's equity accounts, and income accounts, things are flip-flopped. A credit balance is the same thing as a positive balance. So an accounts payable credit balance of $2,000 means that you owe your creditors $2,000. A bank loan credit balance of $10,000 means that you owe the bank $10,000. And a sales account credit balance of $60,000 means that you've enjoyed $60,000 of sales.

I know that I keep saying this, but do remember that those income and expense account balances are year-to-date figures. They exist only if the conversion date is after the start of the financial year.

Table 1-2	A "Right Way" Sample Trial Balance	
Trial Balance Information	*Debit*	*Credit*
Assets		
Checking	$5,000	
Fixed Assets	$60,000	
Accumulated Depreciation (fixed assets)		$2,000
Liabilities information		
Loan Payable		$10,000
Owner's equity and income statement information		
Opening Bal Equity		$53,000
Totals	$65,000	$65,000

The mother of all scavenger hunts

Even after you've decided when you want to convert to QuickBooks and have come up with a trial balance, you still need to collect a bunch of additional information. I'm just going to list these items in laundry list fashion. What you want to do is find all this stuff and then pile it up (neatly) in a big stack next to the computer on which you'll install QuickBooks.

- **Last year's federal tax return.** QuickBooks asks which federal income tax form you use to file your tax return and also about your taxpayer identification number. Last year's federal tax return in the easiest place to find this stuff.

- **Copies of your most recent state and federal payroll tax returns.** If you prepare payroll for employees, QuickBooks wants to know about the federal and state payroll tax rates you pay, as well as some other stuff.

- **Copies of all the unpaid invoices that your customers (or clients or patients or whatever) owe you as of the conversion date.** I guess this is probably obvious, but the total accounts receivable balance shown on your trial balance needs to match the total of the unpaid customer invoices.

- **Copies of all unpaid invoices that you owe your vendors as of the conversion date.** Again, this is probably obvious, but the total accounts payable balance shown on your trial balance needs to match the total of the unpaid vendor invoices.

- **A detailed listing of any inventory items you're holding for resale.** This list should include not only inventory item descriptions and quantities but also the initial purchase prices and the anticipated sales prices. In other words, if you sell porcelain wombats and you've got 1,200 of these beauties in inventory, you need to know exactly what you paid for them.

- **Copies of the prior year's W-2 statements, W-4 statements for anybody you've hired since the beginning of the prior year, detailed information about any payroll tax liabilities you owe as of the conversion date, and detailed information about the payroll tax deposits you've made since the beginning of the year.** You need the information shown on these forms to adequately and accurately set up QuickBooks' payroll feature. I don't want to scare you, but this is probably the most tedious part of setting up QuickBooks.

> ✔ **If you're retroactively converting as of the beginning of the year, you need a list of all the transactions that have occurred since the beginning of the year: sales, purchases, payroll transactions, and everything and anything else.** As I mentioned earlier in this chapter, if you do the right way conversion retroactively, you need to re-enter each of these transactions into the new system. You actually enter the information after you complete the EasyStep Interview described later in this chapter. But you may as well get all this information together at the same time you do the rest of the scavenger hunt.

If you take the slightly awkward way, you don't need to find the stuff described in item 7. You can just use the year-to-date income and expense numbers from the trial balance.

Doing the EasyStep Interview

After you decide when you want to convert, prepare a trial balance as of the conversion date, and collect the additional raw data you need, you're ready to step through the EasyStep Interview.

Before you begin the interview, you first have to start QuickBooks 6. To do so, choose Start⇨Programs and then click the menu choices that lead to QuickBooks. (For example, I choose Start⇨Programs⇨QuickBooks Pro⇨ QuickBooks Pro.)

Note: QuickBooks actually comes in two flavors: QuickBooks and QuickBooks Pro. These two programs differ in a couple of significant ways: QuickBooks Pro includes the job-costing and time-estimating features briefly described in Appendix C. It also includes the ability to share a QuickBooks file over a network, as described in Chapter 3. I used QuickBooks Pro for writing this book, by the way, so the figures you see here may look a wee bit different from what you see on your screen. But other than minor cosmetic differences, the two programs work the same way.

If this is the first time you've started QuickBooks, the EasyStep Interview starts automatically, displaying the dialog box shown in Figure 1-1. If this isn't the first time you've started QuickBooks but you want to step through the EasyStep Interview to set up a new company anyway, choose the File⇨New Company command. Or, if you want to step through the Interview for a company you've already set up (but perhaps set up incorrectly or incompletely), choose the File⇨EasyStep Interview command.

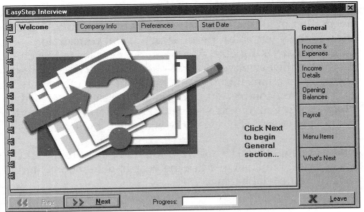

Figure 1-1:
The
EasyStep
Interview
dialog box.

To begin the interview, you click the Next button. The next page of dialog box information asks whether you're upgrading from a previous version of Quicken, QuickBooks, or QuickBooks Pro. You're probably not (or you wouldn't be reading this chapter), so click the option that says, "No, I'm not upgrading," and then continue with the interview by clicking the Next button. Each time you finish a page of the interview, click the Next button to continue.

After QuickBooks starts, you may also see a message box that asks whether you want to register QuickBooks. You can use the product roughly a couple dozen times and then — whammo — either you register it or you can't use it. I don't like being forced to do something, but getting worked up about having to register QuickBooks is a waste of time. The simplest option is to just register. Here's how: When QuickBooks displays the message box that asks whether you want to register, click Register. Then QuickBooks displays another dialog box that gives you a telephone number to call and provides a space for you to enter your customer number. (You can get your customer number from your invoice if you bought QuickBooks from Intuit, or over the phone when you call to register.)

I'm not going to provide you with a blow-by-blow account of what happens when you take the Interview. A much better approach is for me to provide you with a handful of key tips that you can read now and then use later (during the interview) to make the process as easy and as fast as possible.

Tip 1: Learn the interview protocol

For the most part, to complete the EasyStep Interview, all you do is fill in text boxes with the information that QuickBooks requests (as shown in Figure 1-2) or answer questions by clicking buttons clearly marked "Yes" or "No."

Figure 1-2: The dialog box page that the EasyStep Interview uses to get your company's trade name and legal name.

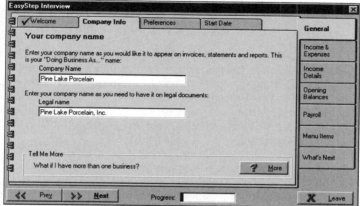

If you ever decide that you want to change some piece of information that you entered on a previous page of the EasyStep Interview's dialog box, you can just click the Prev button to back up. If you get partway through the interview process and decide that it's not worth the time, just click the Leave button in the lower-right corner, and QuickBooks closes the EasyStep Interview dialog box. And, if after leaving the interview, you realize that you've made a mistake, all you have to do is choose File⇔EasyStep Interview and then use the tabs to go back and change something you entered.

Here are a few extra notes that may come in handy:

✔ The EasyStep Interview dialog box appears every time you start a new company (which you do by choosing File⇔New Company).

✔ Note that when you click the tabs on the right side of the EasyStep Interview dialog box, the tabs at the top change accordingly. This change comes in handy when you're leafing through the 60 or 70 pages of information displayed in the EasyStep Interview's dialog box.

✔ QuickBooks purposely makes deleting a company you create in QuickBooks hard, so don't make up an imaginary company to play with unless you're familiar enough with your operating system to delete files.

Tip 2: Take your time

As you step through the Interview process, the EasyStep Interview dialog box displays a bunch of different pages with suggestions, instructions, and advice. Take the time to read this information. Click the Help button if you have questions. If the EasyStep Interview suggests that you view some related document with helpful information, do so.

Tip 3: Get industry-specific advice

One of the handiest features of QuickBooks is the industry-specific advice. For example, are you a rancher or a farmer? QuickBooks includes a detailed online document that describes some of the unique accounting challenges you face, provides tips for making your record-keeping easier, and points out QuickBooks features that may be of particular interest to someone like you. Are you a retailer? A manufacturer? A writer? A consultant? You can get this same sort of information, too.

QuickBooks displays industry-specific tips and tidbits of information throughout the interview. Keep your eyes peeled for the green arrows that mark these little hints. Let me mention one other quick pointer about this industry-specific information stuff: You may not understand everything you read. That's okay. You still want to read the tips and maybe jot them down on a piece of paper as you go along. As you work with QuickBooks and find out more about it, you'll find that more and more of the information provided in the industry-specific tips makes sense.

To view a document of industry-specific information at any time, click the Business Resources tab of the QuickBooks Navigator and click the QuickBooks and Your Industry icon. Then select your industry from the list in the Help window QuickBooks displays. To print a copy of the information, click the Options button and choose Print Topic from the drop-down menu.

Tip 4: Accept the suggested filename and location

A few minutes into the EasyStep Interview, QuickBooks asks you to specify a name and location for the file that it uses to store your accounting information (see Figure 1-3). I can think of no good reason why you should fiddle with or change the suggested filename or location. Don't do it. Let QuickBooks name the QuickBooks file whatever it wants and let QuickBooks store the file wherever it wants.

Figure 1-3:
The Save
As dialog
box lets you
change the
suggested
filename
and
locations,
but I don't
recommend
doing so.

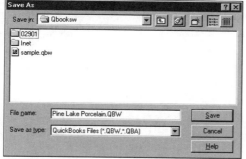

Tip 5: Go with the suggested chart of accounts

Immediately after you name the file that QuickBooks uses for storing your financial information, the EasyStep Interview displays a dialog box that shows a list of accounts that QuickBooks wants to use for tracking your business's financial condition. This dialog box also asks whether the list of accounts is the one you want to use. Unless you know quite a bit about accounting and are willing to learn just as much about QuickBooks, I recommend that you accept the suggested chart of accounts. You make your future record-keeping much easier by doing so.

Tip 6: Consider tracking all your expenses with your checkbook

You get two choices as to how you record your expenses: (1) by using just your checkbook or (2) by creating a "bills-to-pay" list. QuickBooks asks this question in the dialog box page shown in Figure 1-4. I want to be careful about what I say next because the decision you make in this dialog box can really screw up your business. But here's my suggestion: I think that you should consider taking the first option — the one that says you want to record bills by using your checkbook. You choose the first option, which I'm hesitantly recommending here, by marking the Enter the Checks Directly button.

Now before you rush off to the next EasyStep Interview question, confident and happy in my suggestion, let me tell you about the implicit trade-off you're making. If you choose the Enter the Checks Directly option, you do simplify your record-keeping — which is why I suggest that you take this

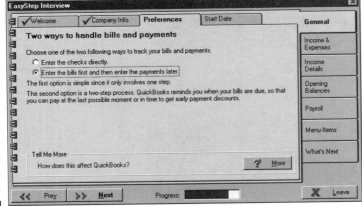

Figure 1-4:
You can
greatly
simplify
your bill-
paying if
you choose
to record
bills when
you write
the checks.

route. But the catch is that you can't track your unpaid bills as closely. Until you sit down to actually write checks for your bills, you don't really know (precisely) how much money you owe vendors. What's more, you can't separate the actual incurring of some expense from the cash outflow that pays the expense. So, by taking the Enter the Checks Directly option, you're unable to do finely-tuned accrual-basis accounting (unless you pay bills when you incur them). And you aren't able to closely monitor the money that you owe to vendors.

In my business, by the way, I do use the Enter the Checks Directly option. I do so to simplify my record-keeping. But I'm probably a little unusual (at least for a small business) for a couple of reasons. First, almost all my expenses get negotiated up front and then get fixed by contract. (With the help of other writers and a team of editors and desktop publishers, I write and package books and technical reference materials.) For this reason, I don't use and don't need to use QuickBooks to keep track of my unpaid bills. In effect, the negotiations and contracts do that.

Second, I've actually been in business for quite a while — more than ten years, in fact. So I don't have the cash flow problems that many (most?) small businesses have, which means that if I want to produce an accurate Profit & Loss statement or an accurate balance sheet — one that includes all my expenses — I can just pay all my unpaid bills.

I guess the bottom line here is this: If you don't need to use QuickBooks to closely monitor your unpaid bills and if you don't mind the profit-calculation precision that you lose because of the lag between the time you incur some expense and the time you pay the bill by writing a check, go ahead and use the Enter the Checks Directly option. This choice greatly simplifies one area of your record-keeping. Otherwise, go with the second option. (To choose the second option, mark Enter the Bills First and Then Enter the Payments Later, shown in Figure 1-4.)

Tip 7: Add accounts you need

As you step through the interview's questions, QuickBooks asks a few times whether you want to add an account (see Figure 1-5). Go ahead and do this — and feel comfortable doing so. Adding accounts isn't hard. (You need an account for each individual asset, liability, income, or expense amount you want to track.)

Figure 1-5: During the EasyStep Interview, QuickBooks asks whether you want to add accounts.

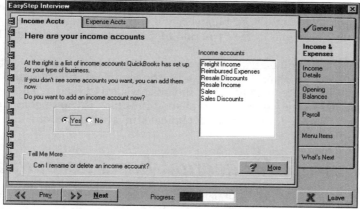

The Rest of the Story

The preceding discussions in this chapter describe how you prepare for and then step through the EasyStep Interview. But even after the EasyStep Interview is over, you probably need to take care of two other little jobs:

1. **If you want to use accrual-basis accounting, you need to make an adjustment.**

2. **You need to describe your current business finances.**

These chores aren't time-consuming, but they are the two most complicated tasks that you need to do to set up QuickBooks. (If you're not sure what the big deal is about accrual-basis accounting, I respectfully suggest that you take a break here and read Appendix B.)

Should you get your accountant's help?

Oh, shoot. I don't know. If you follow my directions carefully and your business's financial affairs are *not* wildly complex, I think that you can probably figure out all this stuff on your own. You don't have to be a rocket scientist.

That said, however, I suggest that you at least think about getting your accountant's help at this juncture. Your accountant can do a much better job of giving you advice that may be specific to your situation. The accountant probably knows your business and can keep you from making a terrible mess of things, just in case you don't follow my directions carefully.

By the way, if you do call upon your accountant to help you with the tasks in this chapter, bookmark the page with the technical stuff sidebar, "For accountants only," and ask your financial wizard to read it. The sidebar summarizes what you've accomplished thus far. (If you're going to do all this stuff yourself, reading the technical stuff sidebar is not a bad idea.)

Adjusting for accrual-basis accounting

If you want to use accrual-basis accounting — and I recommend that you do — you need to camouflage a couple of goofy accounts, called *suspense accounts,* that QuickBooks creates when you set up the Item, Customer, and Vendor Lists.

Figure 1-6 shows the example trial balance after I've entered the inventory, accounts receivable, and accounts payable balances. (These account balances get set up indirectly, as noted in the information for accountants. When you set up your Item, Customer, and Vendor Lists, you also create account balances for inventory, accounts receivable, and accounts payable.)

You can produce your own half-complete trial balance from inside QuickBooks by choosing Reports⇨Other Reports⇨Trial Balance. QuickBooks displays the trial balance report in a document window.

If you need to do so, enter the conversion date in the From and To date boxes by clicking these date boxes and typing the conversion date in MM/DD/YY fashion. Figure 1-6, for example, shows the conversion date 02/01/99 in both boxes. Make a note of the credit and debit balances shown for the Uncategorized Income and Uncategorized Expenses accounts.

If you want, you can print the report by clicking the Print button and then, when QuickBooks displays the Print Report dialog box, clicking its Print button. Yes, you click two Print buttons.

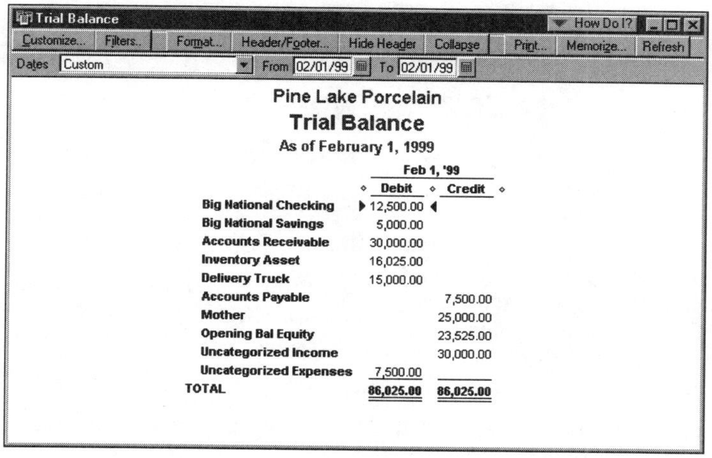

Pine Lake Porcelain

Trial Balance

As of February 1, 1999

	Feb 1, '99	
	Debit	Credit
Big National Checking	12,500.00	
Big National Savings	5,000.00	
Accounts Receivable	30,000.00	
Inventory Asset	16,025.00	
Delivery Truck	15,000.00	
Accounts Payable		7,500.00
Mother		25,000.00
Opening Bal Equity		23,525.00
Uncategorized Income		30,000.00
Uncategorized Expenses	7,500.00	
TOTAL	86,025.00	86,025.00

Figure 1-6: A sample trial balance.

After you have the conversion date balances for the Uncategorized Income and Uncategorized Expenses accounts, you're ready to make the accrual accounting adjustment. To do so, follow these steps:

1. **Display the Chart of Accounts window.**

   Click the Company tab of the QuickBooks Navigator, and then click the Chart of Accounts icon. QuickBooks displays the Chart of Accounts window, shown in Figure 1-7.

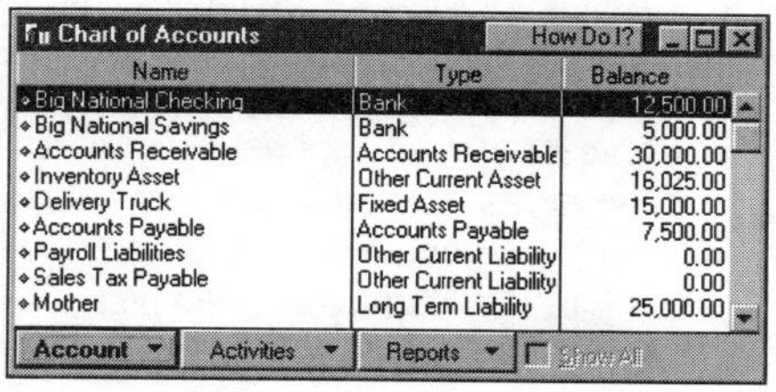

Name	Type	Balance
Big National Checking	Bank	12,500.00
Big National Savings	Bank	5,000.00
Accounts Receivable	Accounts Receivable	30,000.00
Inventory Asset	Other Current Asset	16,025.00
Delivery Truck	Fixed Asset	15,000.00
Accounts Payable	Accounts Payable	7,500.00
Payroll Liabilities	Other Current Liability	0.00
Sales Tax Payable	Other Current Liability	0.00
Mother	Long Term Liability	25,000.00

Figure 1-7: The Chart of Accounts window.

2. **Display the Opening Bal Equity account.**

   Scroll through the Chart of Accounts list until you see the account Opening Bal Equity. (It's after the liability accounts.) Double-click it. QuickBooks displays the *register* — just a list of transactions — for the account named Opening Bal Equity. Figure 1-8, coincidentally, shows this register.

TECHNICAL STUFF

For accountants only

If you're reading this sidebar, I assume that you're an accountant who has been asked to help your client with the last piece of the QuickBooks conversion. I also assume that you understand double-entry bookkeeping and that you're at least passingly familiar with the general mechanics involved in converting to new accounting systems. With those two caveats, you're ready to start.

First, your client has probably already installed QuickBooks and then, by running something called the EasyStep Interview, partially set up a chart of accounts and loaded three master files: the Item List, the Customer List, and the Vendor List. The Item List master file describes the inventory account balances. (QuickBooks uses an average costing assumption.) The Customer List master file describes the accounts receivable balances. The Vendor List master file describes the accounts payable balances. Because your client has set up these master files, QuickBooks has made three journal entries, as described in the following paragraphs. (I'm using *Xs* to represent numbers, in case you're not familiar with this convention.)

To set up the conversion date inventory balance (if inventory exists), QuickBooks has created the following entry:

	Debit	Credit
Inventory Asset	$X,XXX	
Opening Bal Equity		$X,XXX

To set up the conversion date accounts receivable (A/R) balance (if A/R exists), QuickBooks has created the following entry:

	Debit	Credit
Accounts Receivable	$X,XXX	
Uncategorized Income		$X,XXX

To set up the conversion date accounts payable (A/P) balance (if A/P exists), QuickBooks has created the following entry:

	Debit	Credit
Accounts Payable		$X,XXX
Uncategorized Expenses	$X,XXX	

To complete the picture, you need to do two little housekeeping chores. If your client plans to use accrual-basis accounting, you need to get rid of the credit to the Uncategorized Income account and the debit to the Uncategorized Expenses account. (These two accounts are really just suspense accounts.) And you need to load the rest of the trial balance. The steps for accomplishing these tasks are described later in this chapter.

3. **If it isn't already selected — and it probably is — select the next empty row of the register.**

   You can select a row by clicking it, or you can use the up- or down-arrow key to move to the next empty row.

4. **Enter the conversion date in the Date field.**

   Move the cursor to the Date field (if it isn't already there) and type the date. Use the MM/DD/YY format. For example, you can type either **020199** or **2/1/99** to enter February 1, 1999.

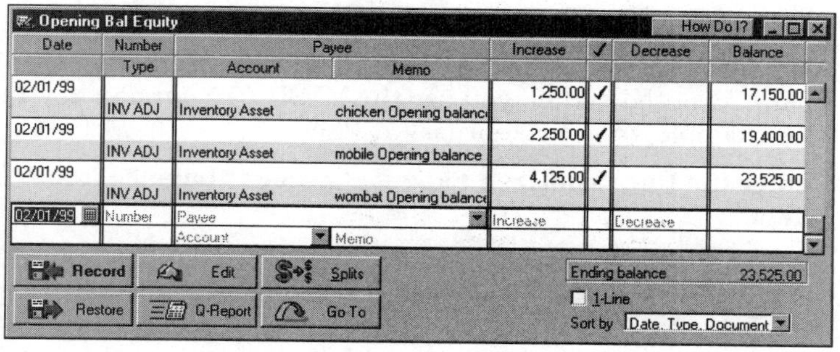

Figure 1-8:
The
Opening Bal
Equity
register.

5. **Enter the Uncategorized Income account balance (from the trial balance report) in the Increase field.**

   In Figure 1-6, for example, the Uncategorized Income account balance is $30,000. In this case, click the Increase field and type **30000** in the field. (You don't need to include the dollar sign or the comma; QuickBooks adds the punctuation for you.)

6. **Type the account name,** Uncategorized Income, **in the Account field.**

   Select the Account field, which is on the row under the word Payee, and begin typing Uncategorized Income, the account name. As soon as you type enough of the name for QuickBooks to figure out what you're typing, it fills in the rest of the name for you. When this happens, you can stop typing. Figure 1-9 shows the Opening Bal Equity register with this Uncategorized Income transaction entered.

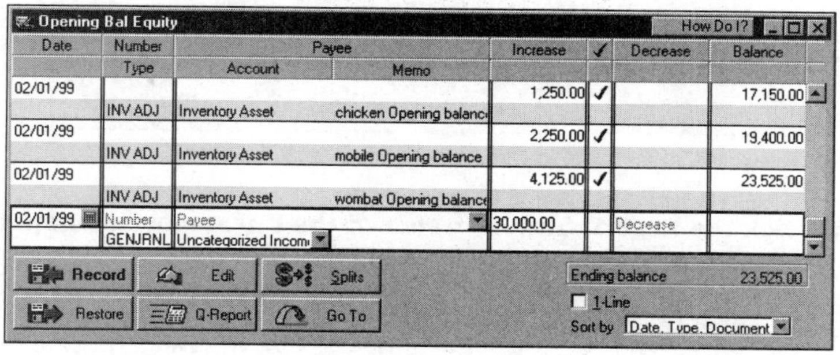

Figure 1-9:
The
transaction
that fixes
the
Uncategorized
Income
account
balance.

7. **Click the Record button to record the Uncategorized Income adjustment transaction.**

8. **Again, select the next empty row of the register.**

   Click it or use the up- or down-arrow key.

9. **Enter the conversion date in the Date field.**

Move the cursor to the Date field (if it isn't already there) and type the date. As noted earlier, you use the MM/DD/YY format. You type 2/1/99, for example, to enter February 1, 1999.

10. **Enter the Uncategorized Expenses account balance in the Decrease field.**

In Figure 1-6, for example, the Uncategorized Expenses account balance is $7,500. In this case, you click the Decrease field and then type **7500** in the field. I've said this before, but I'll say it again because you're just starting out: You don't need to include any punctuation, such as dollar signs.

11. **Type the account name,** Uncategorized Expenses, **in the Account field.**

Select the Account field, which is on the second line of the register transaction, and begin typing Uncategorized Expenses, the account name. As soon as you type enough of the name for QuickBooks to figure out what you're typing, it fills in the rest of the name for you. When this happens, you can stop typing. Figure 1-10 shows the Opening Bal Equity register with this Uncategorized Expenses transaction entered.

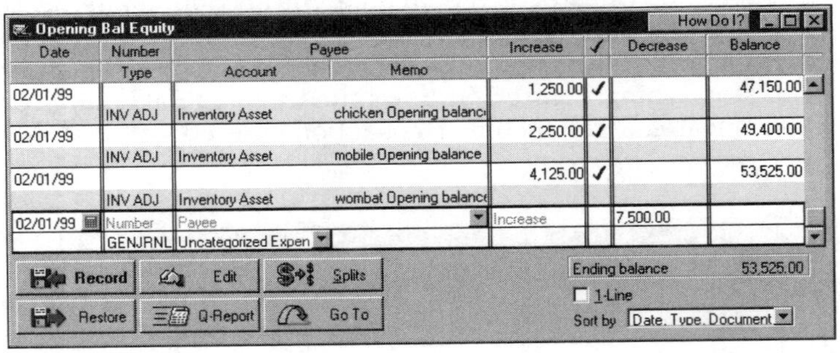

Figure 1-10:
The transaction that fixes the Uncategorized Expenses account balance.

Date	Number	Payee		Increase	✓	Decrease	Balance
	Type	Account	Memo				
02/01/99				1,250.00	✓		47,150.00
	INV ADJ	Inventory Asset	chicken Opening balance				
02/01/99				2,250.00	✓		49,400.00
	INV ADJ	Inventory Asset	mobile Opening balance				
02/01/99				4,125.00	✓		53,525.00
	INV ADJ	Inventory Asset	wombat Opening balance				
02/01/99	Number	Payee		Increase		7,500.00	
	GENJRNL	Uncategorized Expen					

Ending balance 53,525.00

12. **Click the Record button to record the Uncategorized Expenses adjustment transaction.**

You can close the Opening Bal Equity register, too, at this point. You're finished with it. (One way to close it is to click the Close button — this is the little button with an "X" in the upper-right corner of the register window.)

You can check your work thus far — and checking it is a good idea — by producing another copy of the trial balance report. What you want to check are the Uncategorized Income and Uncategorized Expenses account balances. They should both be zero — as evidenced by the fact that neither account shows up in the trial balance — as shown in Figure 1-11.

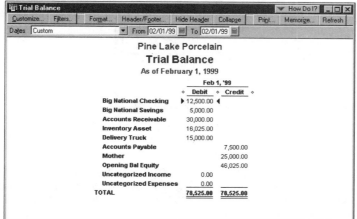

Figure 1-11:
Another
sample trial
balance.

As you may remember, you can produce a trial balance by choosing Reports⇨Other Reports⇨Trial Balance. QuickBooks displays the trial balance report in a document window. If you need to enter the conversion date in the From and To date boxes, click the boxes and type the conversion date in MM/DD/YY fashion in both boxes. Figure 1-11, for example, shows the conversion date 02/01/99 in both boxes.

If the Uncategorized Income and the Uncategorized Expenses account balances don't show zero, it means that you (with my help, of course) botched the accrual adjustment. To fix the mistake, redisplay the Opening Bal Equity register, select the adjustment transactions, and then check the account, amount, and field (increase or decrease). If one of the fields is wrong, select the field and then replace its contents by typing over them.

Supplying the missing numbers

You're almost done. Really. Your only other task is to enter the rest of the trial balance into QuickBooks. To perform this task, of course, you need to already have a trial balance as of the conversion date. But you should have one. (I talked about this earlier in the chapter, remember?) Follow these steps:

1. **Display the General Journal Entry window.**

   Click the Taxes and Accountant tab of the QuickBooks Navigator, and then click the Make Journal Entry icon. QuickBooks displays the General Journal Entry window, shown in Figure 1-12.

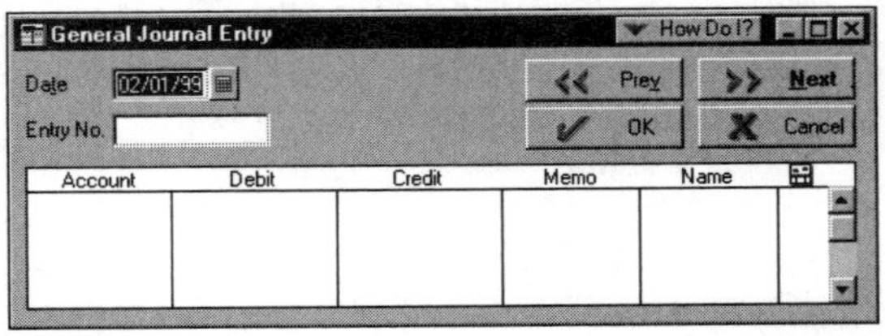

Figure 1-12:
The empty
General
Journal
Entry
window.

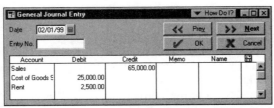

2. **Enter the conversion date.**

   Move the cursor to the Date field (if it isn't already there) and type the date. As you may know by now, you use the MM/DD/YY format. For example, you type 2/1/99 for February 1, 1999. (Or 020199, if you don't want to put the slashes in.)

3. **Enter each trial balance account and balance that isn't already in the half-completed trial balance.**

   Okay. This step sounds confusing. But remember that you already entered your cash, accounts receivable, inventory, and accounts payable account balances, as well as most other liability account balances and a portion of the Opening Bal Equity account balance as part of the EasyStep Interview. So what you need to do now is enter the rest of the trial balance: specifically, the year-to-date income and expense account balances and the remaining portion of the Opening Bal Equity. To enter each account and balance, use a row of the General Journal Entry window's list box. Figure 1-13 shows how this window looks after you enter the rest of the trial balance into the list box rows.

Figure 1-13:
The
completed
General
Journal
Entry
window.

4. **Click OK to record the general journal entries that set up the rest of your trial balance.**

Checking your work one more time

Checking your work again is a good idea. Produce another copy of the trial balance report. What you want to check is that the QuickBooks trial balance is the same one that you want to enter.

Remember that you can produce a trial balance by choosing Reports⇨Other Reports⇨Trial Balance. Be sure to enter the conversion date in the From and To date boxes. If the QuickBooks trial balance report agrees with what your records show, you're finished.

If the QuickBooks trial balance doesn't agree with what your records show, you need to fix the problem. Fixing it is a bit awkward, but it's not complicated. Choose Reports⇨Other Reports⇨Journal. QuickBooks displays a report or journal that lists all the transactions that you or QuickBooks has entered as part of setting up. (The Dates, From, and To text boxes need to specify the conversion date.) Scroll through the list of transactions until you get to the last one. The last transaction is the one that you entered to set up the rest of the trial balance, and it names recognizable accounts and uses familiar debit and credit amounts. Double-click this transaction. QuickBooks redisplays the General Journal Entry window with the botched transaction. Find the mistake and then fix the erroneous account or amount by clicking it and typing the correct account or amount.

Congratulations! You're done.

Chapter 2

Lots of Lists

● ●

In This Chapter

▶ Adding items to the Item list

▶ Adding employees to the Employee list

▶ Adding new customers and jobs

▶ Adding new vendors

▶ Understanding and using the other lists

● ●

*I*f you just finished going through the EasyStep Interview (see Chapter 1), don't look at the title of this chapter and think to yourself that you're ready to throw in the towel because you're sick and tired of creating lists. As a matter of fact, if you just finished the EasyStep Interview and carefully entered the names of all your products, employees, customers, and vendors into lists, you can kick up your heels and relax because you probably don't even need to read this chapter just yet. The lists that you need are already set up. But as time goes by, I bet you anything that you find that your lists need updating. With any luck, you get a new customer or two and maybe a new vendor. You may even hire a new employee. This chapter describes how you add to the lists you created in the EasyStep Interview.

The QuickBooks Navigator is a great little tool that enables you to easily access the features that you use most in QuickBooks. To make moving around in QuickBooks simple for you, I use the QuickBooks Navigator as my starting point whenever I describe how to go somewhere in QuickBooks. So you need to keep in mind, as you go along, how to get to the Navigator from wherever you're working. Getting to the Navigator is really quite simple — to view the QuickBooks Navigator if it isn't already displayed in the middle of your screen, all you have to do is click the QB Navigator button in the upper-right corner of the application window.

The Magic and Mystery of Items

Before you start adding to your Item list, I need to tell you that QuickBooks isn't very smart about its view of what you sell. It thinks that anything you stick on a sales invoice or a purchase order is something you're selling.

If you sell blue, yellow, and red coffee mugs, for example, you probably figure (and correctly so) that you need to add descriptions of each of these items to the Item list: blue mug, yellow mug, and red mug. But if you add freight charges to an invoice, QuickBooks thinks that you're adding another mug. And if you add sales tax to an invoice, well, guess what? QuickBooks again thinks that you're adding another mug.

This wacky definition of items is confusing at first. But just remember one thing, and you'll be okay: You aren't the one who's stupid. QuickBooks is. No, I'm not saying that QuickBooks is a bad program. It's a wonderful accounting program and a great tool. What I'm saying is that QuickBooks is only a dumb computer program. It's not an artificial intelligence program. It doesn't pick up on the little subtleties of business — such as the fact that, even though you charge customers for freight, you're not really in the shipping business.

Each entry on the invoice or purchase order — the mugs you sell, the subtotal, the discount, the freight charges, and the sales tax — is an *item*. Yes, I know. This setup is weird. But getting used to the wackiness now makes the discussions that follow much easier to understand. (If you want to see a sample invoice, take a peek at Figure 2-1.)

Creating invoices is described in Chapter 4. Creating purchase orders is described in Chapter 7.

Adding items you may include on invoices

To add invoice or purchase order items to the Item list, follow these steps:

1. **Click the Sales and Customers tab of the QuickBooks Navigator, and then click the Items & Services icon.**

   QuickBooks, with restrained but obvious enthusiasm, displays the Item List window (see Figure 2-2).

2. **Click the Item button in the Item List window and choose New from the drop-down menu.**

   QuickBooks displays the New Item window (see Figure 2-3).

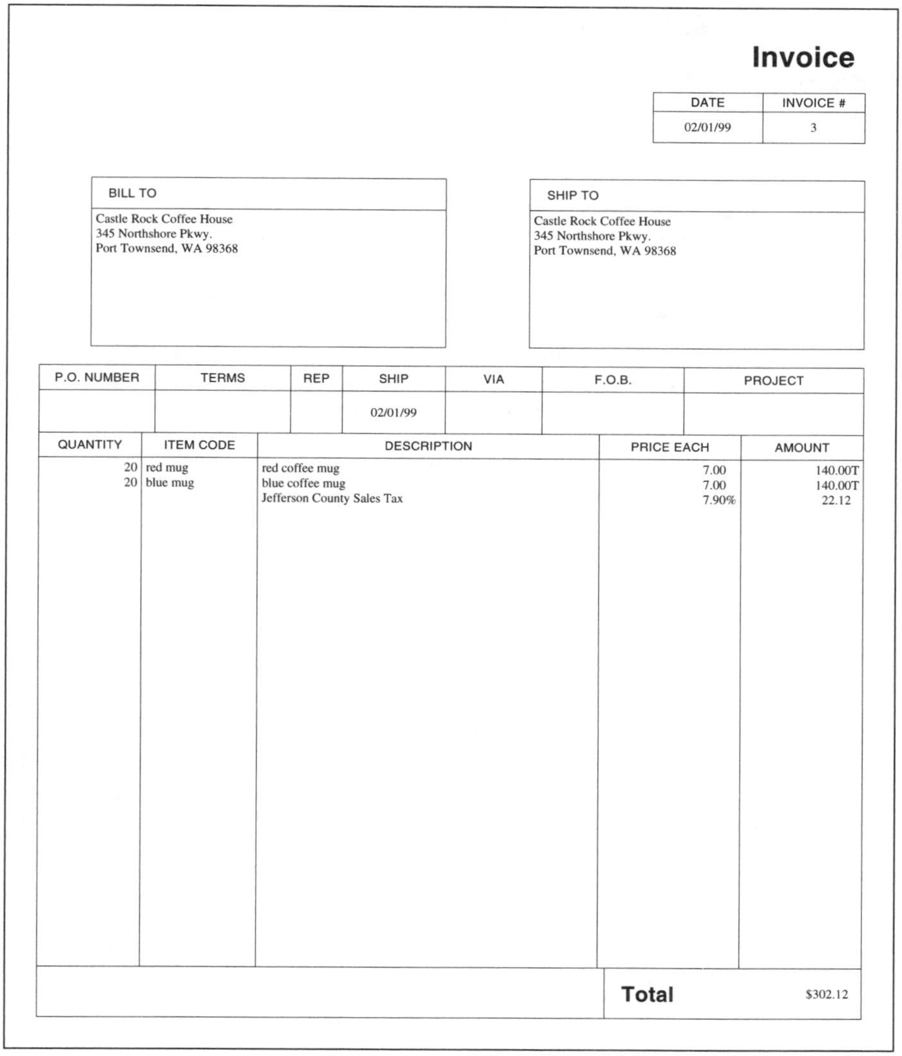

Invoice

DATE	INVOICE #
02/01/99	3

BILL TO

Castle Rock Coffee House
345 Northshore Pkwy.
Port Townsend, WA 98368

SHIP TO

Castle Rock Coffee House
345 Northshore Pkwy.
Port Townsend, WA 98368

P.O. NUMBER	TERMS	REP	SHIP	VIA	F.O.B.	PROJECT
			02/01/99			

QUANTITY	ITEM CODE	DESCRIPTION	PRICE EACH	AMOUNT
20	red mug	red coffee mug	7.00	140.00T
20	blue mug	blue coffee mug	7.00	140.00T
		Jefferson County Sales Tax	7.90%	22.12

	Total	$302.12

Figure 2-1:
A sample
invoice
form.

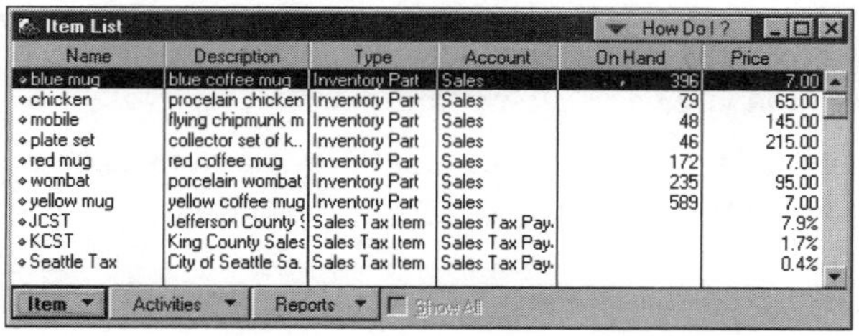

Figure 2-2:
The Item
List
window.

	Item List		▼ How Do I ?	_ □ ×
Name	Description	Type	Account	On Hand	Price
◆ blue mug	blue coffee mug	Inventory Part	Sales	396	7.00
◆ chicken	procelain chicken	Inventory Part	Sales	79	65.00
◆ mobile	flying chipmunk m	Inventory Part	Sales	48	145.00
◆ plate set	collector set of k..	Inventory Part	Sales	46	215.00
◆ red mug	red coffee mug	Inventory Part	Sales	172	7.00
◆ wombat	porcelain wombat	Inventory Part	Sales	235	95.00
◆ yellow mug	yellow coffee mug	Inventory Part	Sales	589	7.00
◆ JCST	Jefferson County S	Sales Tax Item	Sales Tax Pay-		7.9%
◆ KCST	King County Sales	Sales Tax Item	Sales Tax Pay-		1.7%
◆ Seattle Tax	City of Seattle Sa.	Sales Tax Item	Sales Tax Pay-		0.4%

Item ▼	Activities ▼	Reports ▼	□ Show All

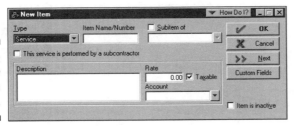

Figure 2-3:
The New
Item
window.

3. **Categorize the item.**

Select an item type from the Type drop-down list box. The Item list you see is dependent upon the type of business you told QuickBooks you were in when you set up the program, so use the following as a sample — the amount and type of items you need depend on the business you're in. Select one of the following item types by clicking the name in the list:

- **Service:** Select this type if you charge for a service — such as an hour of labor or a repair job.

- **Inventory Part:** Select this type if what you sell is something that you buy from someone else. If you sell thingamajigs that you purchase from the manufacturer Thingamajigs Amalgamated, for example, you specify the item type as Inventory Part. (For more information on using QuickBooks to track inventory, see Chapter 7.)

- **Non-inventory Part:** Select this type if what you sell is something that you don't want to track as inventory. (You usually don't use this item type for products that you sell, by the way. Instead, you use it for items that you buy for the business and need to include on purchase orders.)

- **Other Charge:** Select this item type for things such as freight and handling charges that you include on invoices.

- **Subtotal:** This item type adds everything up before you subtract any discount, add the sales tax, and so on.

- **Group:** Use this item type to enter a bunch of items (which are already on the list) at one time. For example, Subtotal and Sales Tax Items appear on every invoice if you charge sales tax. By using Group, you don't have to specify those items individually every time you write an invoice.

- **Discount:** This item type calculates an amount to be subtracted from a subtotal.

- **Payment:** This option is wacky, but if your invoice sometimes includes an entry that reduces the invoice total — customer deposits, for example — select this item type. If you're confused by this item type, just ignore it.

- **Sales Tax Item:** Select this item type for the sales tax that you include on the invoice.

- **Sales Tax Group:** This item type is similar to the Group item type, but you use it only for sales taxes that always appear on the same invoice. It's a very nice time-saver.

4. **Enter an item number or name.**

   Press the Tab key or use your mouse to click the text box to the right of the Type drop-down list box. (The name of the text box changes, depending on the item type.) Then enter a short description of the item.

5. **(Optional) Make the item a subitem.**

   If you want to work with *subitems* — items that appear within other items — check the Subitem Of check box and use the corresponding drop-down list box to specify the parent item to which a subitem belongs. If you set up a parent item for coffee mugs and subitems for blue, yellow, and red mugs, for example, you can produce reports that show parent items (such as mugs) or subitems (such as the different-colored mugs). Subitems are just an extra complexity, so if you're new to this QuickBooks stuff, I suggest that you keep things simple by avoiding them.

6. **Describe the item in more detail.**

   Move the cursor to the Description text box and type a description. This description then appears on the invoice. Note that if you specify the item type as Inventory Part, you see two description text boxes: Description on Purchase Transactions, and Description on Sales Transactions. The purchase description appears on purchase orders, and the sales description appears on sales invoices.

7. **If the item type is Service, Non-Inventory Part, or Other Charge, tell QuickBooks how much to charge for the item, whether the item is taxable for sales tax purposes, and which income account to use for tracking the income that you receive from selling the item.**

   - For a Service type, use the Rate text box to specify the price you charge for one unit of the service. If you charge by the hour, for example, the rate is the charge for an hour of service. If you charge for a job — such as a repair job or the completion of a specific task — the rate is the charge for the job or task.

- For a Non-Inventory Part type, use the Price text box to specify the amount you charge for the item.

- For an Other Charge type, use the Amount or % text box, which replaces the Rate text box, to specify the amount you charge for the item. You can enter an amount, such as "20 for $20.00," or you can enter a percentage. If you enter a percentage, QuickBooks calculates the Other Charge Amount as the percentage multiplied by the preceding item shown on the invoice. (You usually put in an Other Charge after using a Subtotal Item — something I talk about later in this chapter.)

- For all three types, use the Taxable check box to indicate whether the item is taxed. (Note that the Taxable check box only appears if you told QuickBooks in the EasyStep Interview that you charge customers sales tax.)

- For all three types, use the Account drop-down list to specify which income account you want to use to track the income that you receive from the sale of this item.

8. **If the item type is Inventory Part, tell QuickBooks how much to charge for the inventory part, how much the inventory part costs, and which income account to use for tracking the product sales income.**

   For an Inventory Part item type, QuickBooks displays the New Item window, shown in Figure 2-4.

Figure 2-4:
The New Item window that QuickBooks displays when the item type is Inventory Part.

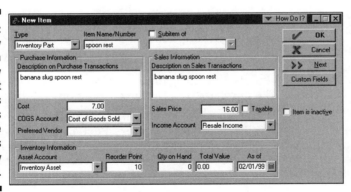

You use the extra fields that this special version of the window displays to record the following information:

- **Description on Purchase Transactions:** Describe the part. This description appears on the documents (such as purchase orders) used when you buy items for your inventory.

- **Cost:** Specify the average cost per unit of the items you currently have.

- **COGS (Cost of Goods Sold) Account:** Specify the account you want QuickBooks to use for tracking this item's cost when you sell it. (QuickBooks may fill in this field for you if you currently have only one Cost of Goods Sold account on the chart of accounts.)

- **Preferred Vendor:** Specify your first choice when ordering the item for your business. (If the vendor is not on your Vendor list, QuickBooks asks you to add it, either through the QuickAdd option or the more detailed Set Up option. Your decision depends on either the detail in which you plan to use QuickBooks or whether you're trying to make an appointment that was scheduled for 10 minutes ago.)

- **Description on Sales Transactions:** Type in a description of the item that you want to appear on documents, such as invoices and so on, that are seen by your customers. (QuickBooks may suggest the same description you used in the Description on Purchase Transactions text box as a default.)

- **Sales Price:** Enter the amount that you charge for the item.

- **Taxable:** Indicate whether the item is taxed.

- **Income Account:** Specify the account that you want QuickBooks to use for tracking the income from the sale of the part. This will probably be the Resale Income or Sales account. You typically use the Resale Income account to track wholesale (non-taxable) sales and the Sales account to track retail (taxable) sales.

- **Asset Account:** Specify the other current asset account that you want QuickBooks to use for tracking this inventory item's value.

- **Reorder Point:** Specify the lowest inventory quantity of this item that can remain before you order more. When the inventory level drops to this quantity, QuickBooks displays the Reminders window to remind you that you need to reorder the item.

- **Qty on Hand:** Leave this field at zero. To enter a number now is to record an uncategorized transaction, and you don't want to do that. (I cover uncategorized transactions in Chapter 1.)

- **Total Value:** Leave this field at zero, too.

- **As Of:** Enter the current date.

9. **If the item type is Sales Tax Item, tell QuickBooks what sales tax rate to charge and what government agency to pay.**

   If the item type is Sales Tax Item, QuickBooks displays the New Item window shown in Figure 2-5. You use this version of the New Item window to record the following information:

- **Tax Name** and **Description:** Specify further details for later identification.

- **Rate:** Specify the sales tax rate as a percentage.

- **Tax Agency:** Name the state or local tax agency that gets all the loot you collect.

Figure 2-5:
The New
Item
window for
the Sales
Tax Item.

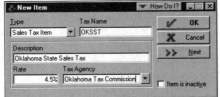

10. **If the item type is Payment, describe the payment method and how you want QuickBooks to handle the payment.**

    If you're setting up a Payment item, you see a Payment Method drop-down list box. After you name and describe the payment item, you use the Payment Method drop-down list to specify the method of payment. QuickBooks provides a starting list of several of the usual payment methods. (Activate the Payment Method drop-down list box to see the list.) You can easily add more payment types by choosing <Add New> from the drop-down list box. When you choose this entry, QuickBooks displays the New Payment Method dialog box. In the dialog box's only text box, identify the payment method: cows, beads, shells, or some other what-have-you.

    After you're finished, use the area in the lower-left corner of the New Item window to either group the payment with other undeposited funds or, if you use the drop-down list box, deposit the payment to a specific account.

11. **Click OK or Next when you're finished.**

    When you finish describing one item, click OK to add the item to the list and return to the Item List window. Click Next to add the item to the list and keep the New Item window displayed on your screen so that you can add more items.

12. **If you added a new Inventory item, record the purchase of the item.**

    After you've finished describing any new inventory items, you need to make another transaction in order to categorize the purchase of the items (unless they just showed up one morning on your doorstep). For an explanation of these transactions, turn to Chapter 7.

Creating other wacky items for invoices

The preceding discussion does not describe all the items that you can add. Some lines on invoices are actually calculations. For example, an invoice usually shows a subtotal of the items already listed. (You usually need this subtotal when you want to calculate a sales tax on the invoice's items.) The invoice also may contain other wacky items, such as discounts. The next few paragraphs describe these special types of items.

Creating subtotal items to stick subtotals on invoices

You need to add a subtotal item if you ever want to apply a discount to a series of items on an invoice. To add a subtotal item to your Item list, click the Sales and Customers tab of the QuickBooks Navigator, click the Items & Services icon, and then click the Item button and choose New from the drop-down menu. This displays the New Item window — the same one you've seen several times already in this chapter. Specify the item type as Subtotal and then provide an item name (such as "Subtotal").

When you want to subtotal items on an invoice, all you do is stick this subtotal item on the invoice after the items you want to subtotal. Keep in mind, though, that QuickBooks doesn't set up a subtotal feature automatically — you have to add a subtotal item; otherwise, you can only apply a discount item you create to the single item that immediately precedes the discount.

Creating group items to batch stuff you sell together

You can create an item that puts one line on an invoice that's actually a combination of several other items. If you purchase three inventory parts — a blue mug, a red mug, and a yellow mug — but sell the items in a set, for example, you can create an item that groups the other three items.

To add a group item, display the New Item window and specify the item type as Group. QuickBooks displays the New Item window shown in Figure 2-6. Use the Item/Description/Qty list box to list each item included in the group. When you click an item line in the Item/Description/Qty list box, QuickBooks places a downward-pointing arrow at the right end of the Item column. You click this arrow to open a drop-down list of items. (If the list is longer than can be shown, you can use the scroll bar on the right to move up and down the list.) If you click the Print Items in Group check box, QuickBooks lists all the items in the group on invoices. (In the case of the mugs, invoices would list the individual blue, red, and yellow mugs instead of just listing the group name, such as "mug set.")

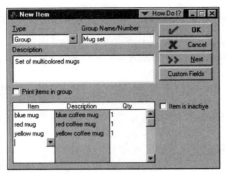

Figure 2-6:
The New
Item
window for
the Group
Item.

Creating discount items to add discounts to invoices

You can create an item that calculates a discount and sticks the discount on
an invoice as another line item. To add a discount item to the list, display
the New Item window, specify the item type as Discount, and provide an
item name or number and a description.

Use the Amount or % text box to specify how the discount is calculated. If
the discount is a set amount (such as $50.00), enter an amount. If the
discount is calculated as a percentage, enter the percentage, including the
percent symbol. When you enter a percentage, QuickBooks calculates the
Discount amount as the percentage multiplied by the preceding item shown
on the invoice. (If you want to apply the discount to a group of items, you
need to use a subtotal item and follow it with the discount.)

Use the Account drop-down list to specify the expense account that you
want to use to track the cost of the discounts you offer.

Click Apply Discount Before Taxes if you want to use this option. (This
option appears only if you indicated in the EasyStep Interview that you
charge sales tax.) If you need to collect sales tax and you didn't set this
function up in the EasyStep Interview, click the Company tab of the
QuickBooks Navigator and then click the Preferences icon. Click the Sales
Tax icon from the list on the left and mark the Yes option button in the Do
You Charge Sales Tax? area. (If you set up the QuickBooks file for multiple
users, this option is on the Company Preferences tab.) Then add the sales
tax item(s) to your Item List.

Creating Sales Tax Group items to batch sales taxes together

Sales Tax Groups enable you to batch several sales taxes that you're supposed to charge as one sales tax so that they appear as a single sales tax on
the invoice. Combining the taxes is necessary — or at least possible — when
you're supposed to charge, say, a 6.5 percent state sales tax, a 1.7 percent
county sales tax, and a 0.4 percent city sales tax, but you want to show one,
all-encompassing 8.6 percent sales tax on the invoice.

To add a Sales Tax Group item, display the New Item window and specify the item type as Sales Tax Group. QuickBooks displays the New Item window, shown in Figure 2-7. Use the Tax Item/Rate/Tax Agency/Description list box to list the other sales tax items that you want to include in the group. When you click an item line in the list box, QuickBooks places a down arrow at the right end of the Tax Item column. You can click this arrow to open a drop-down list of Sales Tax items.

Figure 2-7:
The New Item window for the Sales Tax Group Item.

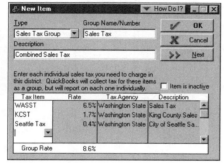

Editing items

If you make a mistake, you can change any piece of item information by displaying the Item List window and double-clicking the item so that QuickBooks displays the Edit Item window. You then can use the Edit Item window to make changes.

Adding Employees to Your Employee List

If you do payroll in QuickBooks or if you track sales by employees, you need to describe each employee. Describing employees is pretty dang easy. Click the Company tab of the QuickBooks Navigator and click the Employees icon to display the Employee List window, shown in Figure 2-8. Then click the Employee button and choose New from the drop-down menu to have QuickBooks display the New Employee window, shown in Figure 2-9.

Figure 2-8:
The Employee List window.

See Figure 2-9? It's pretty straightforward, right? You just fill in the fields to describe the employee.

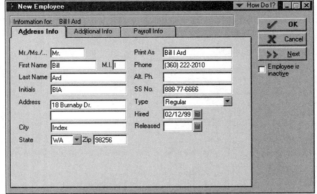

Figure 2-9:
The
Address
Info tab of
the New
Employee
window.

Lesser computer book writers would probably provide step-by-step descriptions of how you move the cursor to the First Name text box and enter the person's first name, how you move the cursor to the next text box, enter something there, and so on. Not me. No way. I know that you can tell just by looking at this window that all you do is click a text box and type the obvious bit of information. Right?

Note that QuickBooks automatically types the employee's initials in the Initials text box. When you later describe your customers, you can use employee initials to identify the sales representatives assigned to them.

Note, too, that you can include the information shown in Figure 2-10 by clicking the Payroll Info tab. Again, what you need to do in this tab is fairly straightforward. The Additional Info tab enables you to create customizable fields, in case you want to keep information that isn't covered by the QuickBooks default fields — favorite color and that type of thing.

After you finish describing an employee, click OK to add the employee to the list and return to the Employee List window. Or click Next to add the employee to the list but leave the New Employee window displayed on the screen so that you can add more employees.

You can also inactivate an employee from your list if it starts to get cluttered with names of employees who may not work for you very often. Read about inactivating items, employees, customers, and vendors in the sidebar "Inactivating list items" later in this chapter.

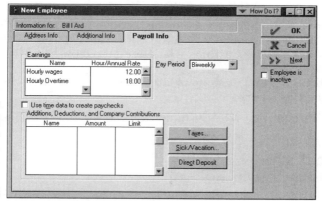

Figure 2-10:
The New
Employee
Payroll Info
tab.

Customers Are Your Business

This is sort of off the subject, but I read about a survey that some business school had done. In the survey, people who wanted to start a business were asked what is the most important thing that a person needs to start a business. Almost all of them answered, "Cash." The same survey also asked a large number of people who had already started businesses — many of whom had been running their businesses successfully for years — what is the most important thing that a person needs to start a business. They all answered, "Customers."

Inactivating list items

One of the neat features in QuickBooks is that it lets you simplify your lists by hiding items that are no longer active, including those that you expect to be active again later. If you have seasonal employees, you can hide them from your Employee list for the times of the year when they don't work. Or if you sell commemorative keychains only every five years, you can keep them from cluttering your Item list in the off years. You can also inactivate customers and vendors from their respective lists.

To inactivate something from a list, all you have to do is open the list and double-click the item. When QuickBooks opens the item,

employee, customer, or vendor that you want to inactivate, check the Item Is Inactive box (the name of the box changes, depending on what you're trying to inactivate). Then click OK. QuickBooks hides this member from your list. The next time you display the list, the Show All box appears.

To view and edit hidden members of your list, just click the Show All box. Any inactive members show up with little ghost figures beside them. If you want to reactivate a member, all you have to do is click the ghost figure, and the member is reactivated.

Weird, huh? I do think that those survey results are true, though. You need customers to get into business. Everything else — including cash — is secondary. But I've sort of gotten off the track. I'm supposed to be describing how you add to your Customer List. Here's the blow-by-blow:

1. **Click the Sales and Customers tab of the QuickBooks Navigator and click the Customers icon.**

   QuickBooks displays the Customer:Job List window (see Figure 2-11).

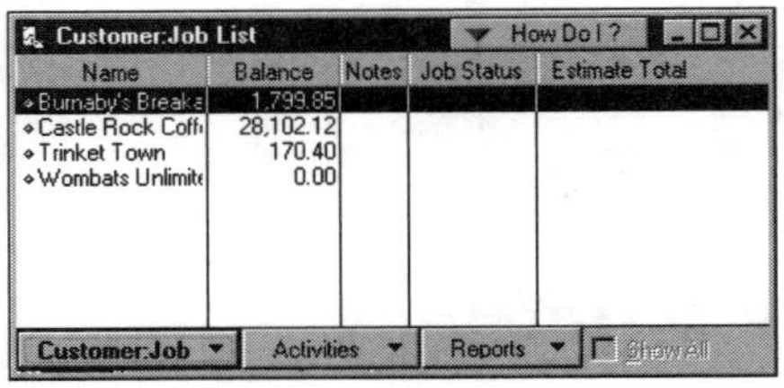

Figure 2-11: The Customer: Job List window.

2. **Click the Customer:Job button and choose New from the drop-down menu.**

   QuickBooks displays the Address Info tab of the New Customer window (see Figure 2-12). Use this window to describe the customer in as much detail as possible.

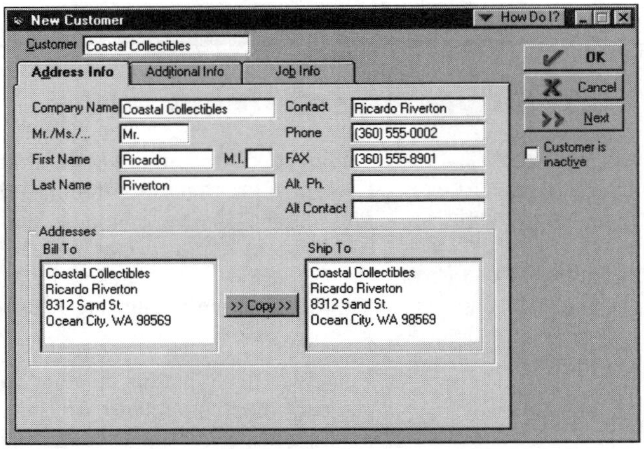

Figure 2-12: The Address Info tab of the New Customer window.

3. **Give the customer's name.**

This step is pretty obvious, right? The cursor is already in the Customer text box. All you have to do is type the customer's name. Hunt, peck, hunt, peck, hunt, peck. If you make a mistake, use Backspace to backspace over or erase your mistake.

4. **Give the company name.**

That's right, type the customer's company name.

5. **(Optional) Give the name of your contact, along with other pertinent information.**

Move the cursor to the Mr./Ms. text box and type the appropriate title. Same with the First Name, M.I., and Last Name text boxes. (QuickBooks automatically types the names into the Contact text box as you type them. Nice touch, eh?)

Go ahead and fill in the Phone, FAX, and Alt. Ph. (alternate phone) text boxes while you're at it.

6. **(Really optional) Give the name of your alternate contact.**

Move the cursor to the Alt. Contact text box and type the name of the alternate contact.

7. **Give the billing address.**

You can use the Bill To text box to provide the customer's billing address. QuickBooks copies the Customer name to the first line of the billing address, so you probably need to enter only the address. To move from the end of one line to the start of the next, press Enter.

8. **Give the shipping address.**

You can use the Ship To text box to provide the customer's shipping address if this address differs from the Bill To address. (If it's the same, just click Copy.) You enter this information in the same way that you enter the Bill To address. A few deft mouse clicks. Some typing. You're done.

9. **Click the Additional Info tab.**

If you don't, you'll wonder where in the world is the rest of the stuff I'm talking about. Your screen changes to look like Figure 2-13. Enter an account number (or name, as the case may be) in the Account text box.

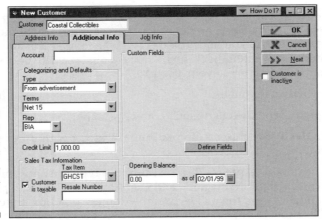

Figure 2-13:
The
Additional
Info tab of
the New
Customer
window.

10. (Massively optional) Categorize the customer.

See that Type drop-down list box? You can use it to assign the customer a particular type. If you want to add to your list of customer types, choose <Add New> from the drop-down list (so QuickBooks displays the New Customer Type dialog box) and then fill in the dialog box blanks. If you have some clever scheme you want to use for categorizing customers, hey, be my guest. If not, don't worry about the customer type.

11. Specify the payment terms that you want the customer to observe.

Did I say "observe"? I guess that word's not really accurate, is it? You want the customer to do more than just observe, by golly. You want the customer to honor the terms. To specify the payment terms, activate the Terms drop-down list and click one of its terms. QuickBooks has already set up all the usual terms. (If you want to, you can choose <Add New> to set up additional payment terms.)

12. (Optional) Name the sales representative.

QuickBooks lets you assign each customer to a sales representative by clicking the sales representative's initials from the Rep drop-down list. (To activate the Rep drop-down list box, click the down arrow at the right end of the Rep box.)

13. (Optional) Specify the customer's credit limit, if you've set one.

Move the cursor to the Credit Limit field. Hmmm. I know. How about clicking it? Then type the credit limit. (The *credit limit,* as you probably know, is just a record of the amount of credit that you've decided to extend to the customer.) QuickBooks helps you track this amount by monitoring the customer's remaining credit limit and alerting you when the customer reaches the limit. If you leave this field blank, QuickBooks figures that you don't care about this customer's limit and so ignores the credit limit.

14. **Identify the sales tax item that you use to track the sales taxes that you collect and later pay.**

    Activate the Tax Item drop-down list and click the sales tax item that you use to calculate sales tax on sales to this customer.

15. **Store the resale number, if you're supposed to do so.**

    If you're supposed to collect resale certificate numbers for customers who don't pay sales tax, move the cursor to the Resale Number text box and enter the number.

16. **Indicate whether the customer is taxable.**

    Click the Customer Is Taxable check box if the customer is, well, taxable.

17. **Enter the Opening Balance as zero.**

    If you enter an amount in this text box, it shows up later as an uncategorized transaction. What you need to do is enter the opening balance as zero and then bill the customer and categorize the sale in another transaction. (See Chapter 4.)

18. **Enter the date on which you created an account for the customer.**

    Move the cursor to the As Of field and enter the date you began doing business with the customer.

19. **(Optional) Add specific job information.**

    Because you're creating a new customer account, not invoicing by jobs, I'll wait and explain this step in the next section. If you're the "can't-wait" type, feel free to take a look. You can add a specific job to the new customer's information.

20. **Save the customer information.**

    When you finish describing a customer, click OK to add the customer to the list and return to the Customer:Job List window. Or click Next to add the customer to the list and keep the New Customer window displayed on the screen so that you can add more customers.

If you want to change some bit of customer information, display the Customer:Job List window, double-click the customer account you want to change, and then make changes using the Edit Customer window.

It's Just a Job

In QuickBooks, you can track invoices by customer or by customer and job. Doing so sounds kooky, I know, but tracking invoices makes sense in businesses that invoice customers, often several times, for specific jobs.

The little things do, too, matter

If you're not familiar with how payment terms work, you can get a bird's-eye view here. For the most part, payment terms just tell the customer how quickly you expect to be paid. At the bottom of the invoice is a phrase that states the payment terms. For example, *Net Due Upon Receipt* means that you expect to be paid as soon as possible. If Net is followed by some number, as in *Net 15* or *Net 30,* the number indicates the number of days after the invoice date within which the customer is supposed to pay. So Net 15 means that the customer is supposed to pay within 15 days of the invoice date.

Some payment terms, such as *2% 10 Net 30,* include early payment discounts. The percentage and first number indicate that the customer can deduct the percentage from the payment if the payment is made within the first number of days. The payment term *2% 10 Net 30* means that the customer can deduct 2 percent from the bill if it's paid within 10 days and the customer must pay the bill within 30 days. For more information on how to make early payment discounts work for you, see Chapter 18.

Take the case of a construction subcontractor who does foundation work for a handful of builders of single-family homes. This construction subcontractor invoices his customers by job, and he invoices each customer several times for the same job. For example, he invoices Poverty Rock Realty for the foundation job at 1113 Birch Street when he pours the footing, and then again when he lays the block. At 1028 Fairview, the same foundation job takes more than one invoice, too.

To set up jobs for customers, you need to first describe the customers (as I explain in the preceding section). Then follow these steps:

1. **Click the Sales and Customers tab of the QuickBooks Navigator and click the Customers icon.**

   QuickBooks displays the Customer:Job List window.

2. **Select the customer for which you want to set up a job.**

   This step is simple. Just click the customer name.

3. **Click the Customer:Job button from the bottom of the window and choose Add Job from the drop-down menu.**

   QuickBooks displays the New Job window (see Figure 2-14). You use this window to describe the job. A great deal of the information in this window appears on the invoice.

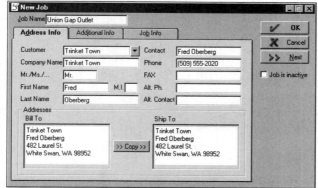

Figure 2-14:
The
Address
Info tab
of the
New Job
window.

4. **Give the job name.**

   The cursor is in the Job Name text box. Just type the name of the job or project.

5. **Identify the customer.**

   Just on the off chance that you selected the wrong customer in Step 2, take a peek at the Customer drop-down list box. Does it name the correct customer? If not, activate the drop-down list and click the correct customer.

6. **(Optional) Name your contact and fill in other relevant information.**

   You can enter the name of your contact and alternate contact in the Mr./Ms., First Name, M.I., and Last Name text boxes. QuickBooks fills in the Contact text box for you. You probably don't need to be told this, but fill in the Phone and FAX text boxes just so that you have that information on hand. If you want to get really optional, fill in the Alt. Ph. and Alt. Contact text boxes. Go ahead, take a walk on the wild side.

7. **Give the job's billing address.**

   You can use the Bill To text box to provide the customer's job billing address. Because chances are good that the job billing address is the same as the customer billing address, QuickBooks copies the billing address from the Customer list. But, if need be, make changes.

8. **Give the Ship To address.**

   You can use the Ship To text box to provide the job's shipping address. Click the Copy button if the shipping address is the same as the Bill To address.

   Click the Additional Info tab. Figure 2-15 illustrates the resulting screen quite admirably.

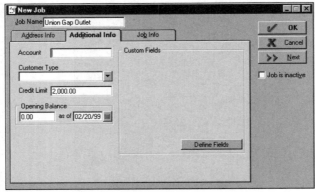

Figure 2-15:
The
Additional
Info tab
of the
New Job
window.

9. **(Massively optional) Categorize the job.**

   You can use the Customer Type drop-down list box to give the job type. As noted earlier in the chapter, the only initial type in the default list is From Advertisement. You can create other types by choosing <Add New> so that QuickBooks displays the New Customer Type dialog box, and then filling in the dialog box blanks.

10. **Set the customer's credit limit.**

    That is, if you've set one — which I strongly recommend.

11. **Enter zero for the Opening Balance.**

    Move the cursor to the Opening Balance text box and enter zero.

12. **Enter the current date.**

    Move the cursor to the As Of text box and enter the current date.

13. **(Optional) Add specific job information.**

    Click the Job Info tab and fill in the information about the job. You can use the Job Status drop-down list box to choose None, Pending, Awarded, In Progress, Closed, or Not Awarded, whichever is most appropriate. The Start Date is (I know that this one is hard to believe) the day you start the job. As anyone knows, the Projected End and the End Date are not necessarily the same. Don't fill in the End Date until the job is actually finished. The Job Description field can contain any helpful information you can fit on one line, and the Job Type is an extra field you can use. (If you do use this field, you can add a new job type by choosing <Add New>.)

14. **Save the job information.**

    After you finish describing the job, click OK to add the job to the list and return to the Customer:Job List window. Or click Next to add the job to the list and keep the New Job window displayed on the screen so that you can add more jobs.

You can edit job information the same way that you edit customer information. Display the Customer:Job List window by clicking the Sales and Customers tab of the QuickBooks Navigator and clicking the Customers icon. When QuickBooks displays the list, double-click the job and use the Edit Job window QuickBooks displays to make the changes.

Adding Vendors to Your Vendor List

Adding vendors to your Vendor list works the same basic way as adding customers to your Customer list does. Here's how to get the job done:

1. **Click the Purchases and Vendors tab of the QuickBooks Navigator and click the Vendor icon.**

   QuickBooks displays the Vendor List window (see Figure 2-16). Along with listing your vendors, it lists any sales tax agencies that you identified as part of setting up Sales Tax items.

Figure 2-16:
The Vendor
List
window.

2. **Click the Vendor button and choose New from the drop-down menu.**

   QuickBooks displays the Address Info tab of the New Vendor window (see Figure 2-17). You use this window to describe the vendors and all their little idiosyncrasies.

3. **Give the vendor's name.**

   The cursor is already in the Vendor text box. All you have to do is type the vendor's name.

4. **(Optional) Give the name of your contact.**

   Fill in the Mr./Ms., First Name, M.I., and Last Name text boxes. QuickBooks fills in the Contact text box for you automatically.

5. **Give the address to which you're supposed to mail checks.**

   You can use the Address text box to provide the vendor's address. QuickBooks copies the vendor's name to the first line of the address, so you probably need to enter only the street address, city, state, and zip code. To move from the end of one line to the start of the next, press Enter.

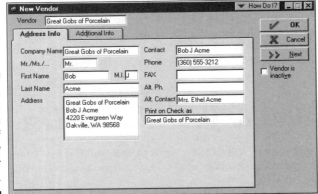

Figure 2-17:
The
Address
Info tab of
the New
Vendor
window.

6. **(Optional) Give the vendor's telephone and fax numbers.**

   If you want, provide the vendor's telephone and fax numbers. The window also has an Alt. Ph. text box for a second telephone number. Hey. They thought of everything, didn't they?

7. **Verify the Print On Check As text box.**

   QuickBooks assumes that you want the company name to appear on any checks you write for this vendor. If not, change the text box to whatever you feel is more appropriate.

   At this point, click the Additional Info tab. The window you see on your screen should now bear an uncanny resemblance to Figure 2-18.

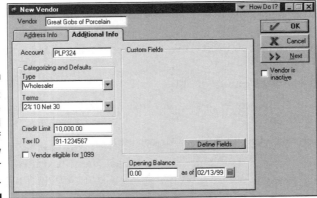

Figure 2-18:
The
Additional
Info tab of
the New
Vendor
window.

8. (Optional) Give your account number.

If the vendor has assigned account numbers or customer numbers to keep track of customers, enter your account or customer number in the Account text box. You can probably get this piece of information from the vendor's last invoice. An account number is required if you want to use QuickBooks' online bill payment feature (described in Chapter 11) to pay the vendor

9. Categorize the vendor.

See that Type drop-down list box? You can use it to assign the vendor a type. If you activate the drop-down list by clicking its arrow, you see the initial QuickBooks list of vendor types. You can pick any of these types, but my suggestion is that you diligently identify any vendor to whom you need to send a 1099 as a 1099 contractor. (A *1099 contractor* is any unincorporated business to whom you pay more than $600 during the year.)

Note: You can create a new vendor type by choosing <Add New> from the drop-down list and filling in the blanks in the New Vendor Type dialog box that QuickBooks displays.

10. Specify the payment terms that you're supposed to observe.

Activate the Terms drop-down list and click one of its terms. QuickBooks has already set up all the usual ones. (If you want to, you can choose <Add New> to set up additional payment terms.)

If a vendor offers an early payment discount, it's usually too good of a deal to pass up. Interested in more information about early payment discounts? Is yours an inquiring mind that needs to know? Refer to Chapter 18 to find out about the advantages of early payment discounts.

11. (Optional) Specify your credit limit, if the vendor has set one.

This procedure is obvious, right? You click the Credit Limit text box and enter the number.

12. (If applicable) Store the vendor's federal tax identification number and check the Vendor Eligible for 1099 check box.

This number may be the vendor's social security number if the vendor is a one-man or one-woman business. If the vendor has employees, the federal tax identification number is the vendor's employer identification number. You need this information only if you're required to prepare a 1099 for the vendor.

13. Enter zero in the Opening Balance text box.

You do not want to enter the amount you owe the vendor because you do that later, when you pay your bills.

14. Enter the date you opened an account with the vendor.

Move the cursor to the As Of field and enter the date you first purchased goods from the vendor.

15. Save the customer information.

After you finish describing the vendor, click OK to add the vendor to the list and return to the Vendor List window. Or click Next to add the vendor to the list and leave the New Vendor window displayed on the screen so that you can add more vendors.

You should periodically check your trial balance, especially after you (or someone else!) add to your lists, to make sure that you haven't created uncategorized transactions by entering balances for inventory items, customers, or vendors. You can produce a trial balance by choosing Reports➪Other Reports➪Trial Balance.

The Other Lists

I've covered almost all the most important lists. A few others I haven't talked about yet: Classes, Other Names, Ship Via, Customer Messages, Purchase Orders, Memorized Transactions, and Reminders. I'm not going to give blow-by-blow descriptions of how you use these lists because you don't really need them. The other QuickBooks lists are generally more than adequate. You can usually use the standard lists as is, without building other lists.

Just so I don't leave you stranded, however, I want to give you quick-and-dirty descriptions of these other lists and what they do.

The Class list

Classes are another way to organize your income and expenses. Classes are cool, really cool. But they add another dimension to the accounting model that you use in QuickBooks. So I'm not going to describe them here. I urge you — nay, I implore you — to get comfortable with how the rest of QuickBooks works before you begin mucking about with classes. If, after finding out how the rest of QuickBooks works, you want to wrestle with classes, you can get whatever help you need from the user's guide. I'll just tell you that you can display the Class list by clicking the Company tab of the QuickBooks Navigator and then clicking the Classes icon.

Whatever you want to do with classes, though, you can probably do it easier and better with a clever chart of accounts or a Customers:Jobs list.

The Other Names list

QuickBooks provides an Other Names list that works as a watered-down, wimpy Vendor and Employee list combination. You can write checks to people named on this Other Names list. But you can't do anything else. You can't create invoices or purchase orders for them, for example. And you don't get any of the other information that you want to collect for vendors or employees.

You're really better off working with good, accurate, rich Vendor and Employee lists. If you don't like this suggestion, however, just choose Lists⇨Other Names to display the Other Names List window, click the Other Names button, choose New from the drop-down menu, and then fill in the blanks in the New Name window.

The Ship Via list

QuickBooks provides descriptions for the usual shipping methods. These descriptions are probably entirely adequate. If you need to add more, however, you can do so by using the Lists⇨Other Lists⇨Ship Via command. When you choose the command, QuickBooks displays the Ship Via List window, which lists all the shipping methods that you or QuickBooks has said are available. To add more methods, click the Shipping Method button, choose New from the drop-down menu, then fill in the window that QuickBooks displays. Friends, it doesn't get much easier than this.

The Customer Message list

This list is another minor player in the QuickBooks drama. You can stick messages at the bottom of invoices if you first type the message in the Customer Message list. QuickBooks provides a handful of boilerplate messages. You can add more messages by choosing the List⇨Other Lists⇨Customer Messages command. When QuickBooks displays the Customer Message List window, click its Customer Message button and choose New. Then use the New Customer Message window that QuickBooks displays to create a new message.

The Purchase Orders list

Click the Purchases and Vendors tab of the QuickBooks Navigator and click the PO List icon to display the Purchase Orders window. You can add purchase orders to the list by clicking the window's Purchase Orders button and then choosing New from the drop-down menu. If you're interested in using purchase orders or want to set up any existing purchase orders, refer to Chapter 8 for the straight scoop.

The Memorized Transaction list

The Memorized Transaction list isn't really a list. At least, it's not like the other lists I've described thus far. The Memorized Transaction list is a list of accounting transactions — invoices, bills, checks, purchase orders, and so on — that you've asked QuickBooks to memorize. To display the Memorized Transaction list, choose Lists⇨Memorized Transactions.

You can have QuickBooks memorize transactions so that you can reuse them. QuickBooks uses this list for QuickFill operations. (QuickFill is that nifty little feature in QuickBooks that fills things in for you as you start to type. This feature can save you lots of time, especially for transactions you regularly make.) Say, for example, you're writing a check to a vendor. QuickBooks recognizes the vendor's name after you type just a couple of letters and then pulls up the last check you wrote for that vendor.

The Reminders list

QuickBooks keeps track of a bunch of different stuff that it knows you need to monitor. If you click the Company tab of the QuickBooks Navigator and click the Reminders icon, QuickBooks displays the Reminders window. On it you see entries such as invoices and checks that need to be printed, inventory items you should probably reorder, and so on.

Working with Your Lists

QuickBooks lets you organize and print lists and enter notes for list items. The way you do these tasks works the same for all lists.

Organizing lists

To organize a list, you must be in single-user mode if you aren't already. (Multi-user mode is described in Chapter 3.) To move an item and all of its subitems, just click the diamond beside the item and drag the item up or down the list to a new location. To make a subitem its own item, click the diamond beside the item and drag it to the left. To make an item a subitem, first move the item so that it's directly beneath the item you want it to fall under. Then click the diamond beside the item and move it to the right. To alphabetize a list, click the button in the lower-left corner of the list window. (The name of this button changes depending on the list you're displaying.) Then choose Re-sort List from the pop-up menu. Sensing that you definitely mean business and don't want it fooling around, QuickBooks displays a message box that asks whether you're sure you want to re-sort your list. Click OK to alphabetize. (Note that you cannot reorganize the Vendor list.)

Jotting down notes for list items

To enter more information about a list item, display the list and select the item. Then click the button in the lower-left corner of the list window. (The name of this button changes depending on the type of list.) Choose Notepad from the pop-up menu. In the Notepad dialog box for the item, enter your notes and click OK. You can also click Date Stamp to stamp the current date on the note.

Printing lists

You can print a list by displaying the list, clicking the button in the lower-left corner of the list window, and choosing Print List. However, the best way to print a list is often to print a list report. You can create, customize, and print a list report by choosing Reports⇨List Reports and then choosing the list you want to print. You can also create one of a handful of different list reports by clicking the Reports button in the list window and choosing a report from the pop-up menu. For more information on printing reports, see Chapter 14.

Click the Activities button in a list window to quickly access common activities associated with the items on that list.

Exporting list items to your word processor

If you use QuickBooks to store the names and addresses of your customers, vendors, and employees, you can create a text file of the contact information for these people. You can then export this file to another application, like a word processor, to create mass mailings or mailing labels. To do this, click the Company tab of the QuickBooks Navigator and then click the Mail Merge icon. In the Select Names for Mail Merge dialog box, select the list of names you want to export, and then click OK. QuickBooks displays the Save Mail Merge Data File dialog box. Enter a name for the text file in the File Name text box and describe where you want to store the file using the Save In boxes. After you export the file from QuickBooks, you can import it into the other application (this process differs depending on the program you use).

Chapter 3

Sharing QuickBooks Files

● ●

In This Chapter

▶ Understanding how QuickBooks works on a network

▶ Installing QuickBooks for network use

▶ Setting up user permissions

▶ Specifying multi-user mode

▶ Working with a shared QuickBooks file

● ●

*O*kay, here's a cool deal: You can now use the standard version of QuickBooks to set up *user permissions,* which lets you specify who has access to which areas of your QuickBooks file. And if you have the Pro version of QuickBooks, you can also work with your QuickBooks file on a network and in a multiple-user environment, using a powerful new feature called record-locking.

Note: If you work on a network and need to make use of or just want to learn about QuickBooks network features, you should read this chapter. If your computer isn't connected to a network but you want to designate unique permissions for different people using a QuickBooks file on a single computer, you should still read the Setting Up User Permissions section in this chapter. And if you're the only one using QuickBooks, you can skip this chapter.

This entire chapter is devoted to these features new to QuickBooks 6 — I just couldn't put this icon on every paragraph!

Sharing a QuickBooks File on a Network

Two important features power QuickBooks Pro's multi-user network capability: user permissions and record locking. User permissions lets multiple users of a QuickBooks file have unique permission settings to access different areas of QuickBooks. (User permissions is also included in the standard version of QuickBooks and can be used on a stand-alone computer, but it's especially pertinent for network users of QuickBooks.) Record locking, a feature specific to the Pro version, allows more than one person to log on to and work with a QuickBooks file at once.

User permissions

QuickBooks now lets you set user permissions so that you can give different QuickBooks users different privileges. For example, Jane Owner might be able to do anything she wants because metaphorically speaking, she's "Da Man." But Joe Clerk might only be able to enter bills. Joe, a lowly clerk of perhaps dubious judgment and discretion, might not have the ability to view the company's Profit & Loss Statement, print checks, or record customer payments. This makes sense at a practical level, right? In a situation where you've got a bunch of different people accessing the QuickBooks file, you want to make sure that confidential information remains confidential.

You also want to make sure that people can't intentionally or unintentionally corrupt your financial records. For example, you don't want someone to enter incorrect data (perhaps because they stumble into some area of the QuickBooks program where they have no business being). And you don't want someone fraudulently recording transactions — like fake checks that they then go cash.

I think if you reflect on this user permissions stuff, you'll realize, "Hey, yeah, that only makes sense!" So I'm not going to talk a bunch more about it. But let me conclude by throwing out a couple of general observations about how you decide which user permissions are appropriate.

- **Data confidentiality:** This issue probably has the most to do with your management philosophy. The more open you are about stuff, the less you probably have to worry about people snooping around for stuff. I should point out, however, that payroll is always a touchy subject. If everybody knows what everyone else is paid, some interesting discussions occur. But you already know this. . . .

- **Data corruption:** Regarding data corruption, you should know that people usually apply two general rules: First, don't give people access to tools they don't know how to use. That's only asking for trouble. Second, as a general rule, make sure that no one person gets to muck around unsupervised in some area of the accounting system — especially if that person records or handles cash. If at all possible, employ a "buddy" system where people do stuff together so that people always double-check — even if only indirectly — other people's work. Maybe Joe records a bill, for example, but Jane always cuts the check to pay the bill. Maybe Raul records customer invoices, but Chang sends them out. Maybe Saul records cash receipts but Britt deposits them. You see the pattern, right? If two people deal with a particular economic event — again, especially one that involves cash — it's a really good idea for Joe and Jane, Raul and Chang, and Saul and Britt to look over each other's shoulders.

Just what is a network, anyway?

A network is just a set of computers that some-one has cabled together so that the people who use the computers can share information. Uh, well, er, this is somewhat self-serving, but let me say that if you don't currently use a network, *Small Business Windows 95 For* *Dummies* and *Small Business Windows 98 For Dummies* (both written by me and published by IDG Books Worldwide, Inc.) explain how to set up a small business network in a couple of hours and live to tell about it.

Record locking

You can most easily understand what record locking is by comparing it to the other variety of locking, file locking. Most of the other programs that you use — perhaps even every one but QuickBooks — use file locking. What file locking means is this: If one person on the network has, for instance, a word-processing document open, nobody else on the network can open that document. Other people may be able to open a copy of the document that they can save on their own computers, but they can't edit the original document. The operating system "locks" the original document, or file, so that only one person can fool around with the file at a time. This locking assures the integrity of the data and the changes that people make to the data. (If this business about assuring integrity seems weird, think about how difficult it would be to make sure that both people's changes ended up in a word-processing document if both people were simultaneously editing a document.)

Record locking works differently. With record locking, more than one person on the network can open and edit the same file at once. But only one person can work with a specific record. A record is just a part of a file. For example, in a file of bills you owe to vendors, the file is the entire collection of bills. The individual bills are records within the file. So more than one person can open the file of bills. But individual bills — the individual records that make up the file — are locked when a person grabs a record.

This sounds like only too much confusion, but differentiating between files and the records within a file makes it possible to share files. In QuickBooks, for example, this means that if Jane is entering one bill for the Alpha Company in a file, Joe can edit a bill for Beta Corporation because the two bills are different records. However, Jane can't — because of record locking — fool around with the Beta Corporation bill that Joe's editing. And Joe can't — again because of record locking — fool around with the Alpha Company bill that Jane is entering. Restated more generally, no two people can edit the same record in the file at the same time. Record locking makes it possible to use a file in a multiple-user environment because it lets more than one person work with a file.

Installing QuickBooks for Network Use

To install QuickBooks Pro for network use, you must first install QuickBooks on all the computers on the network that need to access and work with the QuickBooks file. There's no trick to this. You don't need to install QuickBooks in any fancy way to be able to share QuickBooks files. (Note that you do need to purchase a copy of QuickBooks Pro for each computer that you want to be able to run the program. So if you have five computers on which you want to use QuickBooks, you need to buy five copies of QuickBooks — or the special five-pack version of QuickBooks.)

When you create the file you want to share, however, you need to make sure that you store the file in a location where the other QuickBooks users can access it. This might mean storing the file on a server. You can also store the file on a client computer as long as you designate sharing permissions for either the folder or the drive on which you save the QuickBooks file.

Another important thing: Whoever creates the QuickBooks file automatically becomes the file administrator. The file administrator has access to all areas of the file and sets up the other file users. So you don't want to have just anybody set up the QuickBooks file. Either the business owner or the head of accounting would be better suited for this. In any case, the person who sets up the file should be trustworthy, regularly around the office, and easy to reach for any questions or problems that arise; and should preferably have a strong background in accounting.

Designating the QuickBooks Administrator

Before you can begin sharing a QuickBooks file, either over a network or on a single computer, you need to first set up a name and password for the QuickBooks administrator. To do this, follow these steps:

1. **Choose File⇨Set Up Users and Passwords⇨Set Up Users.**

   This displays the Set Up QuickBooks Administrator dialog box shown in Figure 3-1.

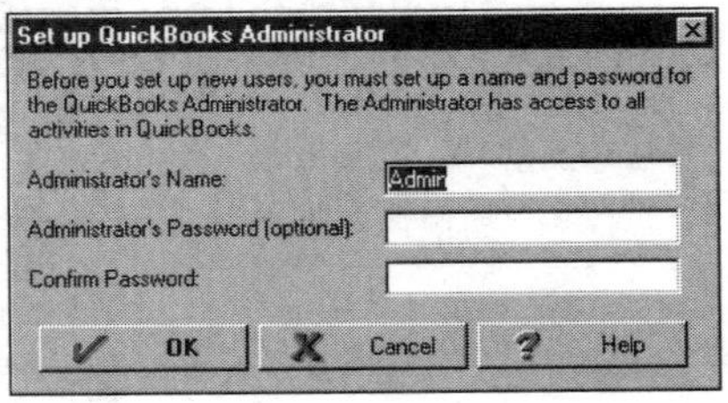

Figure 3-1:
Setting up a user name and password for the QuickBooks administrator.

> **Set up QuickBooks Administrator**
>
> Before you set up new users, you must set up a name and password for the QuickBooks Administrator. The Administrator has access to all activities in QuickBooks.
>
> Administrator's Name: `Admin`
>
> Administrator's Password (optional): [   ]
>
> Confirm Password: [   ]
>
> ✓ OK   ✗ Cancel   ? Help

Choosing a good password

The administrator has access to all areas of QuickBooks, so picking a good password for the administrator is especially important. Other users (especially those with higher levels of access permission) also need to carefully select their passwords.

A good password is one that you can easily remember but others can't easily guess. Combinations of letters and numbers are the best way to go. For example, use your grade-school nickname plus the number of your favorite basketball player. Or a random number combined

with the name of your favorite restaurant (as long as you don't walk around all day talking about your love of this particular eatery). Avoid using telephone numbers, family names, and family dates (such as the birthday of a family member or spouse). And absolutely do not use banking PIN numbers or Social Security numbers.

One last tip: QuickBooks lets you create passwords from zero to 16 characters in length. As a general rule, choose a password that's five or more characters in length.

2. **Enter a name for the administrator in the Administrator's Name text box.**

   You can also choose to keep the default administrator name, "Admin."

3. **Enter a password for the administrator in the Administrator's Password text box.**

   Keep in mind that the password you enter is case sensitive. So you probably want to make sure that you don't have Caps Lock on. And in any case, you need to remember the password exactly as you enter it.

4. **Re-enter the password in the Confirm Password text box.**

   This confirms that you entered the password correctly the first time.

5. **Click OK.**

Again, the business owner should be the administrator. If the business owner isn't the administrator — for example, because he or she doesn't possess the QuickBooks skills — someone else who is deeply trusted, such as the firm's CPA, can fulfill this role.

Setting Up User Permissions

After you set up the administrator's password, you're ready to tell QuickBooks who else will use the file and set permissions for these other people. To do so, use the User List dialog box shown in Figure 3-2.

Figure 3-2:
Use this
dialog box
to add new
users and
change
permissions
for existing
users.

If you just set up the QuickBooks administrator, this dialog box is already displayed. If this dialog box isn't currently displayed, choose File⇨Set Up Users And Passwords⇨Set Up Users. Then follow these steps:

1. **Click Add User.**

   This displays the first dialog box of the Set Up User Password and Access wizard, as shown in Figure 3-3. You use this wizard to add new users and specify user permissions.

Figure 3-3:
Adding
a new
user and
entering the
new user's
password.

2. **Enter a user name and password for the additional person you want to be able to use the QuickBooks file, and then re-enter the password in the Confirm Password box.**

   The password you enter is case sensitive, so make sure that you don't have Caps Lock on. Re-entering the password confirms that you typed the password correctly the first time.

   From now on, when someone opens the QuickBooks file, QuickBooks will ask for a user name and password. So in order for another person to access the QuickBooks file, he or she must enter the user name and password you set.

3. Click Next.

QuickBooks displays a dialog box (not shown here) asking whether you want the person to have access to all areas of the QuickBooks file or only some areas.

4. Click All Areas or click Selected Areas. And then click Next.

If you specify that you want to give access to only some areas, QuickBooks displays a series of dialog boxes (starting with the Sales and Accounts Receivable dialog box shown in Figure 3-4) allowing you to set permissions for each area.

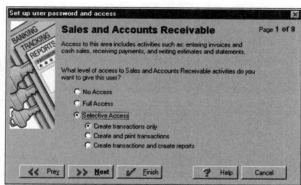

Figure 3-4:
Designating
access
permissions
to each
individual
area.

5. Designate the access permission level for each area in pages one through seven of the Set Up User Password and Access wizard.

Click No Access to make the area off-limits for the user. Click Full Access to give the user permission to create and print transactions and reports in the area, or click Selective Access to give partial access to the area. If you click Selective Access, specify the limited access. Click Next after supplying each area's access information to proceed to the next area. The other areas' dialog boxes look and work the same way.

6. Tell QuickBooks whether you want the user to be able to change or delete existing transactions and those recorded before closing dates you specify.

After you've gone through the access permissions for all the areas, QuickBooks displays the dialog box shown in Figure 3-5. Use this dialog box's option buttons to restrict user access to existing transactions. By specifying a closing date, you can prevent users — for example, new QuickBooks users or new employees — from altering data before a given date.

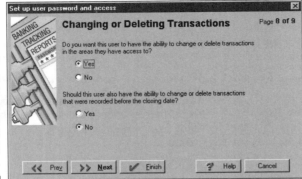

Figure 3-5:
Granting
permissions
to change
existing and
historical
transactions.

To set a closing date, log on to the QuickBooks file as the administrator. Then, make sure that you're working in single-user mode. (If you aren't, choose File⇨Switch To Single User Mode.) Then choose File⇨Set Up Users and Passwords⇨Set Up Users and click the Closing Date button. In the Set Closing Date dialog box, enter the date before which you want to restrict changes to transactions and click OK.

7. Click Next.

Review the permissions you have granted the new user, as shown in Figure 3-6. Click Prev if you need to go back and change permissions for an area.

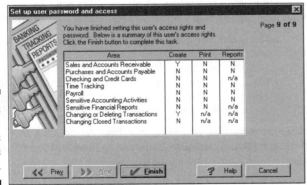

Figure 3-6:
Reviewing a
new user's
access
rights.

8. Click Finish to finish setting up the new user.

QuickBooks redisplays the User List dialog box with the new user added. Click Add User to add another new user, click Edit User to edit the selected user, or click Close to close the dialog box.

A user can log on and open a QuickBooks file from any computer on the network, as long as the computer has QuickBooks installed and has network access to the QuickBooks file. If a person attempts to open a restricted area or perform an unauthorized action, QuickBooks displays a message box similar to the one shown in Figure 3-7.

Figure 3-7:
Access is
forbidden.

Individual users can specify and save their own personal preferences for working with QuickBooks. For example, a user can decide to display and even customize the QuickBooks iconbar, or set options for graphs, reminders, and warnings. Users can access their individual preference settings by clicking the Company tab of the QuickBooks Navigator and then clicking the Preferences icon. Click the My Preferences tab if it isn't already selected.

Specifying Multi-User Mode

In order for more than one person to work with the QuickBooks file at once, the users must work with the QuickBooks file in what is called multi-user mode. The first person who opens the file needs to specify multi-user mode for others to be able to open the file. To specify multi-user mode, choose File⇨Switch to Multi-User Mode. When you choose this command, QuickBooks displays a dialog box alerting you that you've switched to multi-user mode. Then it redisplays the QuickBooks file. You can tell that you're working in multi-user mode because the QuickBooks title bar indicates so, as shown in Figure 3-8. When other people open the QuickBooks file, it automatically opens in multi-user mode. For another user to work in single-user mode, the other users must close the QuickBooks file.

The application window title bar is the only clue that you're working in multi-user mode.

Figure 3-8:
Multi-user
mode looks
almost
exactly the
same as
single-user
mode.

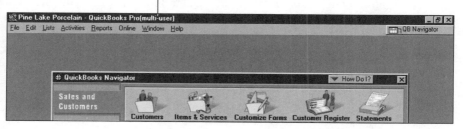

Working in Multi-User Mode

There are a couple of tricks when it comes to sharing a QuickBooks file over a network. First, you need to make sure that no one is using the file you want to open in single-user mode. If someone is, and you try to open the file, QuickBooks displays the message shown in Figure 3-9. Tell the person to switch to multi-user mode, and then click Try Again.

Figure 3-9:
You can't
open a file
in multi-
user mode
in this
case.

QuickBooks Pro multi-user

Another user is currently using this company file in single-user mode.

They must be in multi-user mode so you can also use this company file.

Ask them to switch to multi-user mode by selecting 'Switch to multi-user mode' from the QuickBooks File menu on their computer.

[Try Again]   [Cancel]

As soon as you begin creating or editing a transaction, QuickBooks locks the transaction. This way, no one else can edit the transaction as you work on it. You can tell if you have a transaction open in edit mode because QuickBooks indicates this in the title bar at the top of the form, as shown in Figure 3-10. Other users can open the transaction as you edit it in edit mode, but they can't make changes to it until you're through.

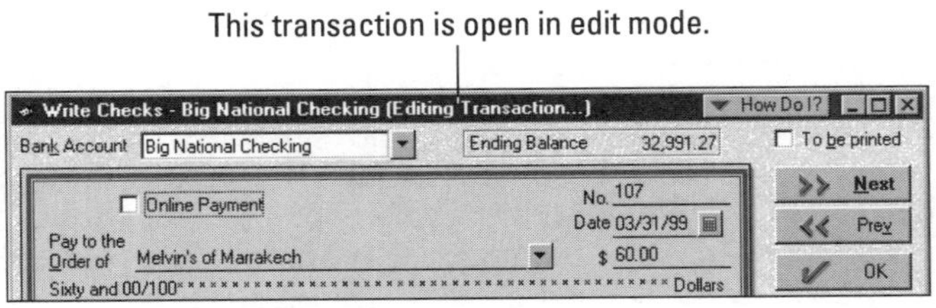

This transaction is open in edit mode.

Figure 3-10:
A form in
edit mode.

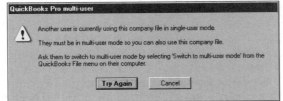

For example, if you attempt to edit a transaction that your coworker Harriet already has open in edit mode, QuickBooks displays the message shown in Figure 3-11.

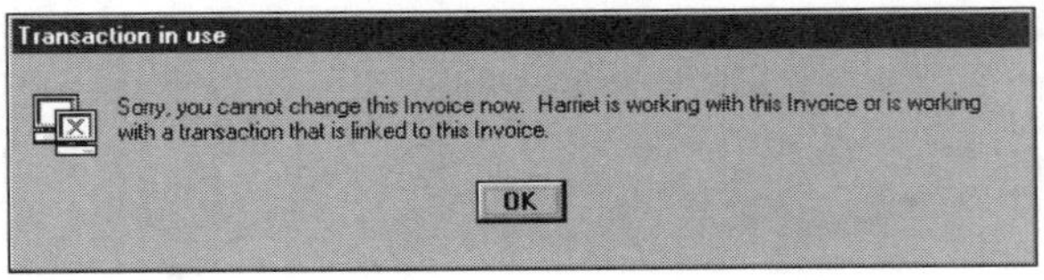

Figure 3-11:
You can't
edit this
transaction.

Transaction in use

Sorry, you cannot change this Invoice now. Harriet is working with this Invoice or is working with a transaction that is linked to this Invoice.

[OK]

Part II
Daily Chores

The 5th Wave   By Rich Tennant

"I'm not sure — I like the wage statements with rotating dollar signs, although the dancing sales receipts look good, too."

In this part . . .

Okay. You've got QuickBooks set up. Or maybe you were lucky enough to have someone else do all the dirty work. But all that doesn't matter now. It's in this part where the rubber really hits the road. You need to start using QuickBooks to do a bunch of stuff on a regular, and maybe daily, basis. Invoice customers. Record customer payments. Pay bills. This part describes how you do all these things.

Chapter 4

Invoices and Credit Memos

. . . .

. . . .

*T*his chapter — you'll be surprised to hear — describes how you create and print invoices in QuickBooks, in addition to telling you how to create and print credit memos.

You use the QuickBooks invoice form to "bill" customers for the goods you sell. You use its credit memos form to handle returns, overpayments, and canceled orders for which you've received payments.

Making Sure That You're Ready to Invoice Customers

I know that you're probably all set to go. But first, you need to check a few things, okay? Good.

You already should have installed QuickBooks, of course. (Appendix A describes how.) You should have set up a company, a chart of accounts, and all of your lists in the EasyStep Interview. You also should have entered your starting trial balance or talked your accountant into entering it for you, as described in Chapter 1.

As long as you have all this prerequisite stuff done, you're ready to start. If you don't have one of the prerequisites done, you need to complete it before going any further.

Sorry. I don't make the rules. I just tell you what they are.

Preparing an Invoice

After you complete all the preliminary work, preparing an invoice with QuickBooks is a snap. If clicking buttons and filling in text boxes are becoming old hat to you, skip the following play-by-play commentary and simply display the Create Invoices window — by clicking the Sales and Customers tab of the QuickBooks Navigator and then clicking the Invoices icon, for example — and then fill in this window and click the Print button. If you want more help than a single sentence provides, keep reading for step-by-step instructions.

Note: The following steps describe how to create the most complicated and involved invoice there is: a product invoice. Some fields on the product invoice don't appear on the service or professional invoice, but don't worry if your business is a service or professional one. Creating a service or professional invoice works basically the same way as creating a product invoice — you just fill in fewer fields. And keep in mind that you start with Steps 1 and 2 no matter what type of invoice you create.

1. **Display the Create Invoices window.**

   You display this window by clicking the Sales and Customers tab of the QuickBooks Navigator and then clicking the Invoices icon. QuickBooks then displays the Create Invoices window, shown in Figure 4-1.

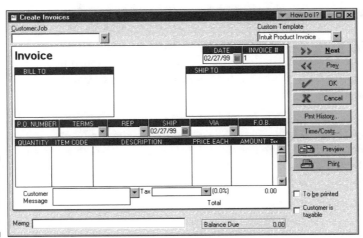

Figure 4-1:
The Create Invoices window.

2. Select the template, or invoice form, you want to use from the Custom Template drop-down list box.

QuickBooks comes with three pre-defined invoice forms: Product, Professional, and Service. Which one appears by default depends on which one you told QuickBooks you wanted to use in the EasyStep Interview. You can, however, also create your own custom invoice template by choosing Customize from the drop-down list box. Customizing invoice forms is described later in this chapter.

3. Identify the customer and, if necessary, the job.

Activate the Customer:Job drop-down list by clicking the down arrow at the right end of the box. Scroll through the Customer:Job list until you see the customer or job name, and then click it.

4. Give the invoice date.

Press Tab to move the cursor to the Date text box. Then enter the correct date in MM/DD/YY format. You also can use the following secret codes to change the date:

- Press + (the plus symbol) to move the date ahead one day.

- Press – (the minus symbol) to move the date back one day.

- Press T to change the date to today's date (as specified by the system time that your computer's internal clock provides).

- Press M to change the date to the first day of the month (because *M* is the first letter in the word *month*).

- Press H to change the date to the last day of the month (because *H* is the last letter in the word *month*).

- Press Y to change the date to the first day of the year (because, as you've no doubt guessed, *Y* is the first letter in the word *year*).

- Press R to change the date to the last day of the year (because *R* is the last letter in the word *year*).

You can also click the button on the right side of the date field to display a small calendar. To select a date from the calendar, just click the date you want. Or click the arrows on the top left and right sides of the calendar to display the previous or next month.

5. (Optional) Enter an invoice number.

QuickBooks suggests an invoice number by adding 1 to the last invoice number that you used. You can accept this addition, or, if you need to have it your way, you can tab to the Invoice # text box and change it to whatever you want.

6. **Fix the Bill To address, if needed.**

   QuickBooks grabs the billing address from the Customer List. You can change the address for the invoice, however, by replacing some portion of the usual billing address. You can, for example, insert another line that says, "Attention: William Bobbins," if that's the name of the person to whom the invoice should go.

7. **Fix the Ship To address, if needed.**

   I feel like a broken record, but here's the deal: QuickBooks also grabs the shipping address from the Customer List. So, if the shipping address has something unusual about it for just this one invoice, you can change it by replacing or adding information to the Ship To address block.

8. **(Optional . . . sort of) Provide the purchase order number.**

   If the customer issues purchase orders, enter the number of the purchase order that authorizes this purchase in the P.O. Number text box. Just for the record, *P.O.* is pronounced *pee-oh.* Not *poh* or *poo.*

9. **Specify the payment terms.**

   To specify the payment terms, activate the Terms drop-down list box and select something from it. I have only one request to make: Don't offer a customer an early payment discount without reading the first couple of sections in Chapter 18. Please. I'm only looking out for your welfare. Really.

10. **(Optional) Name the sales representative.**

   Rep does not stand for *Reputation,* so don't put three-letter editorial comments in here. (Although I can't, for the life of me, imagine what you could do with three letters.) If you want to track sales by sales representative, use the Rep drop-down list box. Simply activate the list box by clicking its arrow, for example, and then pick a name. I don't want to do the "I told you so" routine, but to specify sales representatives, you need to have set up the Employee List (see Chapter 2).

11. **Specify the shipping date if it's something other than the invoice date.**

   To specify the date, simply move the cursor to the Ship text box and then type the date in MM/DD/YY fashion. You can move the cursor by pressing Tab or by clicking the text box. Oh — one other quick point: Remember all those secret codes I talked about in Step 4 for changing the invoice date? They also work for changing the shipping date.

12. **Specify the shipping method.**

   You can probably guess how you specify the shipping method. But parallel structure and a compulsive personality force me to continue. So, to specify the shipping method, move the cursor to the Via drop-down list, activate the list, and then select a shipping method.

By the way, you can add new shipping methods to the list by choosing <Add New> and then filling out the cute little dialog box that QuickBooks displays. Setting up new shipping methods is really easy. Really easy.

13. Specify the FOB point using the F.O.B. text box.

FOB stands for *free-on-board.* The FOB point is more important than it first seems — at least in a business sense — because the FOB point determines when the transfer of ownership occurs, who pays freight, and who bears the risks of damage to the goods during shipping.

If a shipment is free-on-board at the shipping point, the ownership of the goods being sold transfers to the purchaser as soon as the goods leave the seller's shipping dock. (Remember that you're the seller.) This means that the purchaser pays the freight and bears the risk of shipping damage. The FOB shipping point can be specified either as FOB Shipping Point or by using the name of the city. If the shipping point is Seattle, for example, FOB Seattle is the same thing as FOB Shipping Point. Most goods are shipped as FOB Shipping Point, by the way.

If a shipment is free-on-board at the destination point, the ownership of the goods that are being sold transfers to the purchaser as soon as the goods arrive on the purchaser's shipping dock. The seller pays the freight and bears the risk of shipping damage. The FOB destination point can be specified either as FOB Destination Point or by using the name of the city. If the destination point is Omaha, for example, FOB Omaha is the same thing as FOB Destination Point.

14. Enter each item that you're selling.

Move the cursor to the first row of the Quantity/Item Code/Description/ Price Each/Amount/Tax list box. Okay, I know that isn't a very good name for it, but you know what I mean, right? You need to start filling in the line items that go on the invoice. After you move the cursor to a row in the list box, QuickBooks turns the Item Code field into a drop-down list box. Activate the Item Code drop-down list box of the first empty row in the list box and then select the item.

When you select the item, QuickBooks fills in the Description and Price Each text boxes with whatever sales description and sales price you entered in the Item List. (You can edit the information for this particular invoice if you need to.) Enter the number of items sold in the Quantity text box. (After you enter this number, QuickBooks calculates the amount by multiplying Quantity by Price Each.) If you need other items on the invoice, use the remaining empty rows of the list box to enter each one. If you checked the Taxable check box when you added the item to the Item List, a small *T* appears in the Tax column to indicate that the item will be taxed.

Note: You can put as many items on an invoice as you want. If you don't have enough room on a single page, QuickBooks just adds as many pages as are needed to the invoice. The invoice total information, of course, goes only on the last page.

15. Enter any special items that should be included on the invoice.

If you haven't worked much with the QuickBooks item file, then you have no idea what I'm talking about. But here's the scoop: QuickBooks thinks that anything you stick on an invoice is something that you're selling. If you sell blue, yellow, and red mugs, you obviously need to add each of these items to the Item List. But if you add a freight charge to your invoice, QuickBooks thinks that the freight charge is just another mug and requires you to add a freight charge item to the list. The same is true for a volume discount that you want to stick on the invoice. And if you add sales tax to your invoice, well, guess what? QuickBooks again thinks that it is just another item. (For more information about adding to and working with lists in QuickBooks, cruise through Chapter 2.)

To describe any of the special items, activate the Item Code drop-down list box of the next empty row in the list box and then select the special item. After QuickBooks fills in the Description and Rate text boxes, edit this information, if necessary. Describe each of the other special items — subtotals, discounts, freight, and so on — that you're itemizing on the invoice by filling in the empty rows in the list box.

If you want to include a discount item and have it apply to multiple items, you need to stick a subtotal item on the invoice after the inventory or other items you want to discount. Then stick a discount item directly after the subtotal item. QuickBooks calculates the discount as a percentage of the subtotal.

16. (Optional) Add a customer message.

Click the Customer Message box, activate its drop-down list, and select a clever customer message. You can add customer messages to the customer message list. Choose <Add New> and then fill in the dialog box that QuickBooks displays. (I know that I talk about the Customer Message box in Chapter 2, but I want to quickly describe how to add a customer message again so that you don't have to flip back a bunch of pages.)

17. Specify the sales tax.

If you have only one sales tax, QuickBooks uses it as a default. If it isn't correct, move the cursor to the Tax list box, activate the drop-down list, and select the correct sales tax.

18. (Truly optional) Add a memo.

You can add a memo description to the invoice if you want to. This memo isn't for your customer. It doesn't even print. It's for your eyes only. Memo descriptions give you a way of storing information related to an invoice with that invoice. Figure 4-2 shows a completed Create Invoices window.

Figure 4-2:
A
completed
Create
Invoices
window.

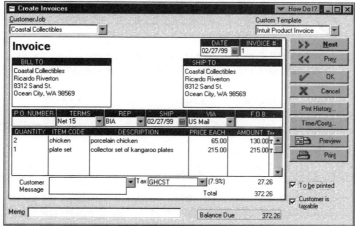

19. If you want to delay printing this invoice, unmark the To Be Printed check box that's below the column of buttons on the right.

I want to postpone talking about what checking the To Be Printed check box does until I finish the discussion of invoice creation. I talk about printing invoices just a little bit later in the chapter. I promise.

20. Save the invoice.

You can save a completed invoice in one of several ways:

- If you want to create more invoices, click Next. QuickBooks saves the invoice that's on the screen and then redisplays an empty Create Invoices window so that you can create another invoice. (Note that you can return to invoices that you created earlier by clicking the Next button's cousin, Prev.)

- If you don't want to create additional invoices, click OK. QuickBooks saves the invoice and closes the Create Invoices window.

- If you want to print the invoice and save it, click the Print button. I discuss printing invoices in detail a little bit later in this chapter.

Fixing Invoice Mistakes

I'm not a perfect person. You're not a perfect person. Heck, very few people are. So everyone makes mistakes. You don't need to get worked up over mistakes that you make while entering information in invoices. Fixing them is easy.

If the invoice is still displayed on the screen

If the invoice is still displayed on the screen, you can just move the cursor to the box or button that's wrong and then fix the mistake. Because most of the bits of information that you enter in the Create Invoices window are short and sweet, you can easily replace the contents of some fields by typing over whatever's already there. To save your correction, click OK, Next, or Prev.

If the invoice isn't displayed on the screen

If the invoice isn't displayed on the screen but you haven't yet printed it, you can use the Next and Prev buttons to page through the invoices. When you get to the one with the error, simply fix the error as described in the preceding section.

If you've printed the invoice, you also can make the sort of change de-scribed in the preceding paragraphs. For example, you can page through the invoices until you find the one (now printed) that has the error. And you can change the error and print the invoice again. I'm not so sure that you want to go this route, however, if you've already sent out the invoice. You may want to consider fixing the invoice by issuing either a credit memo (if the original invoice overcharged) or another invoice (if the original invoice undercharged). The reason I suggest issuing a credit memo or another invoice is that life gets awfully messy if you or your customer has multiple copies of the same invoice floating around and causing confusion.

Deleting an invoice

I hesitate to mention this, but you also can delete invoices. Procedurally, deleting an invoice is easy. You just display the invoice in the Create Invoices window by clicking the Sales and Customers tab of the QuickBooks Navigator and then clicking the Invoices icon. Use the Next and Prev buttons to page through the invoices until you see the invoice that you want to delete. Then choose Edit⇨Delete Invoice. When QuickBooks asks you to confirm your deletion, click Yes. But read the next paragraph first. You may not want to delete the invoice. . . .

Even though deleting invoices is easy, it isn't something that you should do casually or for fun. It's okay to delete an invoice if you've just created it, only you have seen it, and you haven't yet printed it. In this case, no one needs to know that you made a mistake. But the rest of the time — even if you created an invoice that you don't want later — you should keep a copy of the invoice in the QuickBooks system. By doing so, you have a record that the invoice existed, which usually makes answering later questions easier.

"But how am I to correct my books if I leave the bogus invoice?" you ask.

Good question. To correct your financial records for the invoice that you don't want to count anymore, simply void the invoice. The invoice remains in the QuickBooks system, but QuickBooks doesn't count it. To void an invoice, display it in the Create Invoices window and then choose Edit⇨ Void Invoice.

Preparing a Credit Memo

Credit memos can be a handy way to fix data entry mistakes that you didn't find or correct earlier. Credit memos are also handy ways to handle things such as customer returns and refunds. If you've prepared an invoice or two in your time, you'll find that preparing a QuickBooks credit memo is super-easy — and handy.

Note: The following steps describe how to create the most complicated and involved kind of credit memo: a product credit memo. Creating a service or professional credit memo works basically the same way, however. You just fill in fewer fields.

1. **Display the Create Credit Memos/Refunds window.**

   Click the Sales and Customers tab of the QuickBooks Navigator and then click the Refunds and Credit icon. When you do, QuickBooks displays the Create Credit Memos/Refunds window, shown in Figure 4-3. Although you can't see it in the figure, the Credit Memos are brown and the Invoices are blue. This creates a color scheme that brings out the highlights in your hair and throws the emphasis on . . . okay, I'll stop.

2. **Identify the customer and, if necessary, the job.**

   Activate the Customer:Job drop-down list. Then select the customer or job by clicking it.

3. **Give the credit memo date.**

   Press Tab to move the cursor to the Date text box. Then enter the correct date in MM/DD/YY format. You also can use the secret date-editing codes that I described earlier in the chapter in the section on preparing invoices. Oh, boy.

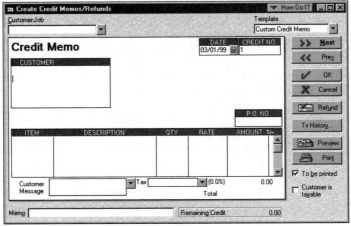

Figure 4-3:
The Create
Credit
Memos/
Refunds
window.

4. (Optional) Enter a credit memo number.

QuickBooks suggests a credit memo number by adding 1 to the last credit memo number you used. You can accept the number or tab to the Credit No. text box to change the number to whatever you want.

5. Fix the Customer address, if needed.

QuickBooks grabs the billing address from the Customer List. You can change the address for the credit memo, however, by replacing some portion of the usual billing address. Typically, you should use the same address for the credit memo that you used for the original invoice or invoices.

6. (Optional . . . sort of) Provide the purchase order number.

If the credit memo adjusts the total remaining balance on a customer purchase order, you should probably enter the number of the purchase order into the P.O. No. text box.

Here's my logic on this suggestion for those readers who care: If you billed your customer $1,000 on P.O. No. 1984, which authorizes a $1,000 purchase, you have "used up" the entire purchase order — at least according to the customer's accounts payable clerk who processes your invoices. If you make sure that a credit memo for $1,000 is identified as related to P.O. No. 1984, however, you essentially free up the $1,000 purchase balance, which may mean that you can use, or bill on, the purchase order again.

7. If the customer is returning items, describe each item.

Move the cursor to the first row of the Item/Description/Qty/Rate/ Amount/Tax text box. In the first empty row of the box, activate the Item drop-down list and then select the item. After you select it,

QuickBooks fills in the Description and Rate text boxes with whatever sales description and sales price you entered in the Item List. (You can edit this information if you want, but it's not necessary.) Enter the number of items that the customer is returning (or not paying for) in the Qty text box. (After you enter this number, QuickBooks calculates the amount by multiplying Qty by Rate.) Enter each item that the customer is returning by filling in the empty rows of the list box.

Note: As with invoices, you can put as many items on a credit memo as you want. If you don't have enough room on a single page, QuickBooks just keeps adding pages to the credit memo until you're finished. The total information, of course, goes on the last page.

8. **Describe any special items that should be included on the credit memo.**

If you want to issue a credit memo for other items that appear on the original invoice — freight, discounts, other charges, and so on — add descriptions of each item to the Item List.

To add descriptions of these items, activate the Item drop-down list of the next empty row in the list box and then select the special item. (You activate the list by clicking the field once to turn it into a drop-down list box and then clicking the field's down arrow to drop down the list box.) After QuickBooks fills in the Description and Rate text boxes, edit this information, if necessary. Enter each special item — subtotal, discount, freight, and so on — that you're itemizing on the credit memo.

If you want to include a discount item, you need to stick a subtotal item on the invoice after the inventory or other items you want to discount. Then stick a discount item directly after the subtotal item. In this way, QuickBooks calculates the discount as a percentage of the subtotal.

9. **(Optional) Add a customer message.**

Activate the Customer Message list and select a clever customer message.

10. **Specify the sales tax.**

Move the cursor to the Tax list box, activate the list box, and select the correct sales tax.

11. **(Optional, but a really good idea. . .) Add a memo.**

You can use the Memo text box to add a memo description to the credit memo. I suggest that you use this description to explain your reasons for issuing the credit memo and to cross-reference the original invoice or invoices. Figure 4-4 shows a completed Create Credit Memos/Refunds window.

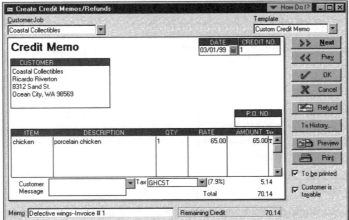

Figure 4-4:
A
completed
Create
Credit
Memos/
Refunds
window.

12. If you want to delay printing this credit memo, clear the To Be Printed check box.

I want to postpone talking about what checking the To Be Printed check box does until I finish the discussion of credit memo creation. Coverage on printing invoices and credit memos comes up in the following section.

13. Save the invoice.

You can save a completed credit memo in one of three ways:

- To create more credit memos, click Next. QuickBooks saves the credit memo that's on the screen and then displays an empty Create Credit Memos/Refunds window so that you can enter another credit memo. (Note that you can return to credit memos that you created earlier by clicking the Prev button.)

- If you don't want to create additional credit memos, click OK. QuickBooks saves the credit memo and closes the Create Credit Memos/Refunds window.

- If you want to print the credit memo and save it, click the Print button. I discuss printing invoices and credit memos a little later in this chapter, in the section cleverly entitled, "Printing Invoices and Credit Memos."

Fixing Credit Memo Mistakes

Sure, I could repeat the same information I gave in the "Fixing Invoice Mistakes" section and leave you with a strange feeling of déjà vu. But I won't.

Here's everything you need to know about fixing credit memo mistakes: You can fix credit memo mistakes the same way that you fix invoice mistakes. If you need more help, refer to the earlier section of this chapter, "Fixing Invoice Mistakes."

Printing Invoices and Credit Memos

As part of setting up QuickBooks, you selected an invoice type. I assume that you have the raw paper stock for whatever invoice type you chose. If you're going to print on blank letterhead, for example, I assume that you have letterhead lying around. If you decide to use preprinted forms, I assume that you've ordered those forms and have received them.

I also assume that you've already set up your printer. If you've ever printed anything, your printer is already set up. Really.

Loading the forms into the printer

This part is easy. Simply load the invoice forms into the printer the same way you always load paper. Because there are about a jillion different printers, I can't give you the precise steps that you need to take, but if you've used a printer a bit, you should have no problem.

Wait a minute. What's that? Your printer is brand new, and you've never used it before? Okay, here's one of my weird ideas: Use a pencil or something else that's heat-resistant (so that it won't melt and gum up the insides of the printer) to draw an arrow on a piece of paper. (Do not, repeat, *do not* use crayon. And don't let your children watch you do this.) Draw the arrow so that it points toward the top edge of the paper. Load the paper in the printer, with the arrow face up, and note which direction the arrow is pointing. Print something. Anything. When the paper comes out, notice whether the image faces the same direction as the arrow and whether it's on the same side of the paper as the arrow. With this information and a little logic, you should be able to figure out how to load forms correctly.

Setting up the invoice printer

You need to set up the invoice printer only once, but you need to specify a handful of general invoice-printing rules. These rules also apply to credit memos and to purchase orders, by the way.

To set up your printer for invoice printing, follow these steps:

1. **Display the Printer Setup dialog box.**

   Choose File➪Printer Setup, and in the Form Name drop-down list box, select Invoice. QuickBooks displays the Printer Setup dialog box, shown in Figure 4-5.

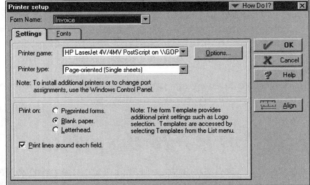

Figure 4-5:
The Printer
Setup
dialog box.

2. **Select the printer that you want to use to print invoices.**

   Activate the Printer Name drop-down list to see the installed printers. Select the one that you want to use for printing invoices and purchase orders.

3. **(Optional) Select the printer type.**

   The Printer Type drop-down list describes the kind of paper your printer uses. You have two choices: Continuous and Page-Oriented. Continuous means that your paper comes as one connected ream with perforated edges. Page-Oriented means that your paper is in single sheets.

4. **Select the type of invoice form.**

   Select the option button that describes the type of form that you want to print on: Preprinted Form, Blank Paper, or Letterhead. Then mark the Print lines around each field check box if you want QuickBooks to draw in nice little boxes to separate each field.

5. **(Optional, but a really good idea. . .) Print a test invoice on real invoice paper.**

   Click the Align button. When QuickBooks displays the Align Printer dialog box, choose the type of invoice you want to print from the list and then click OK. When QuickBooks displays the Fine Alignment dialog box, shown in Figure 4-6, click Print Sample to tell QuickBooks to print a dummy invoice on whatever paper you've loaded in the invoice printer.

Figure 4-6:
The Fine
Alignment
dialog box.

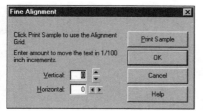

   The dummy invoice that QuickBooks prints gives you a chance to see what your invoices will look like. The invoice also has a set of alignment gridlines that prints over the Bill To text box, as shown in Figure 4-7, which you can use if you need to fine-align your printer.

6. **Fix any form-alignment problems.**

   If you see any alignment problems after you complete Step 5, you need to fix them. (Alignment problems probably occur only with impact printers. With laser printers or inkjet printers, sheets of paper feed into the printer the same way every time, so you almost never need to fiddle with the form alignment.)

   To fix any big alignment problems — like stuff printing in completely the wrong place — you need to adjust the way the paper feeds into the printer. When you finally get the paper loaded as best you can, be sure to note exactly how you have it loaded. You need to have the printer and paper set up the same way every time you print.

   For minor, but nonetheless still annoying, alignment problems, use the Fine Alignment dialog box's Vertical and Horizontal boxes to adjust the form's alignment. Then print another sample invoice. Go ahead and experiment a bit. You need to fine-tune the printing of the invoice form only once. Click OK in the Fine Alignment dialog box when you finish to have QuickBooks redisplay the Printer Setup dialog box.

   Note: Clicking the Options button in the Printer Setup dialog box opens the selected printer's Windows printer setup information. Because this information relates to Windows and not to QuickBooks, I'm not going to explain it. You shouldn't have to worry about these settings. But if you're the curious type or accidentally click it and then have questions about what you see, refer either to your *Windows User's Guide* or to the printer's user guide.

7. Save your printer settings stuff.

After you finish fiddling with all of the Printer Setup dialog box's boxes and buttons, click OK to save your changes.

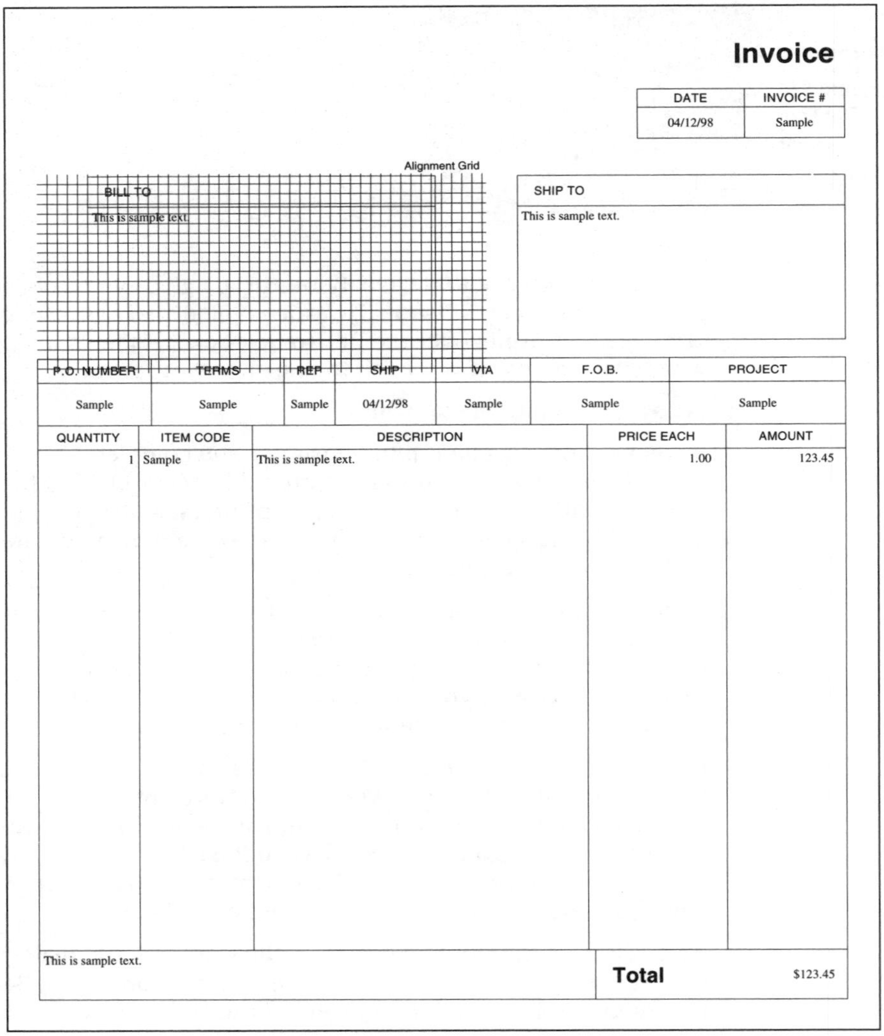

	Invoice

DATE	INVOICE #
04/12/98	Sample

Alignment Grid

BILL TO
This is sample text.

SHIP TO
This is sample text.

P.O. NUMBER	TERMS	REF	SHIP	VIA	F.O.B.	PROJECT
Sample	Sample	Sample	04/12/98	Sample	Sample	Sample

QUANTITY	ITEM CODE	DESCRIPTION	PRICE EACH	AMOUNT
1	Sample	This is sample text.	1.00	123.45

This is sample text.

Total	$123.45

Figure 4-7:
This dummy invoice form has a set of alignment gridlines.

And now for the main event

You can print invoices and credit memos either one at a time or in a batch. How you print them makes no difference to QuickBooks or to me, your humble author and new friend. Pick whatever way seems to fit your style the best.

Printing invoices and credit memos as you create them

If you want to print invoices and credit memos as you create them, follow these steps:

1. **Click the Print button after you create the invoice or credit memo.**

   After you fill in each of the boxes in the Create Invoices window or the Create Credit Memos/Refunds window, click the Print button. QuickBooks, ever the faithful servant, displays either the Print One Invoice dialog box (shown in Figure 4-8) or the Print One Credit Memo/Refund dialog box (which looks almost like the Print One Invoice dialog box).

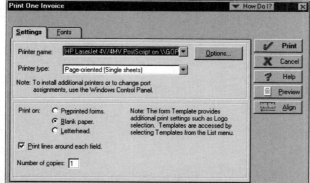

Figure 4-8:
The Print
One Invoice
dialog box.

2. **(Optional) Select the type of invoice or credit memo form.**

   If you're using a different type of invoice or credit memo form than you described for the invoice printer setup, select the type of form that you want to print on in the Print On box. You can choose Preprinted Form, Blank Paper, or Letterhead.

   Note: You shouldn't have to worry about printing test-invoice or credit-memo forms or fiddling with form-alignment problems if you addressed these issues when you set up the invoice printer. So I'm not going to talk about the Align button here. If you want to do this kind of stuff and you need help, refer to the preceding section, "Setting up the invoice printer." It describes how to print test forms and fix form-alignment problems.

3. Print the form.

Click the Print button to send the form to the printer. QuickBooks prints the form (see Figures 4-9 and 4-10).

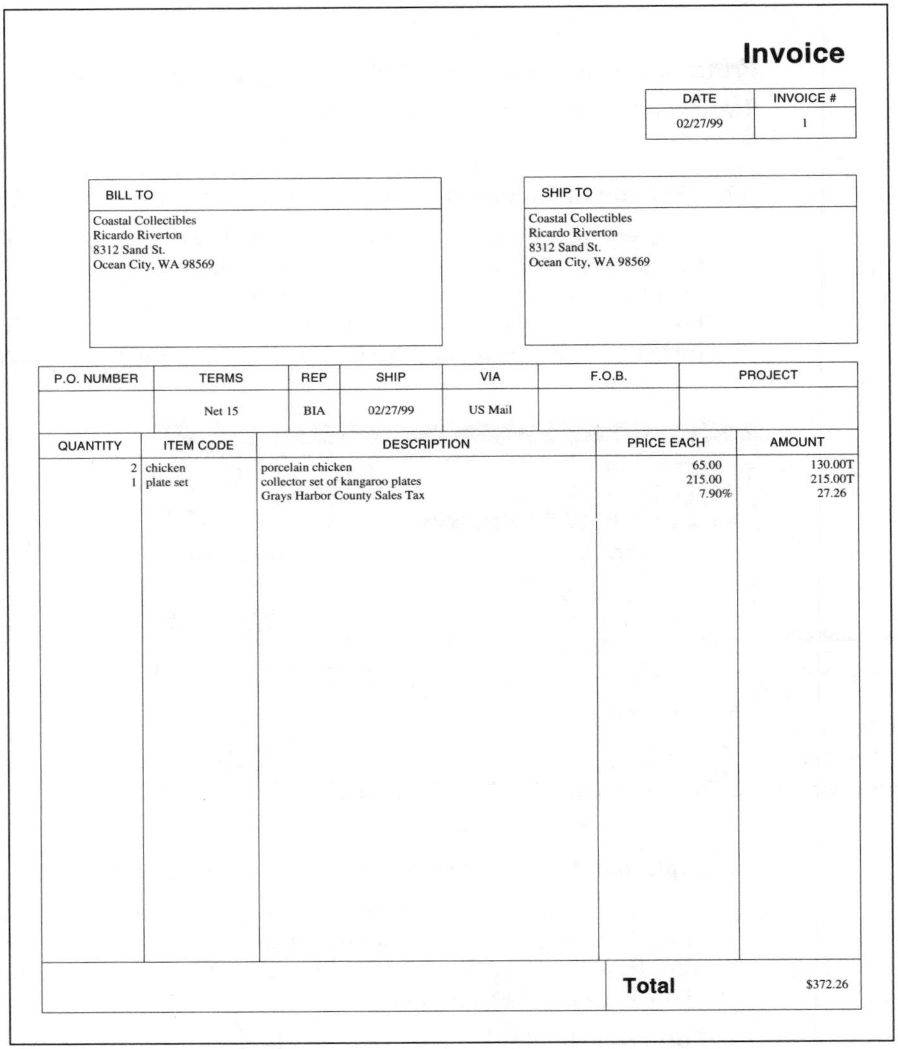

Invoice

DATE	INVOICE #
02/27/99	1

BILL TO

Coastal Collectibles
Ricardo Riverton
8312 Sand St.
Ocean City, WA 98569

SHIP TO

Coastal Collectibles
Ricardo Riverton
8312 Sand St.
Ocean City, WA 98569

P.O. NUMBER	TERMS	REP	SHIP	VIA	F.O.B.	PROJECT
	Net 15	BIA	02/27/99	US Mail		

QUANTITY	ITEM CODE	DESCRIPTION	PRICE EACH	AMOUNT
2	chicken	porcelain chicken	65.00	130.00T
1	plate set	collector set of kangaroo plates	215.00	215.00T
		Grays Harbor County Sales Tax	7.90%	27.26

	Total	$372.26

Figure 4-9:
A printed invoice.

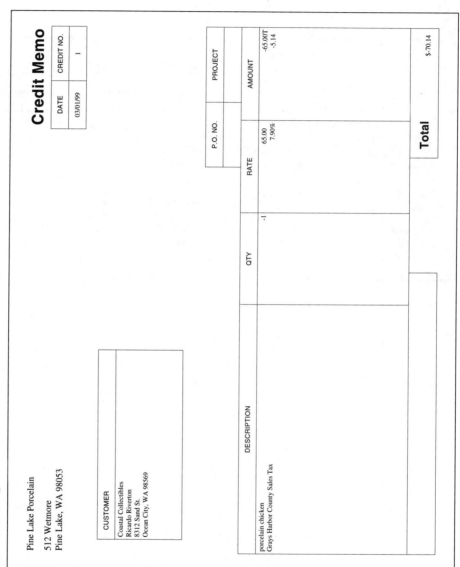

Figure 4-10:
A printed
credit
memo.

What am I printing on?

Sometimes people get confused about pre-printed forms versus letterhead versus plain paper. Here's the scoop: Preprinted forms have your company name, perhaps your logo, and a bunch of other boxes and lines (often in another color of ink) already printed on them. Preprinted forms are often multipart forms. (Examples of preprinted forms come in the QuickBooks box.)

Letterhead is what you usually use for letters that you write. It has your company name and address on it, for example, but nothing else. To

save you from having to purchase preprinted forms, QuickBooks enables you to use letterhead to create invoices and forms. (To make the letterhead look a little more bookkeeperish, QuickBooks draws lines and boxes on the letterhead so that it looks sort of like a preprinted invoice.)

Plain paper is, well, plain paper. Nothing is printed on it. So QuickBooks needs to print everything — your company name, all the invoice stuff, and optionally, lines and boxes.

4. Review the invoice or credit memo and reprint the form, if necessary.

Review the invoice or credit memo to see whether QuickBooks printed it correctly. If the form doesn't look okay, fix whatever problem fouled up the form (perhaps you printed it on the wrong paper, for example) and reprint the form by clicking the Print button again.

Printing invoices in a batch

If you want to print invoices in a batch, you need to check the To Be Printed check box that appears in the lower-right corner of the Create Invoices window. This check mark tells QuickBooks to put a copy of the invoice on a special invoices-to-be-printed list.

When you later want to print the invoices-to-be-printed list, follow these steps:

1. Choose File⇨Print Forms⇨Print Invoices.

QuickBooks displays the Select Invoices to Print dialog box, shown in Figure 4-11. This box lists all the invoices that you marked as To Be Printed that you haven't yet printed.

2. Select the invoices that you want to print.

Initially, QuickBooks marks all the invoices with a check mark, indicating that they will be printed. You can check and uncheck individual invoices on the list by clicking them. You also can use the Select All and the Select None buttons. Click Select All to check all the invoices. Click Select None to uncheck all the invoices.

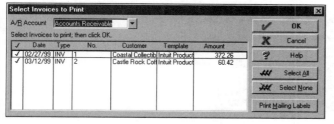

Figure 4-11:
The Select
Invoices
to Print
dialog box.

3. **Click OK.**

   After you correctly mark all the invoices you want to print — and none of the ones you don't want to print — click OK. QuickBooks displays the Print Invoices dialog box, shown in Figure 4-12.

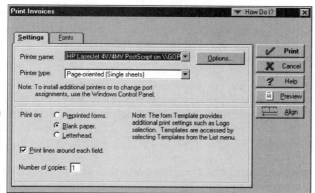

Figure 4-12:
The Print
Invoices
dialog box.

4. **(Optional) Select the type of invoice form.**

   If you use a different type of invoice form than you described during the invoice and PO printer setup, select the type of form that you want to print on using the Print On box. You can choose Preprinted Forms, Blank Paper, or Letterhead.

5. **Print the forms.**

   Click the Print button to send the selected invoice forms to the printer. QuickBooks prints the forms and then displays a message box that asks whether the forms printed correctly (see Figure 4-13).

6. **Review the invoice forms and reprint them if necessary.**

   Review the invoices to see whether QuickBooks printed all of them correctly. If all the forms look okay, click OK in the message box. If one or more forms don't look okay, enter the invoice number of the first bad

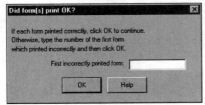

Figure 4-13:
The Did
Form(s)
Print OK?
message
box.

form in the message box. Then fix whatever problem fouled up the form (perhaps you printed it on the wrong paper, for example) and reprint the bad form(s) by clicking the Print button again. (The Print button is in the Print Invoices dialog box.)

Printing credit memos in a batch

If you want to print credit memos in a batch, you need to check the To Be Printed check box that appears in the lower-right corner of the Create Credit Memos/Refunds window. Checking this box tells QuickBooks to put a copy of the credit memo on a special credit-memos-to-be-printed list.

Note: Printing credit memos in a batch works very similarly to printing invoices in a batch. Because the preceding section describes how to print invoices in a batch, I'm going to speed through the following description of printing credit memos in a batch. If you get lost or have questions, refer to the preceding section.

When you're ready to print the credit memos that are on the to-be-printed list, follow these steps:

1. **Choose File⇨Print Forms⇨Print Credit Memos.**

   QuickBooks displays the Select Credit Memos to Print dialog box.

2. **Select the credit memos that you want to print.**

3. **Click OK to display the Print Credit Memos dialog box.**

4. **Use the Print Credit Memos dialog box to describe how you want your credit memos printed.**

5. **Click the Print button to send the selected credit memos to the printer.**

   QuickBooks prints the forms.

Customizing Your Invoices and Credit Memos

QuickBooks makes it really easy for you to customize its invoice and credit menu templates or create new invoices and credit memos based on one of its existing templates. All you have to do is click the Sales and Customers tab of the QuickBooks Navigator and click the Customize Forms icon. (If you already have the form you want to customize open, you can also choose Customize from the Custom Template drop-down list box.) When QuickBooks displays the Templates window, double-click an existing template to edit it, or click the Templates button and choose New to build a new template. Then select the type of template you want to create in the dialog box QuickBooks displays. If you're creating a new invoice form, QuickBooks displays the Customize Invoice dialog box shown in Figure 4-14.

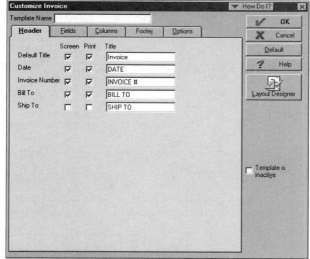

Figure 4-14:
The
Customize
Invoice
dialog box.

You can use the tabs of the Customize Invoice dialog box to customize almost everything on your invoice. You can choose what you want in the header, footer, and fields of your invoice and in what order you want the information. You can also change the fonts or add a logo to your invoice. If you're creating a new invoice template, click the Layout Designer button on the Customize Invoice dialog box to start the Layout Designer, shown in Figure 4-15. In this window, you can become a true layout artist and observe how the overall look of your invoice changes when you move fields around the page using your mouse.

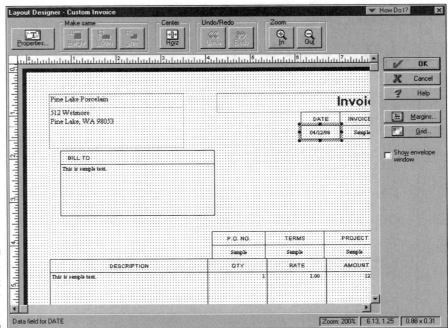

Chapter 5

Reeling In the Dough

· ·

In This Chapter

▶ Recording cash sales

▶ Fixing cash sale mistakes

▶ Recording customer payments

▶ Correcting mistakes in recording customer payments

▶ Tracking customer open invoices and collections

▶ Assessing finance charges

· ·

*Y*ou need to record the amounts customers pay you when they fork over cash, whether it be at the time of a sale or after you invoice them. This chapter describes how to record these payments and explains how to make bank deposits, track the amounts that customers owe and pay, and assess finance charges

Note: If you've been using QuickBooks to prepare customer invoices, you're ready to begin recording payments. You'll have no problem. If you haven't been invoicing customers, you need to make sure you have a couple of things ready to go before you can record cash sales. First, you need to make sure your lists are up to date (updating these lists is described in Chapter 2). And second, if you want to print cash sales receipts, you need to have your printer set up to print them. You do this by choosing File⇨Printer Setup, and then selecting Cash Sales from the drop-down list box. Setting up your printer to print cash sales receipts works just like setting it up to print invoices and credit memos (as described in Chapter 4).

Recording a Cash Sale

You record a cash sale when a customer pays you in full for the goods at the point of sale. Cash sales work similarly to regular sales (for which you first invoice a customer and then later receive payment on the invoice). In fact, the big difference between the two types of sales is that cash sales are recorded in a way that changes your cash balance rather than your accounts receivable balance. (For you accountants, this means that the debit is to cash rather than to accounts receivable.) Don't get confused by the term "cash sale." It doesn't have to do with the method of payment. You can record a cash sale even if a customer pays you by check or credit card. Here's the abridged procedure:

Display the Enter Cash Sales window by clicking the Sales and Customers tab of the QuickBooks Navigator and then clicking the Cash Sales icon. Then fill in the window that appears.

Note: The following unabridged steps describe how to record cash sales for products, which are the most complicated type of cash sale. Recording cash sales for services works basically the same way, however. You simply fill in fewer fields.

1. **Display the Enter Cash Sales window.**

   Click the Sales and Customers tab of the QuickBooks Navigator and then click the Cash Sales icon so that QuickBooks displays the Enter Cash Sales window, shown in Figure 5-1.

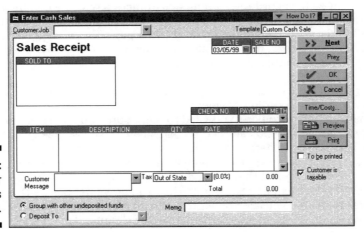

Figure 5-1: The Enter Cash Sales window.

Note: Your Enter Cash Sales window might not look exactly like mine for a couple of reasons. The first is that QuickBooks customizes its forms to fit your particular type of business. The second reason is that forms in QuickBooks are really easy to customize. You can customize the cash sales form by choosing Customize from the Template drop-down list box in the Enter Cash Sales window. Customizing cash sales forms works in a similar way to customizing invoices and credit memos, as described in Chapter 4. If your Enter Cash Sales window includes more fields than I describe here, you can also turn back to that chapter for help on how to fill out the additional fields.

2. Identify the customer and, if necessary, the job.

Activate the Customer:Job drop-down list by clicking the down arrow to the right of the box. Scroll through the Customer:Job list until you see the customer or job name and then click it.

3. Give the cash sale date.

Press Tab to move the cursor to the Date text box. Then enter the correct date in MM/DD/YY format. You can change the date by using any of the date-editing codes. (Chapter 4 and the Cheat Sheet at the front of the book describe these codes.)

4. (Optional) Enter a sale number.

QuickBooks suggests a cash sale number by adding 1 to the last cash sale number you used. Use this number or tab to the Sale No. text box and change it to whatever you want.

5. Fix the Sold To address, if necessary.

QuickBooks grabs the billing address from the Customer list and uses it as the Sold To address. You can change the address for the cash sale, however, by replacing the appropriate part of the usual billing address.

6. Record the check number.

Enter the customer's check number in the Check No. text box. If the customer is paying you with cold hard cash, you can leave the Check No. text box empty.

7. Specify the payment method.

To specify the payment method, activate the Payment Method drop-down list and select something from it: cash, check, VISA, MasterCard, or whatever. If you don't see the payment method that you want to use, you can add the method to the Payment Method list. Choose <Add New> to display the New Payment Method dialog box. Enter a description of the payment method in the dialog box's only text box.

8. Describe each item that you're selling.

Move the cursor to the first row of the Item/Description/Qty/Rate/Amount/Tax list box. When you do, QuickBooks turns the Item field into a drop-down list box. Activate the Item drop-down list of the first empty row in the list box and then select the item. When you do, QuickBooks fills in the Description and Rate text boxes with whatever sales description and sales price you entered in the Item list. (You can edit this information if you want, but it probably won't be necessary.) Enter the number of items sold in the Qty text box. (QuickBooks then calculates the amount by multiplying the quantity by the rate.) Describe each of the other items you're selling by filling in the next empty rows of the list box.

Note: If you've already read the chapter on invoicing customers (Chapter 4), what I'm about to tell you is going to seem very, very familiar. But just in case you haven't already read this in another chapter, you can put as many items on a cash sales receipt as you want. If you don't have enough room on a single page, QuickBooks just adds as many pages as you need to the receipt. The cash sales receipt total, of course, goes on the last page.

9. **Describe any special items that should be included on the cash sales receipt.**

If you didn't set up the QuickBooks item file, you have no idea what I'm talking about. But here's the scoop: QuickBooks thinks that anything that you stick on a receipt (or an invoice, for that matter) is something that you're selling. If you sell blue, yellow, and red thingamajigs, you obviously need to add each of these items to the Item list. But if you add freight charges to your receipt, QuickBooks thinks that these charges are just another thingamajig, so it requires you to enter another item in the list. The same is true for a volume discount that you want to stick on the receipt. And if you add sales tax to your receipt, well, guess what? QuickBooks thinks that the sales tax is just another item that needs to be included in the Item list. (For more information about working with your Item list and adding new items, refer to Chapter 2.)

To include one of these special items, move the cursor to the next empty row in the Item box, activate the drop-down list by clicking the arrow on the right side of the box, and then select the special item. After QuickBooks fills in the Description and Rate text boxes, edit this information, if necessary. Enter each special item — subtotals, discounts, freight, and so on — that you're itemizing on the receipt by filling in the next empty rows of the list box.

If you checked the Taxable check box when you added the item to the Item list, a small *T* appears in the Tax column to indicate that the item will be taxed.

If you want to include a discount item, you need to stick a subtotal item on the receipt after the inventory items or other items you want to discount. Then stick a discount item directly after the subtotal item. In this way, QuickBooks calculates the discount as a percentage of the subtotal.

10. (Optional) Add a customer message.

Click the Customer Message box, activate its drop-down list, and select a clever customer message. To add customer messages to the customer message list, choose <Add New>. When QuickBooks displays the New Customer Message box, fill it in and click OK.

11. Specify the sales tax.

If you specified tax information when you created your company file during the EasyStep Interview — remember how QuickBooks asked whether you charge sales tax? — QuickBooks fills in the default tax information by adding together the taxable items (which are indicated by the little *T* in the Tax column) and multiplying by the percentage you indicated when you created your company file. If the information is okay, move on to Step 12. If not, move the cursor to the Tax box that's to the right of the Customer Message box, activate the drop-down list box, and select the correct sales tax. If you need to add a new sales tax rate, you can choose <Add New> from the list.

12. (Truly optional and probably unnecessary for cash sales) Add a memo in the Memo text box.

You can include a memo description with the cash sale information. This memo isn't for your customer. It doesn't even print on the cash receipt, should you decide to print a cash receipt. It's for your eyes only. Memo descriptions give you a way to store information that's related to a sale with the cash sales receipt information.

13. Decide how you want to handle the resulting payment.

The option buttons in the lower-left corner enable you to designate whether to group the payment with other undeposited funds or deposit it directly to an account. To decide how to handle the payment, look at a previous bank statement. If your bank lists deposits as a transaction total, you should probably click the Group With Other Undeposited Funds button. If your bank lists deposits individually by check, you should probably click the Deposit To option button and use the drop-down list box to designate the account to which you want to deposit the payment. (By the way, I also describe how to handle deposits in this chapter, in the section titled "In the Bank.")

14. Decide whether you're going to print the receipt.

If you're not going to print the receipt, make sure that the To Be Printed check box is empty — if not, click it to remove the check.

Figure 5-2 shows a completed Enter Cash Sales window.

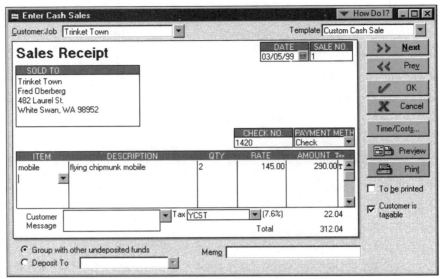

Figure 5-2:
A
completed
Enter Cash
Sales
window.

15. **Save the cash sales receipt.**

You can save the cash sales receipt in one of several ways:

- Click Next. QuickBooks saves the cash sales receipt shown on-screen and then redisplays an empty Enter Cash Sales window so that you can enter another cash sale. If you click Next, you're done with this receipt.

- If you don't want to enter additional cash sales, click OK. QuickBooks saves the cash sales receipt and closes the Enter Cash Sales window. If you click OK, you're done with this receipt.

- If you want to save the cash sale information and print a receipt for the cash sale immediately, click the Print button. After you click it, QuickBooks displays the Print One Sales Receipt dialog box, shown in Figure 5-3. The next section describes how to complete this dialog box.

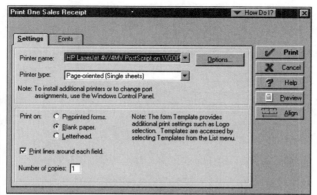

Figure 5-3:
The Print
One Sales
Receipt
dialog box.

Printing a Sales Receipt

To print a single cash sales receipt as you're recording the information, click the Print button in the Enter Cash Sales window. This displays the Print One Sales Receipt dialog box (refer to Figure 5-3). The following steps tell you how to complete this dialog box.

1. **Select the type of cash receipt form.**

   If you're using a different sales receipt form type than you described for the invoice/PO printer setup, select the type of form that you want to print on by clicking an option in the Print On box. You can choose Preprinted Forms, Blank Paper, or Letterhead. (See Chapter 4 for more on these printer options.)

   Note: You shouldn't have to worry about printing test receipts or fiddling with form alignment problems if you addressed these issues during the invoice/PO printer setup, so I'm not going to talk about the Align button here. If you want to print a test receipt or need to change the alignment, refer to Chapter 4 for information on how to proceed.

2. **Print that puppy!**

   Click the Print button to send the form to the printer. QuickBooks prints the sales receipt (see Figure 5-4). Then it displays a message box that asks whether the form printed correctly.

3. **Review the sales receipt and reprint the form, if necessary.**

   Review the cash sales receipt to see whether QuickBooks printed it correctly. If the form looks okay, click OK in the message box. If the form doesn't look okay, enter the form's sales number in the message box. Then fix whatever problem fouled up the printing; perhaps you forgot to include the company name and address, for example. Reprint the form by clicking the Print button again in the Print One Sales Receipt dialog box.

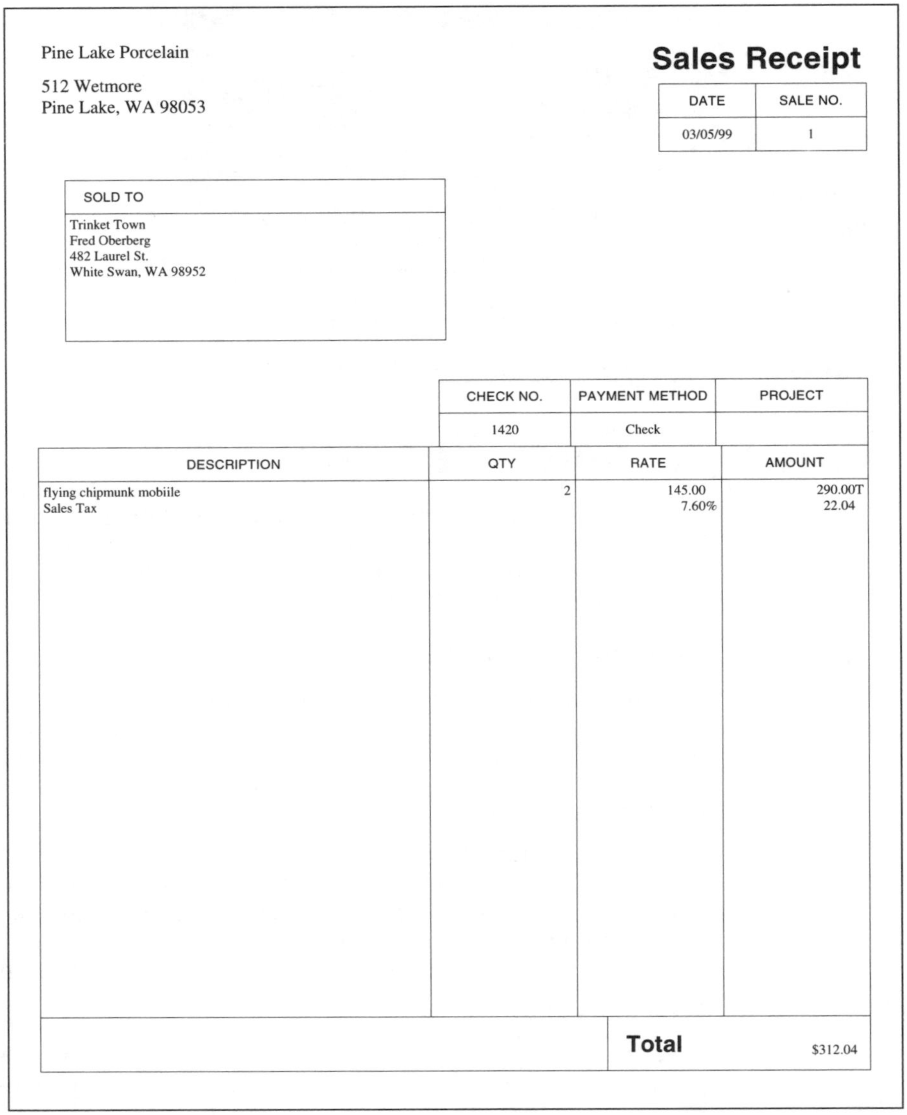

Pine Lake Porcelain

512 Wetmore
Pine Lake, WA 98053

Sales Receipt

DATE	SALE NO.
03/05/99	1

SOLD TO
Trinket Town Fred Oberberg 482 Laurel St. White Swan, WA 98952

CHECK NO.	PAYMENT METHOD	PROJECT
1420	Check	

DESCRIPTION	QTY	RATE	AMOUNT
flying chipmunk mobiile	2	145.00	290.00T
Sales Tax		7.60%	22.04

	Total	$312.04

Figure 5-4:
A printed
sales
receipt.

Note: To print a batch of receipts, make sure that you check the To Be Printed box on each receipt you want to print, and then choose File⇨Print Forms⇨ Print Sales Receipts. After displaying a window that allows you to choose which receipts to print — you choose them by putting a check in the first column and clicking OK — the Print Sales Receipts dialog box appears. This dialog box resembles the Print One Sales Receipt dialog box in just about every way, and the instructions work in exactly the same manner. For help with this dialog box, refer to the sections on printing invoices and credit memos in batches in Chapter 4.

Correcting Cash Sales Mistakes

If you make a mistake in entering a cash sale, don't worry. Fixing it is easy.

If the cash sales receipt is still displayed on the screen

If the cash sales receipt is still displayed on the screen, you can move the cursor to the box or button that's wrong and then fix the mistake. Most of the bits of information that you enter in the Enter Cash Sales window are fairly short or are entries that you've selected from a list. You can usually just replace the contents of some field by typing over whatever's already there or by making a couple of quick clicks. To save a correction, click OK, Next, or Prev.

If the cash sales receipt isn't displayed on the screen

If the cash sales receipt isn't displayed on the screen but you haven't yet printed it, you can use the Next and Prev buttons to page through the cash sales receipts. When you get to the one with the error, fix the error as described in the preceding section.

Even if you've printed the customer's receipt, you can make the sort of change that I just described. For example, you can page through the cash sales receipts by using the Next and Prev buttons until you find the receipt (now printed) with the error. And you can change the error and print the receipt again. I'm not so sure that you want to go this route, however. Things will be much cleaner if you void the cash sale by displaying the cash sales receipt and choosing Edit⇨Void Cash Sale. Then enter a new, correct cash sales transaction.

If you don't want the cash sales receipt

You usually won't want to delete cash sales receipts, but you can delete them. (You'll almost always be in much better shape if you just void the cash sales receipt.) To delete the receipt, display it in the Enter Cash Sales window (click the Sales and Customers tab of the QuickBooks Navigator, click the Cash Sales icon, and then page through the cash sales receipts by using the Next and Prev buttons until you see the cash sale that you want to delete) and then choose Edit⇨Delete Cash Sale. When QuickBooks asks you to confirm the deletion, click Yes.

If you want to see a list of all your cash sales, choose Edit⇨Find from the menu, choose Transaction Type from the Filter list box and Cash Sale from the drop-down list, and then click the Find button. QuickBooks gives you a list of your cash sales.

Recording Customer Payments

If your customers don't always pay you up-front for their purchases, you need to record another type of payment—the ones that customers make to pay off or pay down what you've invoiced them. To record the payments, of course, you need to first record invoices for the customer. (Chapter 4 describes how to record them.) The rest is easy.

All you do is click the Sales and Customers tab of the QuickBooks Navigator and click the Receive Payments icon to display the Receive Payments window. Then describe the customer payment and the invoices paid. If you want the gory details, read through the following steps:

1. **Display the Receive Payments window.**

   Click the Sales and Customers tab of the QuickBooks Navigator and click the Receive Payments icon to have QuickBooks display the Receive Payments window, shown in Figure 5-5.

2. **Identify the customer and, if necessary, the job.**

   Activate the Customer:Job drop-down list. Then select the customer or job by clicking it. QuickBooks lists the open, or unpaid, invoices for the customer in the big Outstanding Invoices/Statement Charges list box at the bottom of the window.

3. **Give the payment date.**

   Press Tab to move the cursor to the Date text box. Then enter the correct date in MM/DD/YY format. To edit the date, you can use the secret date-editing codes that are described in Chapter 4 and on the Cheat Sheet at the front of the book.

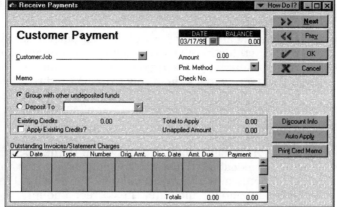

Figure 5-5:
The
Receive
Payments
window.

4. Enter the amount of the payment.

Move the cursor to the Amount line and enter the customer payment amount.

5. (Optional) Specify the payment method.

Activate the Pmt. Method drop-down list and select the payment method.

6. (Optional) Give the check number.

Oh, shoot. You can guess how this works, right? You move the cursor to the Check No. line. Then you type the check number from the customer's check. Do you need to do this? Naw. But this bit of information may be useful if you or the customer later have questions about what checks paid for what invoices. So I would go ahead and enter the check number.

7. (Optional) Add a memo description.

Use the Memo description for storing some bit of information that will help you in some way.

8. Decide how you want to handle the payment.

The option buttons under the Memo field should look somewhat familiar because they were also in the Enter Cash Sales window. These options enable you to designate whether to group the payment with other undeposited funds or deposit it directly to an account.

9. **(Optional) If the customer has any outstanding credits, decide whether to apply them in this payment.**

QuickBooks lists the amounts of any of the customer's existing credits. They could be anything from an overpayment on a previous invoice, to a return credit, to anything else. If you want to include these credits in the current transaction, click the Apply Existing Credits? check box to have the amount added to the Total to Apply amount. If a credit remains on the account, it appears in the Unapplied Amount total.

10. **Identify which open invoices the customer is paying.**

QuickBooks automatically applies the payment to the open invoices, starting with the oldest open invoice. You can change this application by entering amounts in the Payment column. Simply click the open invoice's payment amount and enter the correct amount.

You can leave a portion of the payment unapplied, if you want to. You also can create a credit memo for the unapplied portion of a customer payment by clicking the Print Cred Memo button. (For information on what steps you need to follow next to print a credit memo, refer to Chapter 4.)

If you want to apply the customer payment to the oldest open invoices automatically, click the Auto Apply button. If you want to unapply payments that you've already applied to open invoices, click the Clear Payments button. Clear Payments and Auto Apply are the same button. QuickBooks changes the name of the button depending on whether you've already applied payments.

11. **(Optional) Adjust the early payment discounts, if necessary.**

If you offer payment terms that include an early payment discount, QuickBooks reduces the open invoice original amount (shown in the Orig. Amt. column) by the early payment discount to calculate the adjusted amount due (shown in the Amt. Due column). If this discount is incorrect — or, more likely, if the customer takes the early payment discount even though the payment isn't early — you may need to adjust the early payment discount.

To adjust the discount, select the open invoice that has the early payment discount that you want to change. Then click the Discount Info button. QuickBooks, with little or no hesitation, displays the Discount Information dialog box, shown in Figure 5-6. Enter the dollar amount of the discount in the Amount of Discount text box. Then specify the expense account that you want to use to track early payment discounts by activating the Discount Account drop-down list and selecting one of the accounts. (Interest Expense is probably a good account to use, unless you want to set up a special early discounts expense account

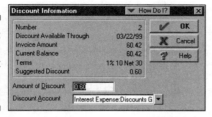

Figure 5-6:
The
Discount
Information
dialog box.

called something like Discount Expense or Discounts Given. After all, early payment discounts amount to interest.) Click OK when you finish to return to the Receive Payments window. (For more information on the costs and benefits of early payment discounts, see Chapter 18.)

12. Record the customer payment information.

When you've identified which invoices the customer is paying — the unapplied amount should probably show as zero — you're ready to record the customer payment information. You can record it in two ways:

- If you want to record more payments, click Next. QuickBooks saves the customer payment shown on the screen and then redisplays an empty Receive Payments window so that you can enter another payment. (Note that you can return to customer payments you recorded earlier by clicking the Prev button.)

- If you don't want to record additional payments, click OK. QuickBooks saves the customer payment information and closes the Receive Payments window.

Correcting Mistakes in Customer Payments Entries

You can correct mistakes that you make in entering customer payments basically the same way that you correct mistakes that you make in entering cash sales. First, you display the window you used to enter the transaction. In the case of customer payments, you click the Sales and Customers tab of the QuickBooks Navigator and click the Receive Payments icon to display the Receive Payments window. Then you use the Next and Prev buttons to page through the customer payments you entered previously until you see the one you want to change. And then you make your changes. Pretty straightforward, right?

In the Bank

Whenever you record a cash sale or a customer payment on an invoice, QuickBooks adds the cash to its list of undeposited funds. These undeposited funds could be a bunch of checks that you haven't yet deposited or currency and coins. (I wanted to use the word *coinage* here, because that's what your bank deposit slip probably uses. My long-suffering editor, however, overruled me, saying *coinage* is a crummy word and overly complex.)

Eventually, though, you'll want to deposit the money in the bank. Follow these steps:

1. **Display the Payments to Deposit dialog box.**

   Click the Sales and Customers tab of the QuickBooks Navigator and click the Deposits icon. QuickBooks displays the Payments to Deposit dialog box, shown in Figure 5-7. This dialog box lists all the payments, regardless of the payment method. Amounts from cash sales are listed as RCPT, and amounts from invoice payments are listed as PMT.

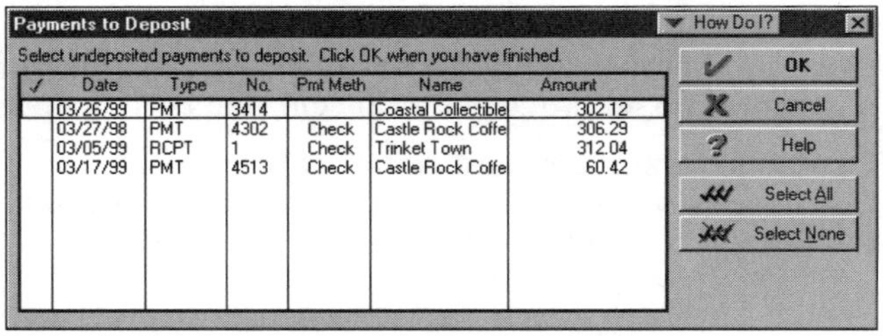

Figure 5-7:
The
Payments
to Deposit
dialog box.

2. **Select the payments that you want to deposit.**

   Click a payment or cash receipt to place a check mark in front of it, marking it for deposit. If you want to uncheck a payment, click it again. To uncheck all the payments, click the Select None button. To check all the payments, click the Select All button.

3. **Click OK.**

   After you indicate which payments you want to deposit, click OK. QuickBooks displays the Make Deposits window, shown in Figure 5-8.

4. **Tell QuickBooks into which bank account you'll deposit the money.**

   Activate the Deposit To drop-down list and select the bank account in which you want to place the funds.

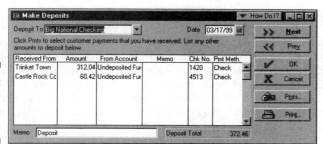

Figure 5-8:
The Make
Deposits
window.

5. Give the deposit date.

Press Tab to move the cursor to the Date text box. Then enter the correct date in MM/DD/YY format. Use the secret date-editing codes if you need to edit the date. (Get these codes from Chapter 4 or the Cheat Sheet at the front of the book if you don't know them.)

6. (Optional) Add a memo description, if you want.

I don't know what sort of memo description you would add for a deposit. Sorry. A bank deposit is a bank deposit. At least to me.

By the way, if you need to redisplay the Payments to Deposit dialog box — like maybe you made a mistake or something and now you need to go back and fix it — click the Pmts button. Note, though, that QuickBooks won't display the Payments to Deposit dialog box unless the undeposited funds list has payments on it.

7. Record the deposit.

Click OK or Next. (Click Next if you want to record another deposit. When you click Next, QuickBooks keeps the Make Deposits window displayed on the screen.)

Improving Your Cash Inflow

I'm not going to provide a lengthy discussion on how to go about collecting cash from your customers. I do, however, want to quickly tell you about a couple of other things. You need to know how to monitor what your customers owe you and how to assess finance charges. Don't worry, though. I explain these two things as briefly as I can.

Tracking what your customers owe

You can track what your customers owe in a couple of ways. Probably the simplest method is to click the Sales and Customers tab of the QuickBooks Navigator and click the Customer Register icon. Then select the customer from the Customer:Job drop-down list box and click the Q-Report button. QuickBooks whips up a quick, on-screen report that shows the invoices you've billed a customer for and the payments the customer has made. Figure 5-9 shows one of these QuickReports.

Figure 5-9:
A
QuickReport
that
describes a
customer.

	Customer QuickReport					▼ How Do I? ▢ ▢ ☒
Customize...	Filters...	Format...	Header/Footer...	Hide Header	Print...	Memorize...	Refresh

Dates [All ▼] From [🔲] To [🔲]

Pine Lake Porcelain
05/12/98 **Customer QuickReport**
All Transactions

◇ Type ◇	Date ◇	Num ◇	Memo ◇	Account ◇	Clr ◇	Split ◇	Amount ◇
Castle Rock Coffee House							
▶ Invoice	12/31/98	1		Accounts Receiva...		Sales	14,000.00 ◀
Invoice	12/31/98	2		Accounts Receiva...		-SPLIT-	13,800.00
Payment	01/17/99	8097		Undeposited Funds	✓	Accounts Re...	14,000.00
Deposit	01/19/99			Big National Check...	✓	Accounts Re...	4,000.00
Payment	01/29/99			Undeposited Funds	✓	Accounts Re...	13,800.00
Invoice	02/01/99	3		Accounts Receiva...		-SPLIT-	302.12
Invoice	03/12/99	2		Accounts Receiva...		-SPLIT-	60.42
Invoice	03/15/99	FC 1	Finance Cha...	Accounts Receiva...		-SPLIT-	4.17
Payment	03/17/99	4513		Undeposited Funds	✓	Accounts Re...	60.42
Cash Sale	03/31/99	3		Undeposited Funds	✓	-SPLIT-	7,930.65
Estimate	04/02/99	1		Estimates		-SPLIT-	75.53

You also should be aware that QuickBooks provides several nifty accounts receivable, or A/R, reports. You get to these reports by clicking the Sales and Customers tab of the QuickBooks Navigator and clicking Accounts Receivable from the Reports area at the bottom of the tab. QuickBooks then displays a list of about half a dozen reports that describe how much money customers owe you. Some reports, for example, organize open invoices into different groups based on how old the invoices are. (These reports are called *agings.*) Some reports summarize only invoices or payments. And some reports show each customer's open, or unpaid, balance.

Chapter 14 describes in general terms how you go about producing and printing QuickBooks reports. So refer to Chapter 14 if you have questions. Let me also say that you can't hurt anything or foul up your financial records just by printing reports. So go ahead and noodle around.

You can print a statement to send to a customer by clicking the Sales and Customers tab of the QuickBooks Navigator and then clicking the Statements icon. Use the Select Statements to Print dialog box to describe which customers you want to print statements for and the date ranges you want the statements to show, and then click OK to print the statements.

Assessing finance charges

I wasn't exactly sure where to stick this discussion of finance charges. But finance charges seem to relate to collecting the cash your customers owe, so I figure that it's okay to talk about assessing finance charges here.

To assess finance charges, follow these steps:

1. **Click the Sales and Customers tab of the QuickBooks Navigator, and click the Finance Charges icon.**

   If you don't have finance charges set up, QuickBooks displays a message box that asks whether you want to set up finance charges now. Click Yes in this message box.

   QuickBooks displays the Preferences dialog box, shown in Figure 5-10. (If you have assessed finance charges before, QuickBooks displays the Assess Finance Charges window. You can display the Preferences dialog box and check or edit your finance charge settings by clicking the Settings button in the Assess Finance Charges window.)

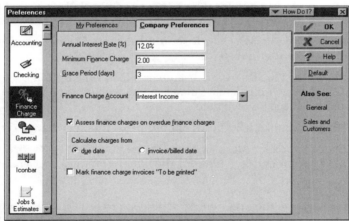

Figure 5-10:
The
Preferences
dialog box
for finance
charges.

2. **Enter the annual interest rate that you want to use to calculate finance charges.**

   Move the cursor to the Annual Interest Rate text box and enter the annual interest rate.

3. **(Optional) Enter the minimum finance charge — if one exists.**

   Move the cursor to the Minimum Finance Charge text box and enter the minimum charge. If you always charge at least $2.00 on a past due invoice, for example, type **2**.

4. Enter the number of days of grace that you give.

Days of Grace. That sounds kind of like an artsy movie or serious novel, doesn't it? Basically, this number is how many days of slack you'll cut people. If you enter 3 in the Grace Period text box, QuickBooks doesn't start assessing finance charges until three days after the invoice is past due.

5. Specify which account you want to use to track the finance charges.

Activate the Finance Charge Account drop-down list and select an account. Finance charges are, essentially, interest that you charge your customers. So unless you have some other account that you want to use, you may just want to use the Interest Income account that appears on most of the standard charts of accounts.

6. Indicate whether you want to charge finance charges on finance charges.

Does this make sense? If you charge somebody a finance charge and they don't pay the finance charge, eventually it becomes past due, too. So then what do you do the next time you assess finance charges? Do you calculate a finance charge on the finance charge? If you want to do this — and state and local laws let you — check the Assess Finance Charges on Overdue Finance Charges check box.

7. Tell QuickBooks whether it should calculate finance charges from the due date or the invoice date.

Select either the Due Date or Invoice/Billed Date option button. As you might guess, you calculate bigger finance charges if you start accruing interest on the invoice date.

8. Tell QuickBooks whether it should print finance charge invoices.

Check the box for Mark Finance Charge Invoices "To Be Printed" if you want to print invoices later for the finance charges that you calculate.

9. Click OK.

After you use the Preferences dialog box to tell QuickBooks how the finance charges should be calculated, click OK. QuickBooks displays the Assess Finance Charges window, shown in Figure 5-11. This window shows all the finance charges that QuickBooks has calculated, organized by customer.

10. Give the finance charge assessment date.

Move the cursor to the Assessment Date text box and enter the date when you're assessing the finance charges, which I'm willing to bet is the current date. (This date is also the invoice date that will be used on the finance charge invoices, if you create them.)

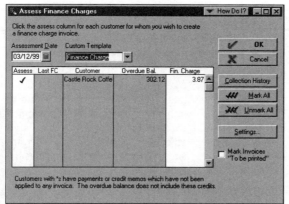

Figure 5-11:
The Assess
Finance
Charges
window.

11. **Confirm which customers you want to be assessed finance charges.**

    QuickBooks initially marks all the finance charges, which means that it sets up a new invoice for each finance charge. (QuickBooks marks finance charges with a little check mark.) If you want to unmark (or later mark) a finance charge, click it. To unmark all the charges, click the Unmark All button. To mark all the charges, click the Mark All button.

    You can produce a collections report for any of the customers or jobs listed in the Assess Finance Charges dialog box by selecting the customer name and then clicking the Collection History button.

12. **Indicate whether you want finance charge invoices printed.**

    If you do, check the Mark Invoices "To Be Printed" check box.

13. **Click OK.**

    When the Assess Finance Charges dialog box correctly describes the finance charges that you want to assess, click OK. You're finished with the finance charge calculations and assessments.

    I'm not going to describe how to print invoices containing finance charges because I already slogged through invoice printing in painstaking detail in Chapter 4. If you have questions about how to print the invoices, you may want to visit that chapter.

A word of advice from an accountant

While I'm on the subject of tracking what your customers owe you, let me share a thought about collecting this money. You should have firm collection procedures that you follow faithfully. For example, as soon as an invoice is past due a week or so, it's very reasonable to place a friendly telephone call to the customer's accounts payable department and verify that the customer has received the invoice and is in the process of paying. You have no reason to be embarrassed because some customer is late in paying you! What's more, you may find out something surprising and essential to your collection. You may discover, for example, that the customer didn't receive the invoice. Or you may find out that something was wrong with the gizmo you sold or the service you provided.

As soon as an invoice is a month or so past due, you need to crank up the pressure. A firm letter asking that the customer call you to explain the past due amount is very reasonable — especially if the customer assured you only a few weeks ago that payment was forthcoming.

When an invoice is a couple of months past due, you need to get pretty serious. You will probably want to stop selling the customer anything more because it's unclear whether you'll be paid. And you may want to start a formal collection process. (Ask your attorney about starting such a process.)

Chapter 6

Paying Bills

· ·

In This Chapter

▶ Using the Write Checks window to pay bills

▶ Using the Accounts Payable method to pay bills

▶ Deleting and editing bill payments

▶ Reminding yourself to pay bills

▶ Paying sales taxes

· ·

*B*enjamin Franklin said, "Nothing is certain except death and taxes and bills." Actually, I added the bills part. Hardly a day goes by that most people don't get at least one bill in the mail. I've been told to look on the bright side: If my business gets a lot of bills, it means that I have a lot of activity and I'm doing pretty well. Okay, looking on the bright side is my specialty, but that still doesn't mean that I like paying bills.

QuickBooks gives you a couple of different ways to pay and record your bills. And you have many options when it comes to deciding when to pay your bills, how to pay your bills, and how to record your bills for the purposes of tracking inventory and expenses.

This chapter explains not only how to pay vendor bills but also how to pay that all-important bill that so many businesses owe to their state and local governments. I'm talking, of course, about sales taxes.

Pay Now or Pay Later?

When it comes to paying bills, you have a fundamental choice to make. You can either record and pay your bills as they come in, or you can delay when payments are recorded and made in order to hang on to your money longer. The second method, called the accounts payable method, gives you more leeway for managing your cash flow. If push comes to shove and you can't cover all your bills, using the accounts payable method enables you to pick and choose which bills to pay. It also gives you a better understanding of how much cash you have on hand and how much you owe.

If you have a small business with little overhead, you may just as well record and pay bills as they arrive. But if you need to juggle cash, I strongly recommend the accounts payable method of paying bills. And besides, using the accounts payable method with QuickBooks is not as difficult as it may seem at first.

The next section of this chapter describes how to pay bills by writing checks. A little later in the chapter, in a section called "Recording Your Bills the Accounts Payable Way," you find out how to pay bills by using the accounts payable method.

Recording Your Bills by Writing Checks

You've just come back from lunch to discover the day's mail waiting on your desk. Naturally, there's a bill. You open it, fire up your computer, and load QuickBooks. Now what? How do you write a check for the bill and then record your payment? Better read on. . . .

Note: When you record bills by writing checks, you're doing cash-basis accounting.

The slow way to write checks

You can write checks either from the register or from the Write Checks window. Using the Write Checks window is the slow way, but it enables you to record your expenses and the items (if any) that you purchase. Using the Write Checks window is the best choice in the following situations:

- ✔ You're paying for something for which you have a purchase order.
- ✔ You plan to be reimbursed for the bill that you're paying.
- ✔ You want to record what job or class this bill falls under.

Follow these steps to use the Write Checks window to write checks:

1. **Click the Checking and Credit Cards tab of the QuickBooks Navigator, and click the Checks icon.**

   The Write Checks window appears on-screen (see Figure 6-1). Notice that this window has three parts:

   - The check part on the top, which you no doubt recognize from having written thousands of checks in the past.
   - The buttons on the right.

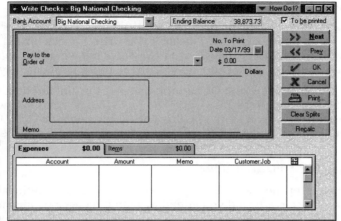

Figure 6-1:
The Write
Checks
window.

- The Expenses and Items tab at the bottom of the window. This
  part is for recording what the check is for, as I explain in Steps 7, 8,
  and 9.

2. **Click the Bank Account drop-down list and choose the account from
   which you want to write this check.**

This is a very important step if you have more than one account. Make
sure you choose the correct account; otherwise, your account balances
in QuickBooks will be incorrect.

3. **Fill in the Pay to the Order Of line.**

If you've written a check to this person or party before, the AutoFill
feature fills in the name of the payee in the Pay to the Order Of line for
you. (AutoFill does this by comparing what you typed with names
shown in the Customer, Vendor, Employee, and Other Names lists.)
AutoFill also puts the payee's address in the Address box. In fact, the
AutoFill feature fills out the entire check for you, based on the last
check that you wrote to this vendor.

Does the check look all right? Maybe all you need to do is tab around,
adjusting numbers. If that's the case, go for it! Otherwise, read the next
12 steps (another 12-step program?). These steps explain how to record
information about a new vendor and pay a check to that vendor in one
fell swoop.

If you've never paid anything to this person before, the program
displays a Name Not Found message box after you enter the name on
the Pay to the Order Of line. You can either click Quick Add or Set Up to
add the payee name to one of your lists. (Check out the sidebar "To
Quick Add or to Set Up" to find out how to do so.)

4. **Enter the amount of the check.**

   Now comes my favorite part. I've always found it a big bother to write out the amount of checks. I mean, if you write a check for $21,457.00, how do you fit *twenty-one-thousand-four-hundred-fifty-seven dollars and no cents* on the line? Where do you put all those hyphens, anyway?

   All you have to do with QuickBooks is enter the amount next to the dollar sign and press Tab. When you press Tab, QuickBooks writes out the amount for you on the Dollars line. At moments like this, I'm grateful to be alive in the late 20th century when computer technology can do these marvelous things for me.

5. **Fill in the Address text box.**

   Filling in this box is optional. You need to fill it in only if the address isn't there already and you intend to send the check by mail using an envelope with a window.

6. **Fill in the Memo line.**

   Filling in the Memo line is optional, too. You can put a message to the payee on the Memo line — a message such as "Quit bleeding me dry." But you usually put an account number on the Memo line so that the payee can record your account number.

   If you try to click OK and close the dialog box now, QuickBooks tells you that you can't and tries to bite your leg off. Why? Because you can't write a check unless you fill out the Expenses and Items tabs. You use these tabs to describe what the check pays.

7. **Move the cursor down to the Account column of the Expenses tab and enter an expense account name.**

   Chances are that you want to enter the name of an account that's already on the chart of accounts. If that's the case, move the cursor to a field in the Account column, and QuickBooks turns the field into a drop-down list box. Click the down arrow to see a list of all your accounts. You'll probably have to scroll down the list to get to the expense accounts. Click the one that this check applies to (most likely it's Supplies or Rent or something like that). If you need to create a new expense account category for this check, choose Add New from the top of the list to see the New Account dialog box. Fill in the information and click OK.

   What if the money that you're paying out with this check can be distributed across two, three, or four expense accounts? Simply click below the account that you just entered. The down arrow shoots down next to the cursor. Click the down arrow and enter another expense account, and another, and another, if you want to.

To Quick Add or to Set Up?

If you click Quick Add in the Name Not Found message box, you see a Select Name Type message box, asking whether the payee is a Vendor, Customer, Employee, or Other. Most likely, the payee is a vendor, in which case you click Vendor (but you can click one of the other three options). The address information that you write on the check goes in the Vendor List — or Customer, Employee, or Other Names List, depending on what you clicked. (Refer to Chapter 2 if you're in the dark about adding to your lists.)

Choosing Set Up in the Name Not Found message box is a little more interesting. When you choose this option, you also see the Select Name Type box. Click Vendor, Customer, Employee, or Other. Click OK, and then you see the New whatever window that you may remember from Chapter 2, if you've already added new vendors, customers, or employees to your lists.

8. **Tab over to the Amount column, if necessary, and change the numbers around.**

   If you're distributing this check across more than one account, you want to make sure that the numbers in the Amount column add up to the total of the check as shown in Figure 6-2. Well, do they?

9. **If you want to, enter words of explanation or encouragement in the Memo column.**

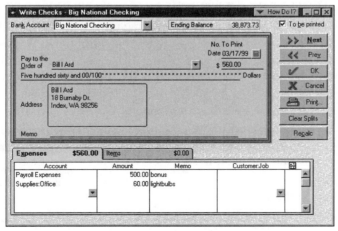

Figure 6-2:
A completed check.

Someday, you may have to go back to this check and try to figure out what these expenses mean. The Memo column may be your only clue. Enter some wise words here: "August rent," "copier repair," or "company party."

10. (Optional) Assign the expense to the Customer:Job column.

If you plan to be reimbursed for these expenses, or if you just want to track your expenses by job, enter the name of the customer who will reimburse you. Click the down arrow to find the customer. Enter an amount for each account, if necessary.

11. (Optional) Assign the expense to a class.

You also can track expenses by class, by making entries in the Class column. Notice the usual down arrow, which you click to see a list of classes. You won't see the Class column, however, unless you told QuickBooks that you want to use classes when you created your company.

If you want to have QuickBooks track expenses by class, you have to set it up to do so. To set up QuickBooks to track expenses, click the Company tab of the QuickBooks Navigator and click the Preferences icon. Then click the Accounting icon from the list on the left and mark the Use Class Tracking check box. (You may need to display the Company Preferences tab to see this check box.)

12. Use the Items tab to record what you're purchasing.

You may already have filled out a purchase order for the items for which you're paying. If so, click the Select PO button to see a list of purchases on order with this vendor. Check the ones for which you are paying and click OK.

If you don't have a purchase order for the items, perform lucky Step 13.

13. Move to the Item column and enter a name for the item.

Notice the down arrow in this column. Click the arrow to see the Items list. Does the item that you're paying for appear on this list? If so, click it. If not, choose <Add New> from the top of the list and fill out the New Item window (refer to Chapter 2).

14. Fill in the rest of the Items columns.

You can enter all the items you're purchasing in this column. Make sure that the Items tab accurately shows the items that you're purchasing, their cost, and the quantity.

When you're done adding items, you may want to use one of the options in the Write Checks window:

- Click the Print button to print the check in the Write Checks window. This does not print all the checks that you have written and marked as to be printed, however. (I explain how to print more than one check at a time in Chapter 10.)

- The Clear Splits button deletes any individual amounts that you've entered for separate expenses or items on the Expenses and Items tabs. QuickBooks then enters the total amount of the check in the Amount column on the Expenses tab.

- The Recalc button totals the items and expenses in the dialog box. It also puts the total on both the numeric and text amount lines of the check.

- The To Be Printed check box designates the check for printing. Check this box if you want to print the check with QuickBooks using your printer and pre-printed check forms. Uncheck this box if you are recording a handwritten check.

15. **Click Next or OK to finish writing the check.**

    Click Next if you want QuickBooks to display another blank check form or click OK if you don't have any more checks to write. If you write check number 101, for example, clicking Next takes you to check 102 so that you can write that one. (Clicking Prev moves you to check 100 in case you need to edit a check you've written earlier.)

Well, that's over with. For a minute there, I thought that it would never end. . . .

The fast way to write checks

If you want to pay a bill that you won't be reimbursed for or that you don't need to track in any way, shape, or form, you can write your check directly from the checking account register. This method is the fast and easy way to write checks.

1. **Open the checking account register.**

   Click the Checking and Credit Card tab of the QuickBooks Navigator and click the Check Register icon. If you have more than one bank account, select the proper account from the drop-down list and click OK. QuickBooks displays the register for the checking account (see Figure 6-3). The cursor is at the end of the register, ready and waiting for you to enter check information.

2. **Fill in the information for the check.**

   Notice that the entries you make are the same ones you would make on a check. You need to note a couple of things about the register:

   - If you enter a Payee name that QuickBooks does not recognize, you see the Name Not Found message box, and you're asked to give information about this new, mysterious vendor. To see what to do next, go back to Step 3 in the instructions on how to write a check the slow way, earlier in this chapter.

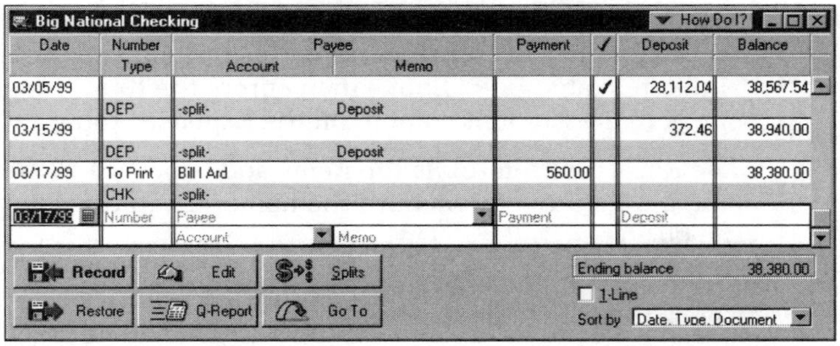

Figure 6-3:
The
checking
account
register.

- You have to choose an account name. Chances are, you can find the right one in the Account drop-down list, but if you can't, enter one of your own. You then see the Account Not Found message box and are asked to fill in the information about this new account.

If you decide, as you fill out the register, that you want to be reimbursed for this check or that you want to track expenses and items, click the Edit button. You see the Write Checks window that you know from Figure 6-1. Follow Steps 3 through 14 in the instructions on how to write a check the slow way (earlier in this chapter) to fill in the Write Checks window. When you're done filling in the Write Checks window, click OK. You're back where you started, in the Register window.

3. When you finish filling in the check information, click Record.

You click Record, of course, to record the check.

By the way, that Restore button is there in case you fill out the register but decide that you want to go back to square one. Clicking Restore blanks out what you just entered so that you can start all over again.

If you want to print the check (or checks) that you've just entered, you need to flip to Chapter 10 for details. In the meantime, Chapter 8 gives you the lowdown on keeping your checkbook — so turn to that chapter if this discussion of checks has you really excited.

Recording Your Bills the Accounts Payable Way

The accounts payable, or A/P, way of paying bills involves two steps. The first is a trifle on the difficult side, and the second step is as easy as pie. First, you record your bills. If you've read the section earlier in this chapter on writing checks the slow way, you're already familiar with using the Expenses tab and the Items tab to record bills. You need to fill out those tabs for the A/P method as well if you want to distribute a bill to accounts, customers, jobs, classes, and items. If you read the first half of this chapter, some of what follows will be old hat.

After you record your bills, you can go on to the second step. All you have to do is tell QuickBooks which bills to pay. QuickBooks then writes the checks. You print them. You mail them.

To make the A/P method work, you have to record your bills as they come in. That doesn't mean that you have to pay them right away. By recording your bills, you can keep track of how much money you owe and how much money your business really has. QuickBooks reminds you when your bills are due so that you don't have to worry about forgetting to pay a bill. Also, by recording bills as they arrive, you can take advantage of early payment discounts. Or, if the vendor allows 60 days for payment, for example, you can hang on to your money for the full 60 days.

When you record bills the accounts payable way, you're using *accrual-basis accounting*. Accrual-basis accounting is described in Appendix B.

Recording your bills

When a bill comes in, the first thing to do is record it. You can record bills through the Enter Bills window or the Accounts Payable register. If you plan to track bills by expense and item, you need to use the Enter Bills window. I describe that method first. If you have a simple bill to pay that doesn't need to be reimbursed or tracked, skip ahead to the "Paying Your Bills" section, later in this chapter.

Follow these steps to record a bill through the Enter Bills dialog box:

1. **Click the Purchases and Vendors tab of the QuickBooks Navigator and click the Enter Bills icon.**

   Figure 6-4 shows the Enter Bills window. You no doubt notice that the top half of this window looks a great deal like a check — that's because much of the information that you put here ends up on the check that you write to pay your bill. (If you see the word Credit in the upper-left box rather than Bill, click the Bill option button at the top of the dialog box. You also can use this screen to enter credit from vendors.)

2. **Select the name of the vendor you're paying.**

   If you want to pay this bill to a vendor who's already on the Vendor list, simply click the down arrow at the end of the Vendor line and choose the vendor. (QuickBooks then automatically fills the Enter Bills window with as much information as it can remember.)

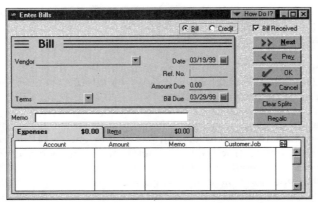

Figure 6-4:
The Enter
Bills
window.

But if this vendor is new, QuickBooks asks you to Quick Add or Set Up some information about the vendor — the address, credit limit, payment terms, and so on. You provide this information in the New Vendor window. If you're not familiar with this window from Chapter 2, make a brief visit to that chapter.

If you have one or more unfilled purchase orders with the vendor you select, QuickBooks asks you if you want to receive against a purchase order. Click Yes if you do or No if you do not. If you choose to receive against a purchase order, QuickBooks displays the dialog box shown in Figure 6-5 (which appears later in this section). When you select one or more purchase orders to receive against, QuickBooks fills in the items and amounts from these orders for you, which you can modify as necessary.

3. Select the payment terms that describe when the bill is due.

In the Terms line, open the drop-down list and select the payment terms (if the information is not already there from when you set up the vendor). If you receive a discount for paying this bill early, QuickBooks calculates the discount automatically.

4. (Optional) Enter a memo to describe the bill.

You can enter a note in the Memo box. The note that you enter appears on the A/P register.

5. Move the cursor down to the Account column of the E̲xpenses tab and enter an expense account name.

Chances are, you want to enter the name of an expense account that's already on the chart of accounts. If that is the case, click the down arrow to see a list of all your accounts. You probably have to scroll down the list to get to the expense accounts (a fast way to move down the list is to start typing the account name — you go straight down the list). Click the account that this bill represents (most likely it's Supplies or something like that).

If you need to create a new expense account category for this bill, choose <Add New> from the top of the list. You see the New Account dialog box. Fill in the information and click OK.

What if the money that you're paying out because of this bill can be split among two, three, or four expense accounts? Simply click below the account that you just entered. The down arrow shoots down next to the cursor. Click the arrow and enter another expense account, and another, and another, if you want to.

6. **Tab over to the Amount column, if necessary, and change the numbers.**

If you're splitting this bill among several accounts, make sure that the numbers in the Amount column add up to the total of the bill. Well, do they?

7. **If you want to, enter words of explanation or wisdom in the Memo column.**

8. **(Optional) Assign the expense to a Customer:Job.**

If you plan to be reimbursed for these expenses, or if you just want to track your expenses by job, enter the customer who will reimburse you. Enter an amount for each account, if necessary. You can use the down arrow to find customers, and then click them.

9. **(Optional) Assign the expense to a class.**

You also can track expenses by class, by making entries in the Class column. Notice the usual down arrow and click it to see a list of classes. (You don't see a Class column unless you've told QuickBooks that you want to use classes this way.)

If you want, click the Recalc button to total the expenses.

If you want to have QuickBooks track expenses by class, you have to set it up to do so. To set up QuickBooks to track expenses by class, click the Company tab of the QuickBooks Navigator and click the Preferences icon. Then click the Accounting icon from the list on the left and mark the Use Class Tracking check box. (You may need to click the Company Preferences tab in order to see this check box.)

10. **Use the Items tab to record the various items that are represented by the bill.**

Click the Items tab. Enter the items you purchased and the prices you paid for them.

TIP

If you realize after partially completing the bill that the bill does indeed pay a purchase order, click the Select PO button in the lower-left corner of the dialog box to see the Open Purchase Orders dialog box (see Figure 6-5).

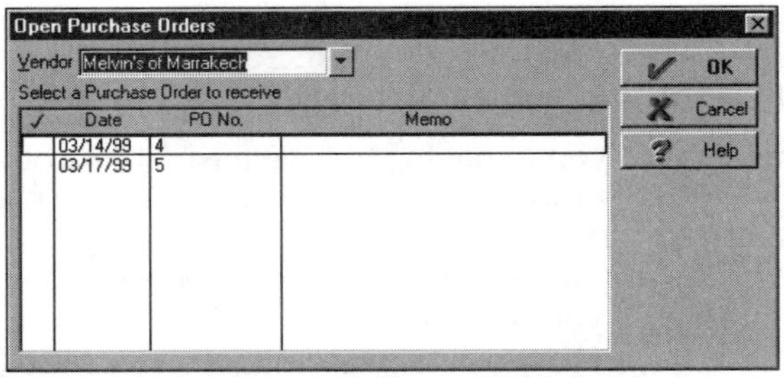

Figure 6-5:
Paying a bill against a purchase order.

From the Vendor drop-down list, click the name of the vendor who sent you the bill. In the list of open purchase orders, click in the column on the left to put a check next to the purchase order (or orders) for which you're paying. Easy enough? Click OK when you're done, and QuickBooks fills the Items tab out for you automatically.

11. Move to the Item column and enter a name for the item.

Notice the down arrow in this column. Click it to see the Item list. Does the item that you're paying for appear on this list? If so, click that item. If not, choose <Add New> from the top of the list and fill out the New Item window (refer to Chapter 2).

12. Fill in the rest of the Item column.

You can enter all the items you're purchasing here. Make sure that the Items tab accurately shows the items that you're purchasing, their costs, and their quantities. If you want to, click the Recalc button to total the items.

13. Click Next, Prev, or OK.

Click Next if you want to enter information on another bill. Clicking OK closes the dialog box and puts all the information that you just entered in the Accounts Payable register. Prev just takes you to the previous bill you entered in case you want to change something there.

Entering your bills the fast way

You also can enter bills directly in the Accounts Payable register. This method is faster, but it makes tracking expenses and items more difficult. Follow these steps if you want to enter bills directly in the Accounts Payable register:

1. Open the chart of accounts.

Click the Company tab of the QuickBooks Navigator and click the Chart of Accounts icon.

Using the Find dialog box

When you can't quite remember the information you need in order to find a particular entry or transaction, you can search for it by using the Find dialog box. For example, if you can't recall when you entered the bill, choose Edit⇨Find to open the Find dialog box, shown in the accompanying figure. Choose a filter (the category to search by). The box to the right changes to include drop-down list boxes or text boxes that you can use to specify what you'd like to search for.

Choose as many filters as you like, but be careful to enter information accurately, or QuickBooks looks for the wrong information.

Also, try to strike a balance, choosing only as many filters as you really need to find your information. The more filters you choose, the more searching QuickBooks does, and the longer the search takes.

After you finish choosing filters, click the Find button, and the transactions that match all your filters appear in the list at the bottom of the window. Click the transaction that you want to examine more closely and then click Go To. QuickBooks opens the appropriate window and takes you right to the transaction. Very snazzy, I do believe.

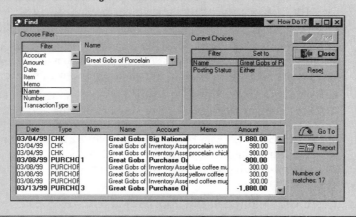

2. **Open the Accounts Payable register.**

   Double-click the Accounts Payable account in the chart of accounts' list of accounts. You see the Accounts Payable register window, shown in Figure 6-6. The cursor is at the end of the register, ready and waiting for you to enter the next bill.

3. **Fill in the information for your bill.**

   Enter the same information that you would if you were filling in the Enter Bills window described at the beginning of this chapter. In the Vendor text box, click the down arrow and choose a name from the Vendor list.

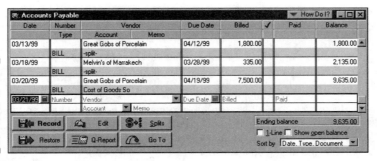

Date	Number	Vendor		Due Date	Billed	✓	Paid	Balance
	Type	Account	Memo					
03/13/99		Great Gobs of Porcelain		04/12/99	1,800.00			1,800.00
	BILL	-split-						
03/18/99		Melvin's of Marrakech		03/28/99	335.00			2,135.00
	BILL	-split-						
03/20/99		Great Gobs of Porcelain		04/19/99	7,500.00			9,635.00
	BILL	Cost of Goods So						
03/21/99	Number	Vendor		Due Date	Billed		Paid	
		Account	Memo					

Ending balance   9,635.00

☐ 1-Line ☐ Show open balance
Sort by [Date, Type, Document]

[Record] [Edit] [Splits]
[Restore] [Q-Report] [Go To]

Figure 6-6:
The
Accounts
Payable
register.

If you enter a vendor name that QuickBooks doesn't recognize, you see the Vendor Not Found message box and are asked to give information about this new, mysterious vendor. Either click Quick Add to have the program collect the information from the register as you fill it out, or click Set Up to see the New Vendor dialog box. (The choice between Quick Add and Set Up is described in the sidebar "To Quick Add or Set Up?" earlier in this chapter. Setting up new vendors is described in Chapter 2.)

You have to choose an account name. You probably can find the right one in the Account drop-down list, but if you can't, then enter one of your own. You see the Account Not Found message box, and QuickBooks asks you to fill in information about this new account.

If you decide as you fill out the register that you want to be reimbursed for this check or that you want to track expenses and items, choose the Edit button to see the Enter Bills window (refer to Figure 6-4). Follow Steps 2 through 12 from the "Recording your bills" section earlier in this chapter to fill in the Enter Bills window. When you've filled in the window, click OK. You're back where you started — in the Accounts Payable window.

4. When you've filled in the information, click Record.

The Restore button, located just below Record, is there in case you fill out the register but decide that you want to begin all over again. Clicking Restore deletes what you just entered, and you have a clean slate.

Deleting a bill

Suppose that you accidentally enter the same bill twice or enter a bill that was really meant for the business next door. (Just because you're tracking bills by computer doesn't mean that you don't have to look over the things carefully anymore.) Here's how to delete a bill that you entered in the Accounts Payable register:

1. **Locate the bill in the Accounts Payable register by using one of the following methods:**

   • If you know roughly what day you entered the bill, you can scroll through the list to find it. The entries are listed in date order. (Click the 1-Line check box to display each bill on one line rather than on two lines to make the scrolling go faster.)

   • If you don't remember the date, use the Edit menu's Find command.

   And now, back to the Accounts Payable register window you have in progress. . . .

2. **Select the bill that you want to delete by putting the cursor anywhere in the bill.**

3. **Choose Edit⇨Delete Bill.**

   QuickBooks confirms that you really truly want to delete the transaction, and if you click OK, it dutifully deletes the bill from the A/P register.

Remind me to pay that bill, will you?

You can tie a string around your finger, but the best way to make sure that you pay bills on time is to have QuickBooks remind you. In fact, you can make the Reminders message box the first thing that comes on-screen when you start QuickBooks.

Click the Company tab of the QuickBooks Navigator and click the Preferences icon. When QuickBooks displays the Preferences dialog box, click the Reminders icon from the list on the left so that the dialog box shown in Figure 6-7 appears. (You may need to click the Company Preferences tab to display this dialog box.) See the seventh item down the list, Bills to Pay?

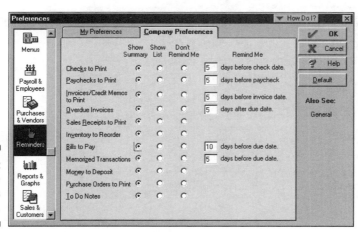

Figure 6-7: The Preferences dialog box.

Make sure that its Show Summary or Show List option button is checked, and then give yourself several days' notice before you need to pay bills by typing a number (10 is the default and usually works well) in the Remind Me text box.

If you click the Show Summary option (the first button to the right of each option), you get a summary of the bills you owe each time you start QuickBooks. If you choose Show List (the second button to the right of each option), you get the details about each bill.

Which reminds me: Be sure to check the Show Reminders List when opening a Company file check box. (This check box may be on the My Preferences tab.) The list pops up whenever you start QuickBooks and tells you which unpaid bills you're supposed to pay. Or you can see the Reminder list at any time by clicking the Company tab of the QuickBooks Navigator and then clicking the Reminders icon. How can you fail to pay your bills now?

Paying Your Bills

If you've done everything right and recorded your bills correctly, writing checks is a snap.

1. **Click the Purchases and Vendors tab of the QuickBooks Navigator and click the Pay Bills icon.**

   You see the Pay Bills window (see Figure 6-8).

2. **Change the Payment Date to the date that you want to appear on the checks.**

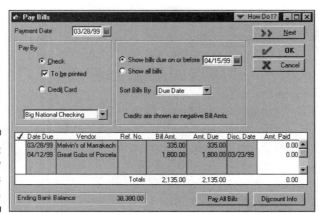

Figure 6-8:
The Pay Bills window.

By default, this box shows today's date. If you want another date on the payment check — for example, if you are postdating the check — change this date. (See the Cheat Sheet at the beginning of this book for some secret date-editing codes.)

3. **Choose a payment method.**

   Click the Check or Credit Card option button. If you have more than one checking or credit card account, click the down arrow next to the drop-down list box and choose the account that you want to use. If you have subscribed to and set up the QuickBooks online bill payment feature, you have another payment method choice, online payment. Making online payments is described in Chapter 11.

4. **If you plan to print the check, put a check mark in the To Be Printed check box.**

   Many businesses use QuickBooks to keep track of checks, but instead of printing the checks, they write them by hand. If your business uses this method, click the To Be Printed check box and remove the check mark.

5. **Set a cutoff date for showing bills.**

   In the Show Bills Due On or Before date box, tell QuickBooks which bills to show by entering a date. If you want to see all the bills, click the Show All Bills option button.

6. **Use the Sort Bills By drop-down list box to tell QuickBooks how to sort the bills.**

   You can arrange bills by due date, with the oldest bills listed first; arrange them alphabetically by vendor; or arrange them from largest to smallest.

7. **Identify which bills to pay.**

   If you want to pay all the bills in the dialog box, click the Pay All Bills button. But if you want to pick and choose, click to the left of the bill's due date to pay the bill. A check mark appears where you click. Note that after you've applied a payment, the Clear Payments button replaces the Pay All Bills button. For this reason, you can't see a Pay All Bills button in Figure 6-9.

8. **Change the Amt. Paid figure if you want to pay only part of a bill.**

   That's right, you can pay only part of a bill by changing the number in the Amt. Paid column.

9. **Get the early payment discount rate on your bills, if any.**

   You may be eligible for an early payment discount on some bills. To find out how much of a discount you get, click the Amt. Paid field and then click the Discount Info button to see the Discount Information dialog box, shown in Figure 6-9.

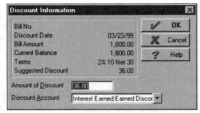

Figure 6-9:
The
Discount
Information
dialog box.

Whether you get a discount depends on the payment terms you entered when you gave QuickBooks information about this vendor. If you do get a discount, this dialog box tells you how much (and you can change the amount if it isn't correct). Choose an account for recording the discount in the Discount Account text box. Then click OK. The discount amount appears in the Amt. Paid column of the Pay Bills window.

10. Click OK to close the Pay Bills window.

QuickBooks makes that cash register *ka-ching* sound and then does two things: It goes into the Accounts Payable register and notes that you paid these bills, and it goes into the Checking register and "writes" the checks. Figures 6-10 and 6-11 show what I mean.

Figure 6-10:
Bills paid
in the
Accounts
Payable
register.

Date	Number	Vendor		Due Date	Billed	✓	Paid	Balance
	Type	Account	Memo					
03/13/99		Great Gobs of Porcelain		Paid	1,800.00			1,913.00
	BILL	-split-						
03/18/99		Melvin's of Marrakech		Paid	335.00			2,248.00
	BILL	-split-						
03/28/99		Great Gobs of Porcelain					1,800.00	448.00
	BILLPMT	Big National Chec						
03/28/99		Melvin's of Marrakech					335.00	113.00
	BILLPMT	Big National Chec						

Ending balance 113.00
☐ 1-Line ☐ Show open balance
Sort by [Date. Type. Document ▼]

Figure 6-11:
Bills paid
in the
Checking
register.

Date	Number	Payee		Payment	✓	Deposit	Balance
	Type	Account	Memo				
03/17/99	To Print	Bill I Ard		560.00			38,493.00
	CHK	-split-					
03/28/99	To Print	Great Gobs of Porcelain		1,800.00			36,693.00
	BILLPMT	Accounts Payable	PLP324				
03/28/99	To Print	Melvin's of Marrakech		335.00			36,358.00
	BILLPMT	Accounts Payable					
03/28/93	Number	Payee		Payment		Deposit	
		Account	Memo				

Ending balance 36,358.00
☐ 1-Line
Sort by [Date. Type. Document ▼]

Note: QuickBooks shows the original bill amount as the amount that's paid, not the original bill amount minus the early payment discount. It needs to use this method to completely pay off the bill.

In the Accounts Payable register, you see BILLPMT in the Type column and the amount paid in the Paid column. The Due Date and Billed columns are now empty.

In the Checking register, you again see BILLPMT in the Type column.

But don't kid yourself; these bills aren't really paid yet. Sure, they're paid in the mind of QuickBooks, but the mind of QuickBooks extends only as far as the metal box that holds your computer. You still have to write or print the checks and deliver them to the payees.

If you're going to write the checks by hand, enter the check numbers from your own checkbook into the QuickBooks Checking register's Number column. You want these numbers to jibe, not jive. (I know, a pun is the lowest form of humor.)

If you plan to print the checks, see Chapter 10.

Paying the Sales Tax

In order to ingratiate itself with your retailers, QuickBooks includes a special dialog box for paying sales taxes. However, to make use of this dialog box, you have to have sales tax items or a sales tax group already set up. See Chapter 2 for a thorough explanation of items and groups.

To see how much sales tax you owe and to write checks to government agencies in one fell swoop, click the Taxes and Accountant tab of the QuickBooks Navigator and click the Pay Sales Tax icon to see the Pay Sales Tax dialog box, shown in Figure 6-12.

Figure 6-12:
The Pay
Sales Tax
dialog box.

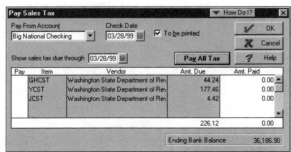

The box is similar to the Pay Bills window (refer to Figure 6-8). The buttons basically work the same way — the only major difference is that this box has a Pay All Tax button. Click this button to put check marks next to all the taxing agencies.

Put a check mark in the Pay column next to all the items that you want to pay by clicking in the Pay column. Checks are written automatically in the Checking register. Your payments are likewise recorded in the Sales Tax Payable register.

Chapter 7
Inventory Magic

● ●

In This Chapter

▶ The Item list and inventory

▶ Keeping inventory as you purchase items

▶ Keeping inventory as you sell items

▶ Using purchase orders to help track inventory

▶ Adjusting inventory records to reflect what's really in stock

● ●

*H*ow many times have you, as a business owner, thought that you had some important item on hand only to discover that you didn't have it after all? How many times have you had to sprint to a hardware store or a stationery shop to get some item that you could have sworn was sitting on the back shelf just a moment ago? Did elves take it?

One of the worst things that can happen to a business is to have customers ask for something and be told, "Sorry, we're all out. But can you check with me next Thursday?" You can bet that those customers will go elsewhere the next time that they need something. The reason that many businesses don't know what they have in stock is that keeping track of inventory is one of the biggest headaches of running a business. But here comes QuickBooks to the rescue. Maintaining inventory levels with QuickBooks keeps this business chore from being a monumental one.

QuickBooks keeps track of your inventory by assessing your sales and purchase orders. The program can tell you what you have on hand and what you need to order, the value of your inventory, and the income from items you've sold.

Setting Up Inventory Items

Before you can track your inventory, you need to create an Item list. This list is simply a description of all items that you might conceivably put on an invoice. In other words, all items that you order and sell belong on the Item list.

You should have set up your initial Item list in the EasyStep Interview. If you need to add an item to your list, click the Purchases and Vendors tab of the QuickBooks Navigator and click the Items & Services icon. Then click the Item button, choose New from the drop-down menu, and fill in the New Item window. If you want the blow-by-blow, go to Chapter 2 and get it straight from the horse's mouth. (Wait a second — did I just say that?)

And that reminds me: You can't track your inventory unless you tell QuickBooks that you want to track inventory. Click the Company tab of the QuickBooks Navigator and click the Preferences icon. When QuickBooks displays the Preferences dialog box, click the Purchases & Vendors icon from the list on the left. Your screen should look remarkably similar to the one in Figure 7-1. (You may have to click the Company Preferences tab first.) Do you see a check in the box for Inventory and Purchase Orders Are Active? If not, better put one there.

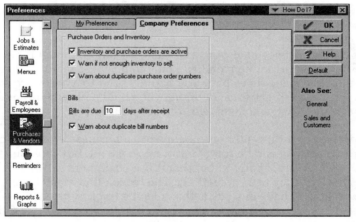

Figure 7-1:
The
Preferences
dialog
box for
Purchases
and
Vendors.

And while you're at it, make sure that the second box is checked. If you're going to the trouble of keeping track of inventory, you may as well have QuickBooks warn you when your stock is running low. If you check this box and you try to fill out a sales receipt or invoice for an item that you don't have enough of, QuickBooks warns you not to do that and bites your leg off (or at least nibbles at your toes).

After your Item list is set up and up-to-date, you can track your inventory.

When You Buy Stuff

As you unload items from a truck, receive them in the mail, or buy them from a peddler, you have to record the items so that QuickBooks can track your inventory. How you record the items and pay for them depends on whether you pay cash on the barrel, receive a bill along with the items, or receive the items without a bill (in which case you'll pay for the items later).

And you may have filled out a purchase order for the items that you're receiving. If that is the case, receiving the items gets a little easier. If you receive items for which you've already filled out a purchase order, see "How Purchase Orders Work" later in this chapter. I strongly recommend filling out a purchase order when you order items that you're going to receive and pay for later.

Recording items that you pay for up front

Okay, you just bought three porcelain chickens in the bazaar at Marrakech, and now you want to add them to your inventory and record the purchase. How do you record inventory you paid for over the counter? Using the Write Checks window, of course — the same way you record any other bills you pay for up front. Just make sure you fill out the Items column as described in "Recording Your Bills by Writing Checks" in Chapter 6.

Recording items that don't come with a bill

What happens if the items come in a big box with a red ribbon around it, and no bill is attached? Lucky you, you've got the stuff, and you don't have to pay for it yet. However, you do have to record the inventory you just received so that you know you have it on hand. You can't do that in the Write Checks window because you won't be writing a check to pay for the stuff — at least not for a while. How do you record items that you receive without paying for them? Read on.

1. **Click the Purchases and Vendors tab of the QuickBooks Navigator and click the Receive Items icon.**

   You see the Create Item Receipts window, shown in Figure 7-2. This window is very similar to the Enter Bills window (see Chapter 6). (You see the Enter Bills window again when you pay the bill for the receipt that you're filling out.)

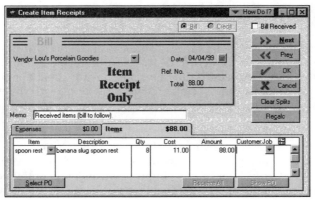

Figure 7-2:
The Create
Item
Receipts
window.

2. Fill in the top part of the window.

If you want to record items from a vendor who's already on the Vendor list, just click the down arrow and choose the vendor. If the vendor is a new vendor, choose <Add New> and click Set Up to set up information about the vendor — the address, credit limit, payment terms, and so on. You enter the information in the New Vendor dialog box.

3. Click the Items tab.

You need to click the Items tab only if it isn't already displayed. It probably is. But the computer book writers' code of honor and a compulsive personality require me to tell you that there's another tab — the Expenses tab — and it's just possible that it could be displayed instead.

4. Move to the Item column and type a name for the item.

Notice the down arrow in the Item column. Click it to see the Item list. Does the item that you're paying for appear on this list? If so, click it. If not, enter a new item name. You see the Item Not Found message box. Click Set Up and fill out the New Item dialog box. (See Chapter 2 for help with describing new items.)

You may just as well go down the packing slip, entering the items in the Items tab. Make sure that the Items tab accurately shows what's on the packing slip. And put a brief description of the items in the Memo field because that description may prove useful later when you want to match up your item receipt with the bill. When you're finished, the Create Item Receipts window should look something like Figure 7-3.

5. Click OK to enter the items you just received on the Item list.

Now the items are officially part of your inventory. The item receipt has been entered on the Accounts Payable register. And not only that, but you're all ready for when the bill comes.

Paying for items when you get the bill

The items arrive, and you fill out an item receipt. Three weeks pass. What's this in your mailbox? Why, it's the bill, of course! (You didn't think that you'd escape, did you?) Now you have to enter a bill for the items that you received three weeks ago. This job is easy.

1. **Click the Purchases and Vendors tab of the QuickBooks Navigator and click the Receive Bill icon.**

   You see the Select Item Receipt dialog box, shown in Figure 7-3.

Figure 7-3:
The Select
Item
Receipt
dialog box.

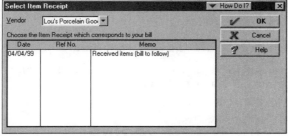

2. **Click the Vendor drop-down list and choose the name of the vendor who sent you the bill.**

   You see one or more item receipts in the box, with the date you put on the receipt, its reference number, and the memo that you wrote on the receipt.

3. **Select the item receipt for which you want to enter a bill, and click OK.**

   The Enter Bills window, shown in Figure 7-4, appears. Does this information look familiar? It should. It's the same information that you put in the Create Item Receipts window, only now you're working with a bill, not a receipt.

4. **Compare the Items tab in the window with the bill.**

   Are you paying for what you received earlier? Shipping charges and sales tax may have been added to your bill. If so, add them to the Items tab. (You can click the Recalc button to add the new items.)

   How many days do you have to pay this bill? Is it due now? Take a look at the Terms line to see what this vendor's payment terms are. Change the payment terms if they're incorrect by selecting a different entry from the drop-down list. Remember, you want to pay your bills at the best possible time, but to do so, the terms in the Enter Bills window must match the vendor's payment terms.

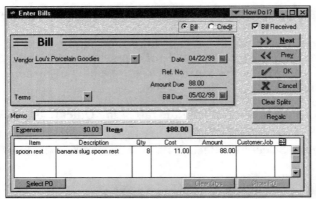

Figure 7-4:
The Enter
Bills
window.

5. **Click OK to record the bill and close the window.**

Of course, you still need to pay the bill to the vendor. Fair enough. Take a look at Chapter 6 if you need help.

Recording items and paying the bill all at once

Suppose that you receive the bill when you receive the goods. The items are unloaded from the elephant's back, and the elephant driver takes a bow and hands you the bill.

1. **Click the Purchases and Vendors tab of the QuickBooks Navigator and click the Receive Items with Bill icon.**

You see the Enter Bills window (refer to Figure 7-4). If you've been reading this chapter from its beginning, you're very familiar with this window and you know exactly what it is and does. If you landed cold turkey on this page by way of the index, you need to know for inventory purposes how to record the items you're paying for.

2. **Fill out the top part of the window.**

This stuff is pretty basic. Choose a vendor from the drop-down list and make sure that the vendor's terms for paying this bill are shown correctly. If this vendor is new, choose <Add New>. QuickBooks asks you to fill in an information dialog box about the vendor. Do it. See that you fill out the Bill Due line correctly.

3. **Click the Items tab and list all the items that you're paying for.**

   To see the Item list, move the cursor to the Item column and click the down arrow that appears. Make sure that the quantity and cost of the items are listed correctly on the Items tab.

4. **Click OK.**

   QuickBooks adds the items you listed to the Item list and makes them an official part of your inventory.

When You Sell Stuff

Chapter 4 tells you how to list the items on the invoice. Maybe you noticed the similarities between the Items tab in the Enter Bills window and the Quantity/Item Code/Description/Price Each/Amount box at the bottom of an invoice. Both are used for keeping inventory.

When you sell stuff, QuickBooks automatically adjusts your inventory. In other words, if you buy 400 porcelain chickens and sell 350 of them, you have only 50 on hand. QuickBooks updates records for this change. No muss, no fuss. Gosh, isn't this great? No more lying awake at night, wondering whether you've got enough chickens or wombats or whatever. The same thing happens when you make cash sales. When you list the items on the sales receipt, QuickBooks assumes that they're leaving your hands and subtracts them from your inventory.

The moral of this story is, "Keep a good, descriptive Item List." And the other moral is, "Enter items carefully on the Items tab of checks and bills and in the Item/Description/Qty/Rate/Amount box of sales receipts and invoices."

How Purchase Orders Work

If you have to order stuff for your business, consider using purchase orders. Create QuickBooks purchase orders even if you order goods by phone or by telegraph or even via the World Wide Web — that is, whenever you don't request goods in writing. Filling out purchase orders enables you to tell what items you have on order and when the items will arrive. All you'll have to do is ask QuickBooks, "What's on order, and when's it coming, anyway?" Never again will you have to rack your brain to remember whether you ordered those thingamajigs and doohickeys.

And when the bill comes, you'll already have it itemized on the purchase order form. Guess what? Having written out all the items on your purchase order, you won't have to fill out an Items tab on your check when you pay the bill. Or, if you're paying bills with the accounts payable method, you won't have to fill out the Items tab in the Enter Bills window. (Look at Chapter 6 if you don't know what I'm talking about here.) When the items arrive, all you have to do is let QuickBooks know — the items are added immediately to your inventory list.

Use purchase orders for items that you order — that is, for items that you'll receive and pay for in the future. If you buy items over the counter or receive items that you didn't order, you obviously don't need a purchase order. What you need to do is just pay the bill and inventory the items you just bought, as explained in the first half of this chapter.

Choosing a purchase order form for you

The first thing to do when you use purchase orders is design a purchase order form for your business. Click the Purchases and Vendors tab of the QuickBooks Navigator and click the Purchase Orders icon. When QuickBooks displays the Create Purchase Orders window, choose Customize from the Template drop-down list box in the upper-right corner of the window. When QuickBooks displays the Customize Template dialog box, choose to either edit QuickBooks' default Custom Purchase Order template for your business or create a new template based on the QuickBooks template. If you're like me and enjoy being able to experiment with things as much as you want, click the New button. This way, you always have a fresh, clean template to start from if you ever want to create more customized Purchase Orders.

QuickBooks displays the Customize Purchase Order dialog box, shown in Figure 7-5. This dialog box has five tabs for determining what your purchase order looks like.

Click the different tabs to see what you can customize. Some options that are listed on the left side apply to the purchase orders for your business; some don't. If you want to use an option on your screen, click the Screen check box next to that option. Likewise, do the same for printed purchase orders. Click the Print check box if you want an option to appear on the order when you print it. In the Title text boxes, type the word or words that you want to see on purchase orders. The Other options on the Fields and Columns tabs are for putting a field or column of your own on the purchase order.

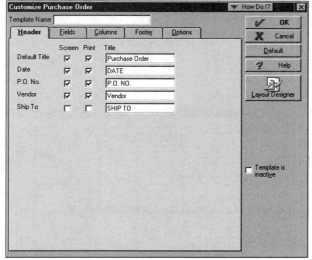

Figure 7-5:
The
Customize
Purchase
Order
dialog box.

Play around with this window for a while until your purchase order comes out just right. To see how your choices look on a purchase order, click the Layout Designer button. Here you can use the mouse to drag-and-drop fields around the page to make it look just the way you want. Click OK to return to the Customize Purchase Order dialog box. If your purchase order doesn't look right, click Cancel and start all over again. And if your purchase order gets too wacky, you can always click the Default button in the Customize Purchase Order window to go back to the default headers, fields, columns, and footers.

When your purchase order looks magnificent, click OK in the Customize Purchase Order dialog box. If you created a brand new template, you also have to give it a name.

QuickBooks returns you to the Create Purchase Orders window. If you later decide that you want to change one of your templates, all you have to do is choose Customize again from the Template drop-down list box and then select the template you want to edit from the list and click the Edit button.

Filling out a purchase order

Perhaps you're running low on gizmos, or doohickeys, or some other item on your Item list, and it's time to reorder these things — whatever they are.

1. **Click the Purchases and Vendors tab of the QuickBooks Navigator and click the Purchase Orders icon.**

   You see the Create Purchase Orders window, which is similar to what's shown in Figure 7-6. Note that the exact details of this window depend on how you customize your purchase order form.

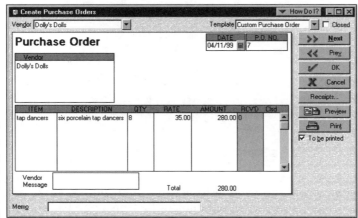

Figure 7-6:
The Create
Purchase
Orders
window.

2. **Choose a vendor from the Vendor drop-down list.**

   Click the down arrow to see a list of your vendors. Click a vendor to see its name and address in the Vendor box. If you can't find the name of the vendor on your list, click Add New and fill in the information about the vendor in the New Vendor dialog box.

3. **If you track your inventory by class, choose a class from the Class drop-down list.**

   The Create Purchase Orders window may not have a Class drop-down list. If it doesn't and you want it to have one, you have to set up QuickBooks to track expenses by class. To do so, click the Company tab of the QuickBooks Navigator and click the Preferences icon. Then click the Accounting icon from the list on the left. (You may also need to click the Company Preferences tab.) Finally, mark the Use Class Tracking check box.

4. **(Optional) Choose a Rep, Expected Date, and FOB (described in Chapter 4) if you're using them on your purchase order.**

   You may have to fill in other fields before you get to the item-by-item descriptions at the bottom. Again, these fields may not appear if you haven't indicated that you want them on your form.

5. Move to the Item column and start entering the items you're ordering.

Entering the items is the most important part of creating a purchase order. When you move into the Item column, it turns into a drop-down list box. Click its down arrow to see the Item List. You may need to scroll to the item that you want to enter. A fast way to scroll to the item is to type the first couple of letters in the item name. If you type the name of an item that isn't on the Item List, QuickBooks asks whether you want to set up this item. Click Set Up and fill in the New Item dialog box.

Enter as many items as you want in the Item column. In the Qty column, indicate how many of each item you need.

6. If you want to, fill in the Vendor Message field — and definitely fill in the Memo field.

The Message field is where you put a message to the party receiving your order. You could write, "Get me this stuff pronto!"

No matter what you do, be sure to fill in the Memo field. What you write in this field appears in the Open Purchase Orders dialog box and is the surest way for you to identify what this purchase order is for. Write something meaningful that you can understand two weeks, three weeks, or a month from now when you pay for the items that you're ordering.

By now, you must have noticed the army of buttons deployed along the right side of the window. Below the buttons is the To Be Printed check box that tells you whether you've printed this purchase order. If you want to print the purchase order, make sure this box is checked. After you print the purchase order, the check disappears from the box.

7. Print the purchase order.

Click Print to print the purchase order. If this purchase order is one of many purchase orders that you've been filling out and you want to print several at once, you have to choose File➪Print Forms➪Print Purchase Orders and fill in the dialog box. Before you print the purchase order, however, click the Preview button to see what the purchase order will look like when you print it. QuickBooks shows you an on-screen replica of the purchase order. I hope that it looks okay.

You use the Receipts button after you receive the items you're so carefully listing on the purchase order. After you receive the items and record their receipt, clicking this button tells QuickBooks to give you the entire history of an item — when you ordered it and when you received it.

As for the top four buttons, I think that you know what those are, and if you don't, go to Step 8.

8. Click Next, Prev, OK, or Cancel to record the purchase order.

The OK button closes the Create Purchase Orders window. The Next button takes you to a new purchase order screen where you can enter another order. Click Prev if you need to see or change the previous order. Click Cancel if you get cold feet and decide not to purchase this stuff after all.

Checking up on purchase orders

You record the purchase orders. A couple of weeks go by, and you ask yourself, "Did I order those doohickeys from Acme?" Click the Purchases and Vendors tab of the QuickBooks Navigator and click the PO List icon to see the Purchase Orders window with a list of outstanding purchase orders (see Figure 7-7). Double-click one of the orders on the list, and it magically appears on-screen.

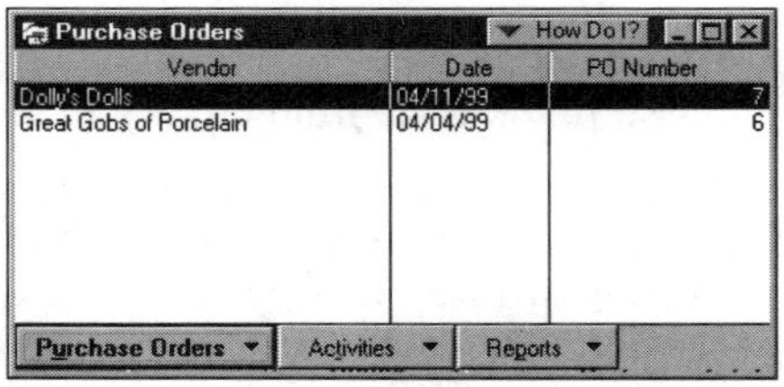

Figure 7-7: The Purchase Orders window.

You can then change any information you need to. Click OK to go back to the Purchase Orders List. You can also enter a new purchase order from this list by clicking the Purchase Orders button and choosing New.

Do you want to delete a purchase order? Just keep the Purchase Orders window open, highlight the purchase order that you want to delete, click the Purchase Orders button, and choose Delete.

Receiving purchase order items

Now that the doohickeys and gizmos have arrived by camel train, you need to record the receipt of the items and add them to your Item list.

The first thing to do is note whether the stuff came with a bill and decide how you want to pay for it. These decisions are the same ones you would have to make if you received the goods without having first filled out a purchase order.

You record purchase order items you receive the same way you record other items you receive. If you pay for purchase order items with a check, you use the Write Checks window. If you receive the purchase order items without a bill, you use the Create Item Receipts window. If you receive the purchase order items with a bill, you use the Enter Bills window. Regardless of the window you're using, when you select the vendor who sold you the purchase order items, QuickBooks alerts you that open purchase orders exist for the vendor and asks you if you want to receive against a purchase order. Of course you do. (*Receive against* simply means to compare what you ordered to what you received.) When you click Yes, QuickBooks displays the Open Purchase Orders dialog box shown in Figure 7-8. Select the purchase order(s) you're receiving against and click OK. QuickBooks fills out the Items tab to show all the stuff you ordered. If it's not what you received, you may have to make adjustments.

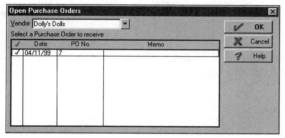

Figure 7-8:
The Open
Purchase
Orders
dialog box.

Time for a Reality Check

QuickBooks does a pretty good job of tracking inventory, but you're still going to have to make that complete annual inventory of what you have in stock. What I'm saying here is that you're going to have to go over everything and count it. Sorry. You just can't avoid that chore.

And when you've made your count, what happens if your inventory figures differ from those QuickBooks has? First, you have to decide who's right — you or a computer program. You're right, probably. Products get dropped. They break. And that means that you have to adjust the QuickBooks inventory numbers.

Click the Purchases and Vendors tab of the QuickBooks Navigator and click the Adjust Qty On Hand icon. The Adjust Quantity/Value on Hand window appears (see Figure 7-9).

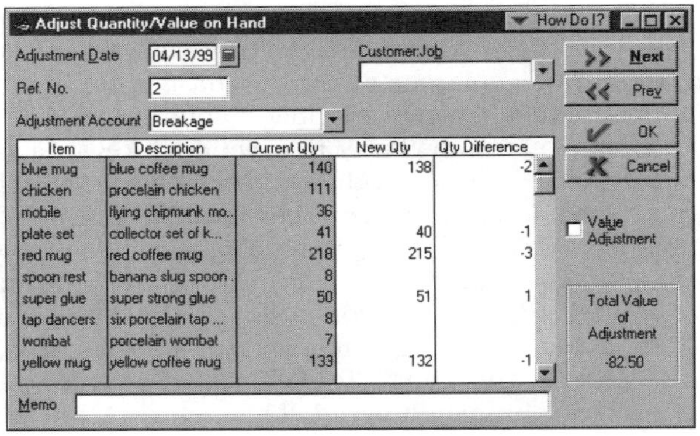

Figure 7-9:
The Adjust
Quantity/
Value on
Hand
window.

The first thing to do is choose an account for storing your inventory adjustments. Choose it from the Adjustment Account drop-down list. You also can
select a class from the Class drop-down list.

Go down the Item column, entering numbers in the New Qty column where
your count differs from the QuickBooks totals. Click OK when you're done.

Chapter 8

Keeping Your Checkbook

. . . .

In This Chapter

▶ Writing checks from the Write Checks window

▶ Writing checks from the Checking register

▶ Recording deposits

▶ Recording transfers

▶ Searching for transactions

▶ Voiding and deleting transactions

. . . .

*T*his is it. You're finally going to do those everyday QuickBooks things: entering checks, deposits, and transfers. Along the way, you also find out about some neat tools that QuickBooks provides for making these tasks easier, faster, and more precise.

Writing Checks

In Chapter 6, you can find out about the two ways to write checks: from the Write Checks window and from the Checking register. In case you were asleep in the back row of the class or your locker got jammed and you couldn't make it in, here's the short version of the instructions for writing checks.

Writing checks from the Write Checks window

You can record handwritten checks and other checks that you want to print with QuickBooks by describing the checks in the Write Checks window. Ah, it all sounds so complicated. But, really, it's not.

To write a check from the Write Checks window, follow these steps:

1. **Click the Checking and Credit Cards tab of the QuickBooks Navigator and click the Checks icon.**

   You see the Write Checks window (see Figure 8-1).

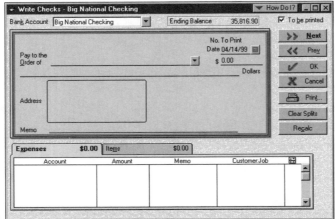

Figure 8-1:
The Write
Checks
window.

2. **Click the Ban<u>k</u> Account drop-down list at the top of the window and choose the account from which you want to write this check.**

   This step is really important and is something you should always check before you write a check.

3. **Enter a check number or mark the check for printing.**

   Check the To Be Printed box if you plan on printing the check with QuickBooks using your printer and preprinted check forms that you've purchased. (I describe this in Chapter 10.) If you're recording a check you wrote by hand, enter the check number you used for the check in the No. box.

4. **Fill in the check.**

   If you've written a check to this person or party before, the AutoFill feature fills in the name of the payee in the Pay to the Order Of line for you. How QuickBooks does this may seem akin to magic, but it's really not that tough. QuickBooks just compares what you've typed so far with names on your lists of customers, employees, and other names. When it can match the letters you've typed so far with a name on one of these lists, it grabs the name. If you haven't written a check to this person or party before, by the way, QuickBooks asks you to Quick Add or Set Up the payee name. Do that. (If you're not sure whether you want to Quick Add or Set Up the payee, refer to Chapter 6.)

Enter the amount of the check next to the dollar sign and press Tab. QuickBooks writes out the amount for you on the Dollars line. It also writes out the address.

5. Fill in the E<u>x</u>penses and Ite<u>m</u>s tabs, if necessary.

Don't know what these are? Chapter 6 explains them in minute detail. Start turning those pages.

6. Click <u>N</u>ext or OK to finish writing the check.

Click Next if you want to write another check or click OK if you're done writing checks for the moment. There you have it. Your check is written, is entered in the Checking register, and is ready to be printed and mailed.

Writing checks from the Checking register

People who've grown accustomed to Quicken, a cousin of QuickBooks, may want to use the Checking register window to write checks. (Quicken users like the register metaphor better, I guess.)

To write a check from the Checking register, follow these steps:

1. Open the Checking register.

Click the Checking and Credit Cards tab of the QuickBooks Navigator and click the Check Register icon. If you have more than one bank account, QuickBooks displays the Open Check Register dialog box. Select from the drop-down list the checking account against which you want to write the check box and click OK. You see the Checking register window (see Figure 8-2). The cursor is at the end of the register, ready and waiting for you to enter check information. (QuickBooks automatically fills in today's date.)

2. Fill in the information for your check.

Notice that the entries you make in this register are the same ones that you would make in the Write Checks window. If you're more comfortable entering checks in that window, you can click the Edit button to see the Write Checks window in all its glory and write a check there. In fact, if you want to enter expenses or itemize what you're paying for with the check, you have to click Edit and get into the Write Checks window.

Date	Number	Payee		Payment	√	Deposit	Balance
	Type	Account	Memo				
03/28/99	To Print	Melvin's of Marrakech		335.00			36,186.90
	BILLPMT	Accounts Payable					
04/03/99	107	Melvin's of Marrakech		90.00			36,096.90
	CHK	Inventory Asset					
04/13/99	To Print	Dolly's Dolls		280.00			35,816.90
	CHK	Inventory Asset					
04/14/99	108	Payee		Payment		Deposit	
		Account	Memo				

Big National Checking — ▼ How Do I?

Record Edit Splits
Restore Q-Report Go To

Ending balance   35,816.90
☐ 1-Line
Sort by [Date, Type, Document ▼]

Figure 8-2: The Checking register window.

Otherwise, just go from field to field and enter the information in the register. Once again, use the drop-down lists to enter the Payee and Account names. If you enter a Payee or Account name that QuickBooks doesn't recognize, the program asks you to give more information.

3. When you're finished filling in the check information, click Record.

Or click the Restore button if you decide that you want to go back to square one and start all over again. Clicking Restore blanks out what you just entered.

If you write checks by hand as opposed to printing them with QuickBooks, make sure that the check numbers in the Checking register and the check numbers in your personal checkbook match up. You may need to go into the QuickBooks Checking register and change numbers in the Number column. When your bank statement comes, reconciling your bank statement and your checkbook is much easier if you entered check numbers correctly.

Paying for items with cash

If you want to track petty cash purchases, you need a petty cash account to do so. You can set up a petty cash account (which works just like a bank account) by following the steps in "Setting up a second bank account" later in this chapter. To record purchases you make from the money in that coffee can beside your desk, use the petty cash register. You can record cash purchases just as you record checks. (Of course, you don't need to worry about using the correct check numbers when you record cash purchases — you can just use the numbers 1, 2, 3, and so on.) To record cash withdrawals to be used for petty cash in the office, just record the withdrawal as a transfer to your petty cash account, as described later in the chapter.

Changing a check that you've written

What if you need to change a check after you have already entered it? Perhaps you made a terrible mistake, such as recording a $52.50 check as $25.20. Can you fix it? Sure. Just go into the Checking register and find the check that you want to change. Go to the Payment or Deposit field and make the change. If you have more extensive changes to make (for instance, if the check is a split transaction), put the cursor where the check is and click Edit. QuickBooks displays the Write Checks window with the original check in it. Make the changes. (Don't forget to make changes on the Items and Expenses tabs, too, if necessary.) When you're finished, click OK. You go back to the Checking register, where you see the changes to the check. Click the Record button or press Enter when you finish.

If you have the Write Checks window displayed, you can also use the Next and Prev buttons to page through your checks and make any changes.

Packing more checks into the register

Normally, QuickBooks displays two rows of information about each check you enter. It also displays two rows of information about each type of transaction that you enter. If you want to pack more checks into a visible portion of the register, check the 1-Line check box at the bottom of the Checking register window. When you check this box, QuickBooks uses a single-line format to display all the information in the register except the Memo field.

Compare Figure 8-2 with Figure 8-3 to see what the 1-Line display looks like. Checking registers can get awfully long, and the 1-Line display is helpful when you're looking through a long register for a check or transaction.

Depositing Money into a Checking Account

You can't write checks unless you deposit some money in your checking account. You didn't know that? Well, the next time you're taking your exercise in the prison yard, give it some serious thought. From time to time, you must deposit money in your checking account and record those deposits in the Checking register.

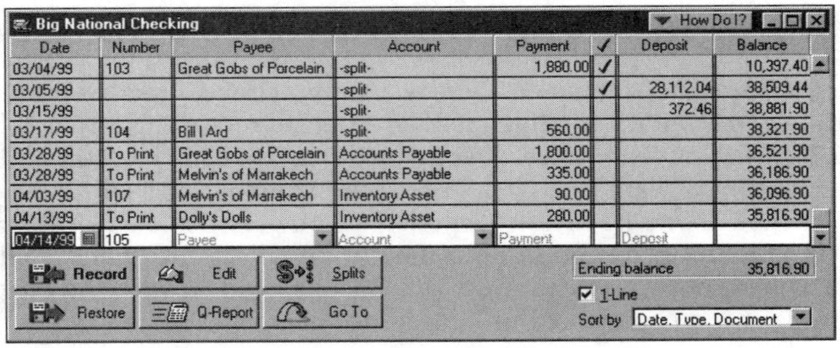

Figure 8-3:
The
Checking
register
window
displays
one
transaction
per line.

Date	Number	Payee	Account	Payment	✓	Deposit	Balance
03/04/99	103	Great Gobs of Porcelain	-split-	1,880.00	✓		10,397.40
03/05/99			-split-		✓	28,112.04	38,509.44
03/15/99			-split-			372.46	38,881.90
03/17/99	104	Bill I Ard	-split-	560.00			38,321.90
03/28/99	To Print	Great Gobs of Porcelain	Accounts Payable	1,800.00			36,521.90
03/28/99	To Print	Melvin's of Marrakech	Accounts Payable	335.00			36,186.90
04/03/99	107	Melvin's of Marrakech	Inventory Asset	90.00			36,096.90
04/13/99	To Print	Dolly's Dolls	Inventory Asset	280.00			35,816.90
04/14/99	105	Payee	Account	Payment		Deposit	

Big National Checking — How Do I?

Record   Edit   Splits

Restore   Q-Report   Go To

Ending balance   35,816.90

☑ 1-Line

Sort by   Date, Type, Document

You can record deposits in two ways. If you have a simple deposit to make — a sum of money that didn't come from one of your customers — just make the deposit directly in the Checking register. For example, suppose that your elderly Aunt Iris sends you $100 with a note explaining how, more than 80 years ago, Great-Uncle Bert started his hammock manufacturing business with only $100, and for good luck she's sending you $100 to help you along.

Recording simple deposits

Recording a simple deposit is, well, pretty simple. Follow these steps:

1. **Open the Checking register.**

   Click the Checking and Credit Cards tab of the QuickBooks Navigator, and then click the Check Register icon. If you have more than one bank account, QuickBooks displays the Open Check Register dialog box. Select the checking account into which you want to make the deposit and click OK. QuickBooks displays the Checking register window (refer to Figure 8-2).

2. **Enter the date on which you made the deposit in the Date column.**

3. **Enter the person or business from whom you received the money in the Payee column.**

   Don't worry if QuickBooks adds a check number in the Number field when you move to the Payee column. When you enter a deposit about, QuickBooks changes the Number field to DEP (for deposit, of course).

4. **Enter the amount that you're depositing.**

   Move the cursor to the Deposit column and enter the amount.

5. **Enter an account for this deposit.**

Move to the Account field, click the down arrow, and choose an account from the list. Most likely, you will choose an account such as Uncategorized Income.

6. **Click the Record button.**

Your deposit is entered, and your checking account's balance is fattened accordingly. Note that all entries in the Checking register are made in chronological order, with deposits first and checks next.

Depositing income from customers

Depositing income from customers is a little more complicated because it involves the Payments to Deposit dialog box. Have you been recording customer payments as they come in? (You do this by clicking the Sales and Customers tab of the QuickBooks Navigator and then clicking the Receive Payments icon or the cash sales icon as described in Chapter 5.) If you've been recording customer payments, QuickBooks has placed these payments in your Undeposited Funds account. Now all you have to do is transfer the undeposited funds to your checking account.

1. **Click the Sales and Customers tab of the QuickBooks Navigator and click the Deposits icon.**

Because you have undeposited funds, you see the Payments to Deposit dialog box (see Figure 8-4). This dialog box lists checks that you've received but haven't put in a checking account or other bank account yet.

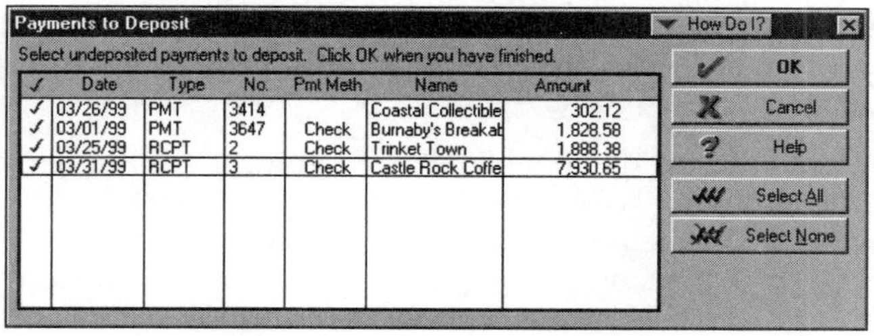

Figure 8-4:
The
Payments
to Deposit
dialog box.

2. **Select the checks that you want to deposit.**

Place a check mark next to the checks that you want to deposit by clicking in the column next to them. Or, if you want to deposit all the checks, click the Select All button. Click OK.

The Make Deposits window appears (see Figure 8-5). Do you recognize the information in the middle of the dialog box? It describes the checks you just selected to be deposited.

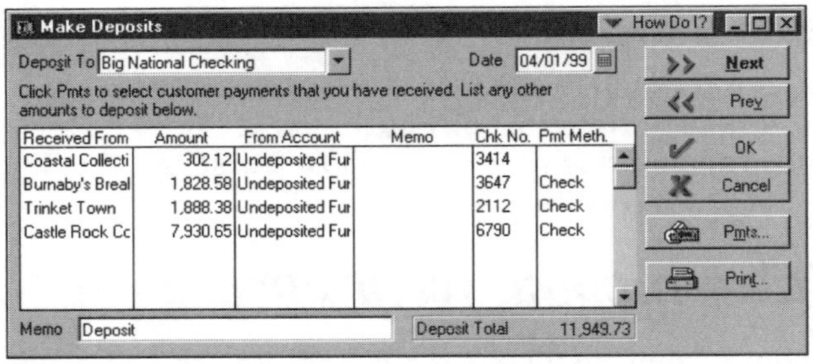

Figure 8-5:
The Make
Deposits
window.

3. **Select the checking account to receive these deposits.**

   Select the account from the Deposit To drop-down list at the top of the dialog box. And while you're at it, check the Date text box to make sure that it shows the date you'll deposit these checks in your checking account. In other words, if you're not going to make it to the bank or the ATM machine until tomorrow, put tomorrow's date in the Date text box.

4. **Add any other non-customer deposits to include on the deposit slip.**

   If your grandma, bless her heart, gave you 1,000 pennies in ten rolls, for example, that's ten extra dollars that you can record on this deposit slip. At the bottom of the slip, enter the name of the person who gave you the cash, the amount, the account, a memo, the payment method (cash in this case), and a class, if you so desire.

5. **Write a note to yourself in the Memo box to describe this deposit, if you want to, and click the Print button to get a hard copy of the deposit slip.**

   Many banks accept this deposit slip, so you can print it and put it in the envelope with your ATM deposit or hand it to the bank clerk. Whatever you write on the memo appears on the Checking register. (You should probably write a memo to yourself in case you need to know what this deposit is years from now when you're old and dotty.)

6. **Click OK.**

   Now the deposit is recorded in QuickBooks. It appears in your Checking register next to the letters *DEP,* which stand for *Deposit.*

Transferring Money between Accounts

Account transfers occur when you move money from one account to another — for example, from your savings account to your checking account. But, jeepers, why am I telling you this? If you have one of those combined savings and checking accounts, you probably do this sort of thing all the time.

Oh, now I remember why I brought this up — QuickBooks makes quick work of account transfers as long as you already have *both* accounts set up.

Setting up a second bank account

If you don't have a second account set up, you need to set one up first. To do so, open the chart of accounts by clicking the Company tab of the QuickBooks Navigator and then clicking the Chart of Accounts icon. Then click the Account button and choose New. Fill in the name of the account and, if you want to, the account number or a description of the account. Then fill in the As Of box with the date you opened the account. Enter the opening balance as zero so that you can record your initial deposit or transfer of money into the account. You record an initial deposits as described earlier in this chapter (either as simple deposits or as customer deposits, whatever the case may be). You record an initial transfer by completing the following steps.

Entering an account transfer

Buckle up. These steps speed through recording an account transfer. For the most part, recording an account transfer works the same way as recording a check or deposit.

1. **Click the Checking and Credit Cards tab of the QuickBooks Navigator and click the Transfer Money icon.**

   You see the Transfer Funds Between Accounts window, shown in Figure 8-6.

2. **Select the bank account that you're going to transfer the money from.**

   In the Transfer Funds From box at the top of the screen, choose the account from the drop-down list.

3. **Select the bank account to which you want to transfer the money.**

   In the Transfer Funds To drop-down list box, select the account that you want to receive the funds.

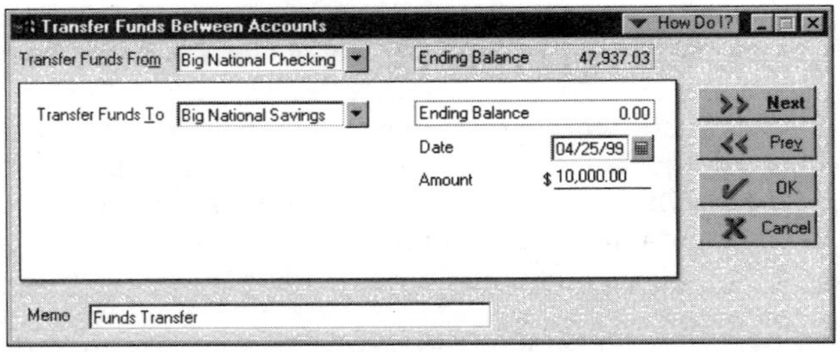

Figure 8-6:
The
Transfer
Funds
Between
Accounts
window.

4. **Enter the amount that you want to transfer and fill in the Memo line.**

   Someday, you may go into the register for the account you're writing this check in and wonder where you transferred this money and why. Filling in the Memo line solves this little mystery beforehand.

5. **Click OK.**

   The transfer is recorded. You can confirm this by opening your Checking register. You see that the transfer has the letters TRANSFR in the Type column and the name of the account to which you transferred the money in the Account column. The amount you transferred shows up in the Payment column (because you transferred the funds out of this account). Figure 8-7 shows a $10,000 transfer from a checking account called Big National Checking to an account called Big National Savings.

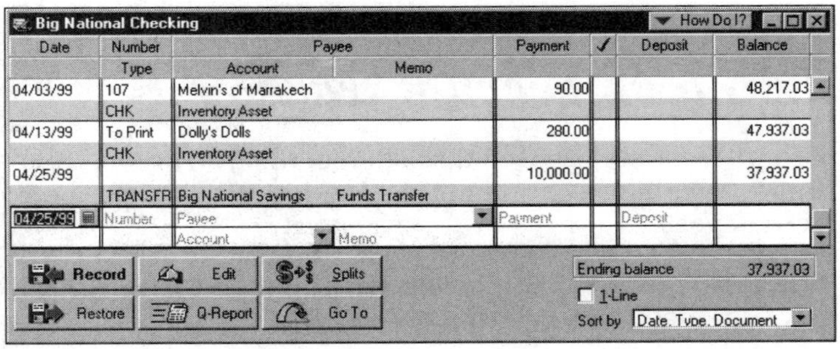

Figure 8-7:
A transfer
payment
in the
Checking
register.

About the other half of the transfer

Here's the cool thing about transfer transactions. QuickBooks automatically records the other half of the transfer for you. Figure 8-8 shows the other half of the transfer from Figure 8-7. This register is for a savings account called, oddly enough, Savings. The $10,000 transfer from your checking account actually made it into your savings account. The transfer once again shows up as a TRANSFR.

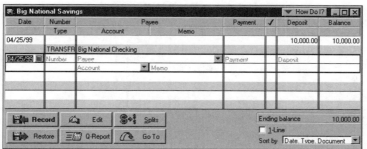

Figure 8-8:
A transfer
deposit in
the Savings
register.

Changing a transfer that you've already entered

Big surprise here, but changing a transfer that you've already entered works just like changing a check. First, you find the transfer in the account register, and then you click Edit. You see the Transfer Funds Between Accounts window with the Transfer check you wrote. Make changes to the check and click OK. You return to the register, where your deposit is adjusted accordingly. Click Record.

To Delete or to Void?

What happens if you put a transaction — a deposit, a check, or a transfer payment — in a Checking register and later decide that it shouldn't be there? You have two ways of handling this situation. If you want to keep a record of the transaction but render it moot, meaningless, or *nada,* you void the transaction. But if you want to obliterate it from the face of the earth as though it never happened in the first place, then you delete it.

Decide whether you want to void or delete the transaction and then follow these steps:

1. **Find the transaction in the register.**

   In the next section of this chapter, "The Big Register Phenomenon," I tell you some quick ways to find transactions.

2. **Choose either Edit➪Delete Check or Edit➪Void Check and click OK.**

   There, the deed is done. Figure 8-9 shows a Checking register window with a voided check. Notice the word VOID. If this check had been deleted, it wouldn't even show up in the register.

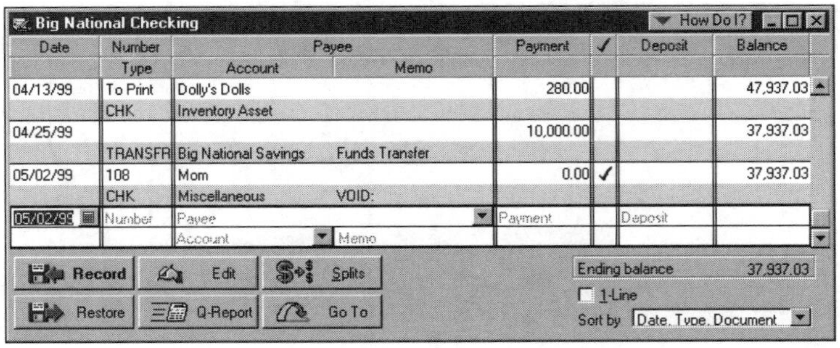

Figure 8-9:
The
Checking
register
shows a
voided
check.

The Big Register Phenomenon

If you start entering checks, deposits, and transfers into your registers, you soon find yourself with registers that contain hundreds, and even thousands, of transactions. You can still work with one of these big registers by using the tools and techniques that I talk about in the preceding paragraphs. Nevertheless, let me give you some more help for dealing with . . . (drumroll, please) . . . *the big register phenomenon.*

Moving through a big register

You can use the Page Up and Page Down keys to page up and down through your register, a screenful of transactions at a time. Some people call this *scrolling.* You can call it whatever you want.

You can also use the Home key to move through the register. Press the Home key once to move to the front of the field you're currently in. Press it twice to move to the first field of the transaction you're on (the Date field) or press it three times to move to the first transaction in the register.

The End key works in a similar fashion. Bet you can guess how this works. Press the End key once to move to the end of the field you're in, press it twice to move to the last field of the transaction you're on (the Memo field), or press it three times to move to the last transaction in the register.

Of course, you can use the vertical scroll bar along the right edge of the Checking register, too. Click the arrows at either end of the vertical scroll bar to select the next or previous transaction. Click either above or below the square scroll box to page back and forth through the register. Or, if you have no qualms about dragging the mouse around, you can drag the scroll box up and down the scroll bar.

QuickBooks 6 now lets you sort your register in different ways, which makes it easier to scroll through and find transactions. To sort your register the way you prefer, choose an option from the Sort By drop-down list box in the lower-right corner of the register window.

Finding that darn transaction

Want to find that one check, deposit, or transfer? No problem. I discuss this technique earlier in the book, but it may be appropriate here, too. The Edit menu's Find command provides a handy way for doing just this. Here's what you do:

1. **Choose Edit⇨Find.**

    QuickBooks, with restrained but obvious enthusiasm, displays the Find window (see Figure 8-10). You use this window to describe the transaction that you want to find in as much detail as possible.

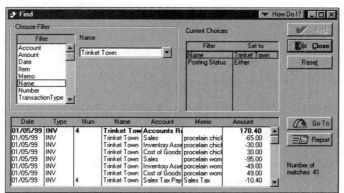

Figure 8-10:
The Find
window.

2. **Choose a filter that describes the information that you already have.**

    In the figure, the Name filter has been chosen. As you click different filters, the upper-right half of the dialog box changes.

3. **Enter the text or number that identifies the transaction that you want to locate.**

    In the upper-right box, which is set to Name in this figure, choose the text or number that describes the subject of your search from the drop-down list. Or just type the information in the box. If more than one field is in the box, use as many as you think help.

By the way, the case of the text doesn't matter. If you type *aunt,* for example, QuickBooks finds AUNT as well as Aunt.

4. Repeat Steps 2 and 3 as needed.

Yes, you can filter through as many fields as you want. In fact, you can filter so much that *nothing* matches your specification. But that defeats the purpose of the whole thing, doesn't it?

5. Let the search begin.

Click the Find button to begin looking.

If QuickBooks finds transactions that match the one you described, it lists them in the bottom half of the dialog box.

Chapter 9
Paying with Plastic

. . . .

. . . .

*Y*ou can use QuickBooks to track your credit cards in much the same way that you use it to keep a checkbook. The process is almost the same, but with a few wrinkles.

Tracking Business Credit Cards

If you want to track credit card spending and balances with QuickBooks, you need to set up a credit card account if you didn't already do so in the EasyStep Interview. (In comparison, you use bank accounts to track things such as the money that flows into and out of a checking, savings, or petty cash account.)

Setting up a credit card account

To set up a credit card account, you follow roughly the same steps that you use to set up a bank account. Here's what you do:

1. **Click the Company tab of the QuickBooks Navigator and click the Chart of Accounts icon.**

   QuickBooks displays the Chart of Accounts window, shown in Figure 9-1.

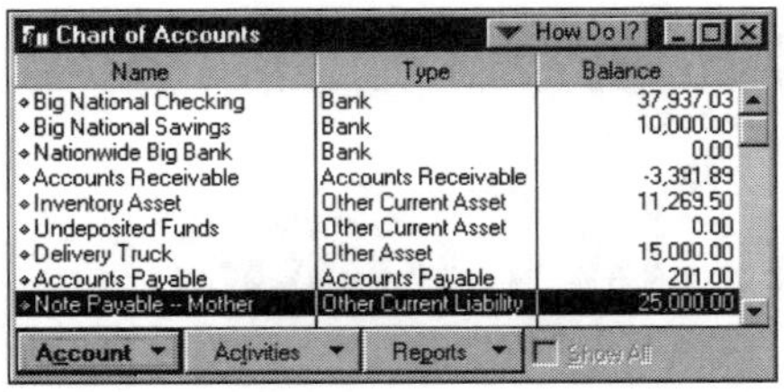

Figure 9-1:
The Chart of
Accounts
window.

2. **Click the Account button in the Chart of Accounts window and choose New.**

   QuickBooks — always sensitive to your feelings — displays the New Account window. Because I'm sensitive to your feelings, too, I include this window as Figure 9-2.

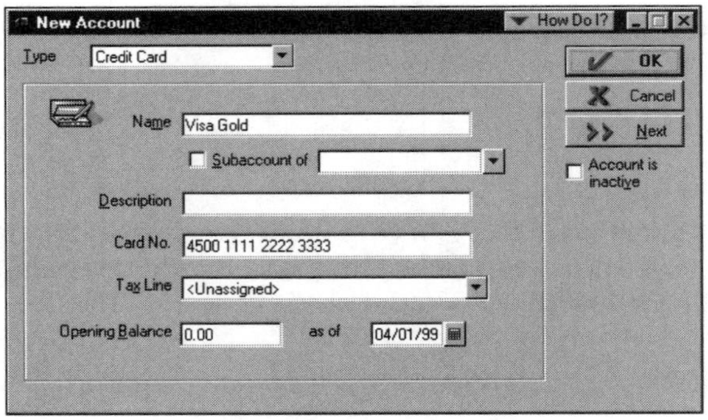

Figure 9-2:
The New
Account
window.

3. **Choose Credit Card from the Type drop-down list.**

   Choosing Credit Card tells QuickBooks that you want to set up a credit card account. I'm sure that you're surprised.

4. **Name the account.**

   Why not do it right? Move the cursor to the Name text box and enter the name of your credit card.

5. **Make this credit card account a subaccount of your all-purpose Credit Card account, if you want to.**

   Why would you want to make it a subaccount? Well, if you have three credit cards, you can call the accounts VISA, MasterCard, and Discover, or neat names like that, and all three of those accounts can be subaccounts of a generic account named Credit Card. That way, you can keep track of your total credit card payments and expenses as well as payments and expenses for individual cards.

To create a subaccount, click the Subaccount Of check box and enter the name of the account that this credit card account goes under. QuickBooks offers a nice generic name for you in the drop-down list: Credit Card. (If you don't see Credit Card in the drop-down list, you can create the account by choosing <Add New> from the list.)

6. **Enter the card number in the Card No. box.**

If you're creating a general Credit Card account for more than one card, leave the Card No. box empty. While you're at it, you can describe the card, too. You might type *Usury!* in the Description box, depending on the interest rate of your card.

7. **Indicate the relationship between the expenses you'll incur and your taxes.**

Use the Tax Line drop-down list box to specify where your purchase amounts can be classified on your tax forms. Chances are, you'll leave this Unassigned because you'll probably be using your credit card for a myriad of items.

8. **Enter the balance that you owed at the end of the last credit card billing period after you made your payment.**

Move the cursor to the Opening Balance text box and use the number keys to enter the balance value. If you just got this credit card and you haven't bought anything with it, leave the box set to 0.00. Otherwise, enter the balance that you currently owe. You enter the balance as a positive number, by the way, even though you owe money.

The only time you should enter a credit card account balance equal to something other than zero is at the time that you start using QuickBooks and are entering your trial balance as of the conversion date. Otherwise, you'll foul up your owner's equity. (Refer to Chapter 1 if you have questions about entering the trial balance or about the conversion date.)

9. **Enter the As Of date on which you'll start keeping records for the credit card account.**

You should probably use the date when you made your most recent payment.

10. **Click OK.**

QuickBooks redisplays the Chart of Accounts window that you saw in Figure 9-1, except this time the window lists an additional account — the credit card account that you just created.

Selecting a credit card account so that you can use it

To tell QuickBooks that you want to work with a credit card account, you use the Chart of Accounts window — the same window that you saw in Figure 9-1. Go figure!

Click the Company tab of the QuickBooks Navigator and click the Chart of Accounts icon to display the Chart of Accounts window. After you display it, double-click the credit card account you want to use. QuickBooks displays the Credit Card register so that you can begin recording transactions.

Entering Credit Card Transactions

After you select a credit card account, QuickBooks displays the Credit Card register (see Figure 9-3). It looks a lot like a Checking register, doesn't it?

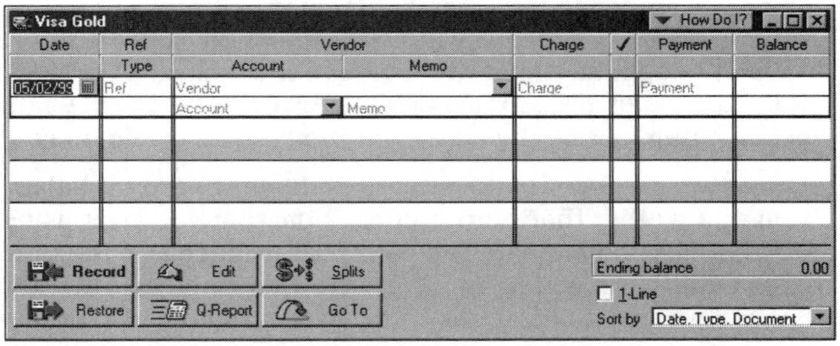

Figure 9-3: The Credit Card register window.

The Credit Card register works like the regular register window that you use for a checking account. You enter transactions in the rows of the register. When you record a charge, QuickBooks updates the credit card balance and the remaining credit limit.

You can use the same icons and commands that you use for your regular ol' bank account register. Earlier chapters cover the icons and commands, so I don't regurgitate them here. Old news is no news. (Refer to Chapter 8 if you need help entering transactions in the register.)

Recording a credit card charge

Recording a credit card charge is similar to recording a check or bank account withdrawal. For the sake of illustration, suppose that you charged

$40.47 for a business lunch at your favorite Mexican restaurant, La Cantina. Here's how you record this charge:

1. **Click the Checking and Credit Cards tab of the QuickBooks Navigator and click the Credit Card icon.**

   You see the Enter Credit Card Charges window (see Figure 9-4).

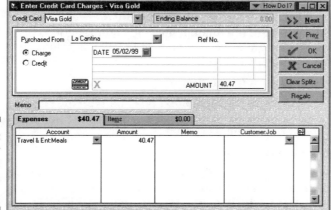

Figure 9-4:
The Enter
Credit Card
Charges
window.

2. **Choose the credit card that you charged the expense against.**

   Click the down arrow next to the Credit Card box and choose a card from the drop-down list.

3. **Record the name of the business that you paid with a credit card.**

   Move the cursor to the Purchased From line and click the down arrow. You see a list of names. Choose one from the list.

   If you've never charged anything on this credit card at this restaurant before, QuickBooks asks you to Set Up or Quick Add the new account. Choose Quick Add and choose an account type. In this case, choose Other because Vendor, Customer, and Employee don't fit the bill. (For help deciding whether to Quick Add or Set Up entries, take a look at Chapter 6.)

4. **Enter whether the transaction is a purchase or a credit.**

   Mark the Charge option button if you want to record a purchase (which is what you do most of the time and what this example shows you). Mark the Credit option button if you want to record a credit on your account (if you returned something, for example).

5. Enter the charge date.

Move the cursor to the Date line (if it isn't already there) and type the date, using the MM/DD/YY format. For example, type either 050299 or 5/2/99 for May 2, 1999. If you're entering this charge two or three days after the fact, don't enter today's date. Enter the date that the charge was made. Using that date makes reconciling your records with your credit card company's records easier when you get the monthly statement.

6. Enter the charge amount.

Move the cursor to the Amount line and enter the total charge amount — 40.47 in this example. Don't type a dollar sign, but do type the period to indicate the decimal place.

7. (Optional) Enter a memo description.

Move the cursor to the Memo text box and type the specific reason that you're charging the item. In this case, you could type *Important Business Lunch* or something like that.

8. Fill in the Expenses tab.

I'm hoping that you read Chapters 6 and 8, that you know all about the Expenses tab, and that you're thoroughly bored by the topic. However, for those of you who opened the book right to this page, you use the Expenses tab to record business expenses.

Move to the Account column of the Expenses tab, click the down arrow, and choose an Expense account from the list (most likely Travel & Ent:Meals, if this is a business lunch). QuickBooks asks you to set up an expense account when you enter a name here that it doesn't know already.

QuickBooks automatically fills in the Amount column when you enter an amount in the Amount line. Type something in the Memo line and assign this expense to a Customer:Job and Class, if you want to. Note that class tracking needs to be turned on if you want to assign the expense to a class.

9. Fill in the Items tab.

Because this charge is for a meal at a restaurant, you don't itemize it (although breaking down the cost of the Mexican lunch into categories might be fun — enchilada, guacamole, red hot chili pepper . . .). But if you were charging lumber, paper supplies, and so on, you'd fill out the Items tab.

If you have a purchase order on file with a vendor that you enter in the Purchased From line, QuickBooks tells you so. Click the Select PO button to see a list of your outstanding purchase orders with the vendor. If you don't know how to handle purchase orders, see Chapter 7.

10. **Record the charge by clicking OK or <u>N</u>ext.**

   Click Next if you want to record a second credit card charge. The charge is recorded in the Credit Card register.

   Figure 9-5 shows what the Credit Card register looks like after I enter a couple of charges.

Figure 9-5: The Credit Card window with a couple of transactions.

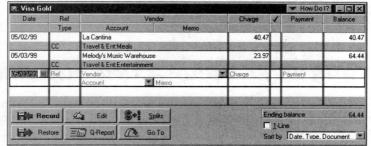

Changing charges that you've already entered

Perhaps you record a credit card charge and then realize that you recorded it incorrectly. Or perhaps you shouldn't have recorded it at all because you didn't pay for the business lunch. (Someone else paid for it after one of those friendly arguments over who should pay the bill. You know the type of argument I mean: "No, I insist." "On the contrary, I insist." You get the picture.)

You have to go into the Credit Card register and either edit or delete the charge.

1. **Click the Company tab of the QuickBooks Navigator and click the Chart of Accounts icon.**

   You see the Chart of Accounts window again.

2. **Open the register.**

   Double-click the credit card account where the faulty charge is. Like magic, the Credit Card register appears on-screen.

3. **Select the credit card transaction that you want to delete or change.**

   That's easy. Just move the cursor to the transaction.

4. **Delete or edit it.**

   To delete it, choose Edit⇨Delete Credit Card Charge. QuickBooks displays a message box that asks whether you really want to delete the transaction. Click OK.

   To edit it, click the Edit button on the bottom of the window. You return to the Enter Credit Card Charges window. Make your changes there and then click OK. You also can make changes inside the Credit Card register and click Restore when you're done.

Reconciling Your Credit Card Statement

You reconcile, or balance, a credit card account the same way you balance a bank account. (For help doing this, see Chapter 13.) After you successfully get the account to balance and click OK, QuickBooks displays the Make Payment dialog box, asking if you want to pay the bill. You can either pay by check or enter a bill to be paid later. (The second option is the accounts payable method, remember?)

If you opt for writing a check, you go straight to the Write Checks window, and the Expenses tab is all filled out for you. Fill in the name of the card issuer, the date, and so on. Click OK when you're done. The payment is recorded in both the Checking register and the Credit Card register.

If you opt to enter the payment as a bill to be paid at a later date, you go to the Enter Bills window. Fill everything out just as you would if you were in the Write Checks window. When you click OK, the transaction is recorded in the Accounts Payable register and the Credit Card register.

See Chapter 6 if you need to know more about either the Enter Bills or Write Checks window.

So What about Debit Cards?

Debit cards, when you get right down to it, aren't really credit cards at all. They're more like bank accounts. Rather than withdrawing money by writing a check, however, you withdraw money by using a debit card.

Although a debit card looks (at least to your friends and the merchants you shop with) like a credit card, you should treat it like a bank account. In a nutshell, here's what you need to do:

  ✔ Set up a bank account with the starting balance equal to the deposit that you make with the debit card company.

  ✔ When you charge something by using the debit card, record the transaction just as you record a regular check.

  ✔ When you replenish the debit balance by sending more money to the debit card company or by making a deposit in your debit card account, record the transaction just as you record a regular deposit.

If all this debit card stuff sounds pretty simple, it is. In fact, I'd go so far as to say that if you've been plugging along, doing just fine with a bank account, you'll find that keeping track of a debit card is as easy as eating an entire bag of potato chips. (Well, maybe not that easy. . . .)

Part III
Stuff You Do Every So Often

The 5th Wave By Rich Tennant

"The first thing you should know about cash-basis accounting is that when you see the exploding bomb icon appear, it's just your computer crashing — not your business."

In this part . . .

After you start using QuickBooks, you need to complete some tasks at the end of every week, month, or year. This part describes these tasks: printing payroll checks, backing up files, printing reports, filing quarterly and annual tax returns. . . . The list goes on and on. Fortunately, QuickBooks comes with some nifty online features to help you get the job done.

Chapter 10
Check Printing 101

*T*his chapter covers the reductivity of the postcolonial implications in Joseph Conrad's *Heart of Darkness.* Oops, only kidding. Guess what I'm going to cover? Gee, you guessed it: how to print checks and checking registers.

Printing checks in QuickBooks is quick — well, it's quick after you set up your printer correctly. If you have a continuous-feed printer, you know by now that these printers have problems printing anything on a form. The alignment always gets screwed up.

QuickBooks has check forms that you can buy, and I recommend using them if you print checks. After all, the QuickBooks checks were made to work with this program. And all banks accept these checks.

If you want help printing reports, refer to Chapter 14, where this topic is covered in almost too much detail.

Getting the Printer Ready

Before you can start printing checks, you have to make sure that your printer is set up to print them. You also have to tell QuickBooks what to put on the checks — your company name, address, logo, and so on. And you might try running a few sample checks through the wringer to see whether they come out all right.

Follow these steps to set up the printer:

1. **Choose File⇨Printer Setup.**

    After you choose this command, choose Check/Paycheck from the Form Name drop-down list box. You see the Printer Setup dialog box, shown in Figure 10-1. In this box, tell QuickBooks about your printer and how you want checks printed.

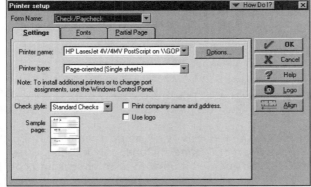

Figure 10-1:
The Printer
Setup
dialog box.

2. **Tell QuickBooks what kind of printer you have.**

    In the Printer Name drop-down list box, click the down arrow and look at the printer names. When you installed QuickBooks, it had a frank, man-to-man talk with Windows to find out what kind of printer you have, among other things. Your printer is probably already selected, but if it's not, select the correct printer.

3. **Set the correct Printer Type option, if necessary.**

    This box is probably already filled in, too, thanks to that frank discussion I mention in Step 2. But if it isn't, click the down arrow and choose Continuous or Page-Oriented. (The former is generally for dot-matrix printers and the latter for laser printers, but it really just depends on what kind of paper you use for your printer.)

4. **Choose a Check Style from the drop-down list.**

    Now you're cooking. This step is where you get to make a real choice. Standard Checks are sized to fit in legal envelopes. Voucher Checks are the same width as standard checks, but they're much longer. When you choose the Voucher Checks option, QuickBooks prints voucher information as well — the items and expenses tabulations from the bottom of the Write Checks window. It also provides information about the checking account that you're writing this check on. The Wallet Checks option is for printing checks that are small enough to fit in — you guessed it — a wallet.

5. **(Optional) Adjust your printer options.**

   Click the Options button. QuickBooks displays your printer's Properties dialog box. Use this dialog box to specify print quality, number of copies, and other options specific to your printer. Click OK to return to the Printer Setup dialog box.

6. **Customize the fonts on your checks.**

   Click the Fonts tab of the Printer Setup dialog box. When you click either the Font button or the Address Font button on this tab, you see the Select Font (see Figure 10-2) or the Select Address Font dialog box. You use the Address Font button to designate how your company's name and address look and the Font button to designate what all other print on your checks looks like. This is your chance to spruce up your checks and make your company's name stand out.

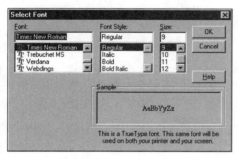

Figure 10-2:
The Select
Font dialog
box.

Experiment for a while with the font, font style, and type size settings. For example, if you have a bookstore, choose the Bookman font (maybe using bold for your company's name and address); if you run a messenger service, choose Courier; Italian mathematicians can use Times Roman. (Just kidding.) You can see what your choices look like in the Sample box. After you're done fooling around, click the OK button to go back to the Printer Setup dialog box.

7. **Choose a Partial Page Printing Style.**

   Click the Partial Page tab of the Printer Setup dialog box. Fortunately, some graphics appear, because otherwise you wouldn't have a clue what these options are, would you? These options are for the thrifty among you. Suppose that you feed two checks to the printer, but the check sheets have three checks each. You have a leftover check.

   Thanks to this option, you can use the extra check. Click one of the options to tell QuickBooks how you'll feed the check to the printer — vertically on the left (the Left option), vertically in the middle (the Centered option), or horizontally (the Portrait option). You feed checks to the printer the same way that you feed envelopes to it.

8. **Enter a company logo or some clip art, if you want.**

   Click the Logo button. In the Logo dialog box, click File and find the directory and .BMP (bitmapped) graphic file that you want to load. Click OK. Only graphics files that are in .BMP format can be used on your checks.

9. **Click OK when you're finished.**

That setup was no Sunday picnic, was it? But your checks are all ready to be printed, and you'll probably never have to go through that ordeal again.

Printing a Check

For some reason, when I get to this part of the discussion, my pulse quickens. It just seems that actually writing a check for real money is terribly serious. I get the same feeling whenever I mail someone cash — even if the amount is nominal.

I think that the best way to lower my heart rate (and yours, if you're like me) is to just print the darn check and be done with it. QuickBooks can print checks in two ways: as you write them and in bunches.

First things first, however. Before you can print checks, you have to load some blank checks into your printer.

This process works the same way as loading any paper into your printer. If you have questions, refer to your printer's documentation. (Sorry I can't help more on this process, but a million different printers are out there, and I can't tell which one you have even when I look into my crystal ball.)

Printing a check as you write it

If you're in the Write Checks window and you've just finished filling out a check, you can print it. The only drawback is that you have to print checks one at a time with this method.

1. **Fill out your check.**

   Yes, I strongly recommend filling out the check before printing it. Turn to Chapter 6 for help with writing checks using QuickBooks.

2. **Click the Print button in the Write Checks window.**

   You see the Print Check dialog box (see Figure 10-3).

Figure 10-3:
The Print
Check
dialog box.

3. **Enter a check number and click OK.**

   After you click OK, you see the similarly named Print Checks dialog box (see Figure 10-4). The settings that you see in this box are the ones that you chose when you first told QuickBooks how to print checks. If you change the settings in the Print Checks dialog box, the changes affect only this particular check. The next time you print a check, you'll see your original settings again.

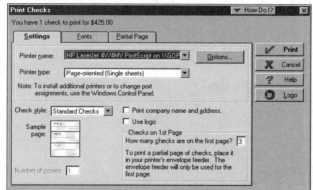

Figure 10-4:
The Print
Checks
dialog box.

4. **Click Print to accept the default settings, or make changes in the dialog box and then click Print.**

   In the Printer Name box, specify which printer you want to print to. In the Check Style box, indicate whether you want to print a Standard, Voucher, or Wallet-sized check. If you're printing a partial page of forms on a laser printer, indicate the number of check forms on the partial page by entering a number in the How Many Checks Are on the First Page? check box. Type **3** if there are three checks, **2** if there are two checks, or **1** if there is one check.

   Check the Print Company Name and Address check box if you want your company's name and address to appear on the check.

   Note that the Number of Copies text box is grayed out. If you want to change these settings, you need to go back to File⇨Printer Setup.

After you click Print, QuickBooks prints the check, and you see the Did Check(s) Print OK? dialog box (see Figure 10-5). Here's your chance to start all over if the check didn't come out right. Type the number of the incorrectly printed check in the text box and click OK. If check number 1005 printed incorrectly, for example, type **1005**. Then click the Print button again, enter the new check number, and click Print again. If the pre-printed check form 1005 is still usable (say, because you acciden-tally printed check 1005 on blank paper instead of on the form) you can reprint the check on check form 1005 by typing **1005** in the Printed Check Number text box. If the incorrectly printed check ruined the check form 1005 (say, because you loaded the form upside-down), load your printer with a fresh check form and verify the new check number, in this case probably 1006.

QuickBooks doesn't automatically keep track of incorrectly-printed check forms, so you have to. If you botched a check form, be sure to write the word VOID in large letters and permanent ink across the face of the check. Then file the check away for your reference. Don't throw the check away.

If you still have questions about how to check mistakes, see the section "What if I make a mistake?" later in this chapter.

Figure 10-5:
The Did
Check(s)
Print OK?
dialog box.

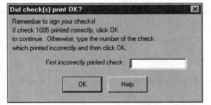

5. If your check looks good, click OK.

This returns you to the Write Checks window. Don't forget to sign the printed check.

Printing checks by the bushel

What if you write a mess of checks and then decide to print them? That's how the process is usually done. Here's how to print a bushel of checks:

1. Go into the Checking register and make sure that the checks that you want to print are marked To Print.

The quickest way to get into the Checking register is to click the Checking and Credit Cards tab of the QuickBooks Navigator and then click the Check Register icon. If you have more than one bank account, select the checking account register you want to open and click OK.

Do the checks that you want to print have To Print in the Number line? If not, place the cursor in the Number line, press T, and then click the Record button. QuickBooks automatically fills the Number field with To Print and then moves on.

2. **Choose File⇨Print Forms⇨Print Checks.**

   You see the Select Checks To Print dialog box, in which you mark which checks to print (see Figure 10-6).

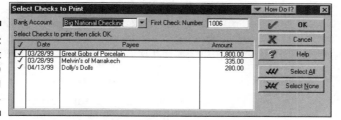

Figure 10-6:
The Select
Checks to
Print dialog
box.

3. **Click the check marks next to the checks that you don't want to print, and then click OK.**

   All the checks are selected at first. If you want to print them all, fine. If not, click the check marks next to the checks that you don't want to print so that QuickBooks removes the check marks. Or, if you want to print only a few of the checks, click the Select None button and then click next to the checks that you want to print so that QuickBooks places a check in the column.

   When only the checks that you want to print are marked with a check mark, click OK to continue with this crazy little thing called check printing. QuickBooks, happy with your progress, displays the Print Checks dialog box (refer to Figure 10-4). Here you see the settings that you chose when you first told QuickBooks how to print checks.

   You can change the settings if you want them to be different. Any changes that you make for a particular batch of checks do not affect the default settings. The next time you print a check, you see your original settings again.

4. **Click Print to accept the default settings, or make changes in the dialog box and then click Print.**

   In the Check Style box, indicate whether you want to print Standard, Voucher, or Wallet-sized checks. If you're printing a partial page of checks, enter the number of checks on the first page in the How Many Checks Are on the First Page? text box.

   Check the Print Company Name and Address check box if you want your company's name and address to appear on the checks.

Note that the Number of Copies text box is grayed out. If you want to change these settings, you need to choose File➪Printer Setup.

QuickBooks prints the checks, and then you see the Did Check(s) Print OK? dialog box (refer to Figure 10-5).

5. **Review the checks that QuickBooks printed.**

If QuickBooks printed the checks correctly, answer the Did Check(s) Print OK? message box by clicking OK. (QuickBooks, apparently thinking that you now want to do nothing but print checks, redisplays the nearly exhausted Write Checks window.)

If QuickBooks didn't print a check correctly, type the number of the first incorrectly printed check in the text box and then click OK. In this case, repeat the steps for check printing. Note, though, that you need to reprint only the first bad check and the checks that follow it. You don't need to reprint good checks that precede the first bad check.

Don't forget to write the word VOID in large letters and permanent ink across the front of incorrectly-printed check forms. Then file the checks for safekeeping. (Don't throw them away.) To record the voided check in QuickBooks, see the section, "What if I make a mistake?" later in the chapter.

If the numbers of the checks you need to reprint aren't sequential and are, in fact, spread all over creation, make it easy on yourself. Click OK to clear the list of checks to be printed, go into the Checking register, and press T in the Number line of the checks you need to reprint. QuickBooks automatically fills these with To Print. Then choose File➪ Print Forms➪Print Checks, as in Step 2, and continue from there.

If your checks came out all right, take the rest of the day off. Give yourself a raise while you're at it.

6. **Sign the printed checks.**

Then — and I guess you probably don't need my help here — put the checks in the mail.

A few words about printing checks

Check printing is kind of complicated, isn't it?

For the record, I'm with you on this one. I really wish it weren't so much work. But you'll find that printing checks gets easier after the first few times.

Pretty soon, you'll be running instead of walking through the steps. Pretty soon, you'll just skate around roadblocks such as check-form alignment problems. Pretty soon, in fact, you'll know all this stuff and never have to read *pretty soon* again.

What if I make a mistake?

If you discover a mistake after you print a check, the problem may not be as big as you think.

If you've already mailed the check, however, you can't do much. You can try to get the check back (if the person you paid hasn't cashed it already) and replace it with a check that's correct. (Good luck on this one.)

If the person has cashed the check, you can't get the check back. If you overpaid the person by writing the check for more than you should have, you need to get the person to pay you the overpayment amount. If you underpaid the person, you need to write another check for the amount of the underpayment.

If you printed the check but haven't mailed it, void the printed check. This operation is in two parts. First, write the word VOID in large letters across the face of the check form. (Use a ballpoint pen if you're using multipart forms so that the second and third parts also show as VOID.) Second, display the Checking register, highlight the check, and then choose Edit⇨ Void Check. (This option marks the check as one that has been voided in the system so that QuickBooks does not use it in calculating the account balance.) If you're voiding an incorrectly-printed check, you need to first create a transaction for the check number that printed incorrectly, and then void that transaction.

Of course, if you want to reissue a voided check, just enter the check all over again — only this time, try to be more careful.

If you notice only after clicking OK in the Did Checks Print OK? dialog box that a check printed incorrectly, you can tell QuickBooks you want to reprint the check in one of two ways. If you have the register window displayed, you can change the check's number from, for example, 007, to To Print. If you have the Write Checks window displayed, you can check the To Be Printed box.

Oh where, oh where do unprinted checks go?

Unprinted checks — those that you entered using the Write Checks window but haven't yet printed — are stored in the Checking register. To identify them as unprinted checks, QuickBooks puts To Print in the Number line. What's more, when you tell QuickBooks to print the unprinted checks, what it really does is print the checks in the register that have To Print in the Number line. All this knowledge is of little practical value in most instances, but it results in several interesting possibilities.

For example, you can enter the checks that you want to print directly into the register — all you need to do is type To Print in the Number line. (Note that you can't enter an address anywhere in the register, so this process isn't practical if you want addresses printed on the checks.)

Printing a Checking Register

You can print a Checking register or a register for any other account, too. Follow these steps to print a register:

1. **Open the account register you want to print.**

   Click the Checking and Credit Cards tab of the QuickBooks Navigator and click the Check Register icon. If you have more than one bank account, select the account register you want to print from the drop-down list box and click OK.

2. **Choose File➪Print Register.**

   You see the Print Register dialog box (see Figure 10-7).

Figure 10-7:
The Print
Register
dialog box.

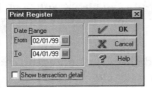

3. **Fill in the Date Range text boxes.**

   To print a register of something other than the current year-to-date transactions, use the From and To text boxes. This step is pretty dang obvious, isn't it? You just move the cursor to the From and To text boxes and type the range of months that the register should include.

4. **If you want, click the Show Transaction Detail check box.**

   As you know, a register doesn't show all the messy details, such as the Items and Expenses tab information. But you can click this check box to include all this stuff on your printed register.

5. **Click OK.**

   You see the Print Lists dialog box (see Figure 10-8).

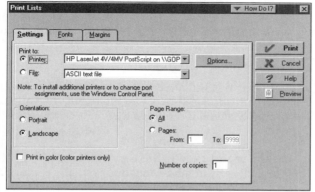

Figure 10-8:
The Print
Lists dialog
box.

6. If everything is cool, click Print.

You don't have to fool around with this dialog box. If you want to print a register pronto, just click Print, and QuickBooks sends the register on its merry way to your printer. Then again, if you're the sort of person who likes to fool around with this kind of stuff, carry on with the rest of these steps.

If you want to see the effect that the different settings in this dialog box have, just experiment. You can't hurt anything or anybody.

7. (Optional) Print the report to disk.

To print the report to disk as a text file, mark the File box and choose one of the following Print To options:

- Choose ASCII Text File if you want to create a text file (for example, when you want to import the register into a word-processing program).

- Choose Excel/Lotus 123 Spreadsheet to import the register into Microsoft Excel or Lotus 1-2-3.

- Choose Tab Delimited File to, for example, import the register into a database program. (Oooh . . . fancy. . . .)

8. Choose the paper orientation.

Which direction do you want the report to be printed — Portrait (regular) or Landscape (sideways)? Just click the appropriate option button.

9. (Optional) Tell QuickBooks which pages to print.

Use the Print Range option buttons and text boxes to limit the pages for QuickBooks to print.

10. **(Optional) Color your world.**

    If you have a color printer and want to print the register in color, click the Print In Color check box.

11. **(Optional) Check it out.**

    To see how your settings will affect the report before you actually print it, click Preview. QuickBooks shows you the results on the screen. This feature has probably saved more trees than can be imagined.

12. **Click Print.**

    After you have the report exactly the way you want it (and not one moment before!), click Print, and QuickBooks finally prints the register.

Chapter 11
Online with QuickBooks

In This Chapter

▶ Using Internet Explorer 4
▶ Web sites you can access from within QuickBooks
▶ Deciding whether to jump onto the electronic banking bandwagon
▶ Signing up for an online service
▶ Making an online payment
▶ Transferring money electronically
▶ Changing payment and transfer instructions
▶ Transmitting payment and transfer instructions
▶ Sending electronic mail to the bank

*T*he first part of this chapter talks about QuickBooks' most popular online features — the fun and useful things you only need a modem and a Web browser (which comes with QuickBooks) to do. Later in this chapter, I talk about deciding whether to use QuickBooks' slightly more complicated online features: online banking and online bill payment. Lastly, I describe how you make online banking and bill payment transactions.

Using Internet Explorer 4

The QuickBooks CD includes Microsoft's Web browser, Internet Explorer 4. If you don't already have Internet Explorer 4 or another Web browser installed on your computer, you probably want to install this one from your QuickBooks CD. You can use Internet Explorer (or the browser of your choice) to browse Intuit Web sites for free. (Intuit is the company that makes QuickBooks, in case you're wondering why I'd suggest such a thing.)

If you have an account with an Internet Service Provider, you also can use Internet Explorer to browse more of the Internet, including the rest of the World Wide Web, FTP sites, and telnet sites (such as those hosted by your local library). You can even use Internet Explorer's add-on components to send and receive e-mail, receive regular newsletters from mailing lists, browse messages posted to newsgroups, create your own home page, and conduct online audio or video conferences with customers or vendors. To be able to use Internet Explorer, you need to have a physical connection to the Internet. For most small businesses, this means that your computer needs a modem connected to a phone line.

Installing Internet Explorer 4

If you accepted the standard installation of QuickBooks, you most likely already installed Internet Explorer 4. If you chose not to install Internet Explorer with QuickBooks, you can install it now by inserting the QuickBooks CD in your CD-ROM drive. In the dialog box Windows displays, click the Install button next to Install Internet Explorer 4.0. If Windows doesn't display a dialog box when you insert the CD, you can use My Computer or Windows Explorer to browse the contents of your CD-ROM drive. Double-click the Autorun application (.exe) file.

Getting set up

If you just installed Internet Explorer 4, or if you want to sign up for and set up an account with an Internet Service Provider, choose Online⇨Internet Connection Setup. The Internet Connection Setup Wizard sets up your modem — and in some cases, your Internet Service Provider account — to work with Internet Explorer 4 and QuickBooks.

Web Sites You Can Access from within QuickBooks

After you install and set up Internet Explorer or another Web browser, you can click icons on the QuickBooks Navigator to launch your Web browser in the background and display Web sites from within the QuickBooks application window. This means that you don't need to leave QuickBooks to browse the Web. When you click one of the icons described below, QuickBooks displays a message box letting you know that it must launch your Web browser and connect to the Internet. Click OK, and QuickBooks is on its way.

Navigating the Web from within QuickBooks is very similar to navigating the Web using your Web browser independently. But just in case you're new to this, here's the run-down: When you run your mouse pointer over a Web page, you'll notice that it sometimes turns into a pointing finger. It often does this when you point to underlined text, for instance. These parts of a Web page are called *hyperlinks*. When you click a hyperlink, your Web browser displays a Web page related to whatever you clicked. For example, if you click a hyperlink that says "Insurance," your Web browser most likely displays a Web page with information about insurance, including more hyperlinks to different types of insurance or to articles relating to insurance issues, and so forth. To move back and forth between the Web pages you visit, you use the Back and Forward buttons. If a Web page seems to take a long time to load (more than about a minute), you can click the Stop button. Then click Refresh to repeat the instruction to display the Web page.

QuickBooks.com

Click the Business Resources tab of the QuickBooks Navigator and click the QuickBooks.com icon to visit the QuickBooks Web site shown in Figure 11-1. (Even though the icon you click says 24-Hour Product Support beneath it, you can access more than product support from the QuickBooks home page, as you can see in Figure 11-1.) You also can visit this Web site if you have your Web browser open independently by typing **www.intuit.com/quickbooks** in your browser's Address or Location text box.

Small Business Tools, Information, and Advice by Quicken.com

Click the Business Resources tab of the QuickBooks Navigator and click the Small Business Tools, Information, and Advice icon to display the Small Business area of the Quicken Web site. Quicken is Intuit's personal accounting program, the popular little cousin of QuickBooks. Take some time to browse the extensive Quicken Web site — it's full of all sorts of helpful information, advice, tools, and resources.

Find an Advisor

Click the Business Resources tab of the QuickBooks Navigator and click the Find an Advisor icon to connect to the Internet and find a financial advisor or a QuickBooks support resource in your area.

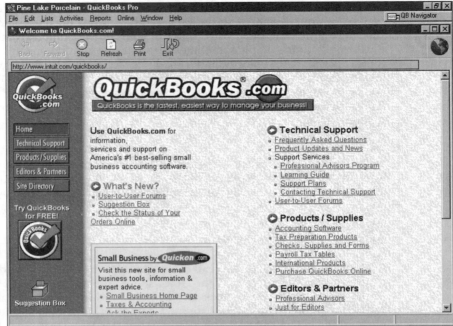

Figure 11-1:
The
QuickBooks
home page.

CashFinder.com

Click the Business Resources tab of the QuickBooks Navigator and click the CashFinder.com icon to access a Web site where you can select and sign up for business loans, lines of credit, credit cards, and leasing from many financial institutions.

QuickBooks Update Service

Click the Company tab of the QuickBooks Navigator and click the QuickBooks Update Service icon to display the dialog box shown in Figure 11-2 and update your copy of QuickBooks online. You update your copy of QuickBooks because some of the information that QuickBooks uses needs to be regularly updated — specifically, the tax table information that QuickBooks uses to make payroll calculations. Therefore, you probably want to use the command every so often — such as every quarter. (At a bare minimum, you want to use this command at the start of each year.) Updating QuickBooks also allows you to download any patches that Intuit creates to fix bugs in the program, as well as additional features created or enhanced after your copy of QuickBooks was shipped.

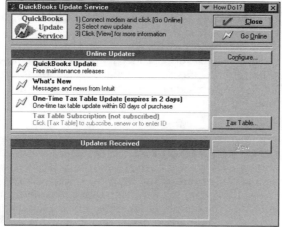

Figure 11-2:
The
QuickBooks
Update
Service.

Order Checks and Forms

Click the Company tab of the QuickBooks Navigator and click the Order Checks and Forms icon to connect to an Intuit Web page from which you can order checks, pre-printed envelopes, business forms, custom stamps, software, and other supplies.

Free Trial for a Friend

If you enjoy using QuickBooks and think another person with a small business would find the program helpful, you can send that person a free trial of both QuickBooks and QuickBooks Pro that can be used up to 25 times. To do this, click the Company tab of the QuickBooks Navigator and click the Free Trial for a Friend icon. When QuickBooks connects you to the Internet and displays a Web page for ordering trial software, fill out the necessary information.

The Online menu offers other commands for accessing various online resources. Choose the Intuit Web Sites command to see a list of more Intuit Web sites you can view from within QuickBooks. Or choose Payroll Tax Tables to download the latest tax table. Choose one of the Payroll Service submenu's commands to learn more about, sign up for, or use QuickBooks' online payroll feature.

Jumping On the Online Bandwagon

Before I talk about how you use QuickBooks' online banking and payment services, you need to consider whether these features even make sense for you and your business. Online banking does make sense for some people — maybe even you. But then again, it may be more like the fins on a '62 Cadillac: cool, but not that cool.

So what's the commotion about?

Although everybody's raving about online banking — especially banks and software companies — I think that it's a service that's still slightly ahead of its time, even though it's had a couple of years to prove itself. QuickBooks defines online banking as including two parts: online banking itself and online bill payment. Basically, online banking enables you to transmit account transfer instructions to your bank and download, or retrieve, account information electronically using your computer and modem. Online bill payment allows you to transmit payment instructions electronically. (You basically tell your bank to write, stamp, and mail a check so that you don't have to.)

And that, my friend, is about all there is to online banking.

Should I get wired?

I don't know whether you should get wired, really. But I'll share some thoughts with you.

On its face, online banking sounds pretty neat. And I guess it is neat — in its own little way. But online banking does have some problems.

Problem one is this: To use the full-blown service, you need to use a bank that has signed up for Intuit's service. Maybe a handful of big banks have signed up. More banks sign up all the time, of course, but many haven't yet. So if your bank hasn't jumped on the bandwagon — that is, Intuit's bandwagon — you can't really jump on the bandwagon either. Or at least not as a full-fledged member of the band. (I talk more about this later in the chapter.)

 To find out whether your bank provides online banking, choose Online⇨ Online Banking⇨Getting Started and click the Financial Institutions button. QuickBooks connects to the Internet (if you're not already connected) and displays a Web page that lists the banks providing the service.

In response to this first problem, people may say, "Well, Dodo-brain, just switch banks." But switching banks is harder than it sounds, especially for small businesses — and often not a smart move. Many factors go into a successful small business banking relationship:

- ✔ **Convenience:** Doing your banking should be easy.

- ✔ **Trust based on a long history:** That way, you can borrow money or set up merchant credit card accounts without using your children for collateral.

- ✔ **Good rapport with a personal banker or loan officer:** If you ever have a problem — and I hope that doesn't happen — you have someone you can talk to.

Sure, online banking is neat. Like Cadillac fins. But online banking isn't the only feature you need to look at when you consider a bank, and it certainly isn't the most important feature of a bank.

And then you have problem number two: Although a totally electronic system sounds really efficient and very slick, you need to realize that online bill payment (a key component of online banking) often isn't that efficient or slick because, to be quite honest, the system isn't totally electronic.

"What the . . ." you're saying. "I thought that was the point." Let me explain: For better or worse, most businesses are still set up and still expect to receive paper checks with remittance advices. So what often happens when you transmit payment instructions is that the bank or online payment service simply writes (and prints) a check for you. Think about that for a minute. If the bank is printing your check, you still have all the disadvantages of a printed check:

- ✔ You still need extra time for mailing.

- ✔ You still have the possibility that the check will get lost.

- ✔ You still have the possibility that the check will be misapplied. (In other words, the check to pay your power bill may instead be applied to your neighbor's account.)

What's more, you also have the extra complication of having your bank mucking all this stuff up instead of you. Best of all, the bank charges for this service. (Remember that banks and software companies are excited about online banking because they think that it's a new way for them to make money.)

And finally, receiving payments from your bank instead of directly from you also often confuses your vendors. This happens because the checks they receive come all bundled up in these cute little envelopes that need to be torn along the perforation on just about all sides. And you can't send a remittance slip with an online payment. So vendors can easily incorrectly credit your account. And this can lead to problems.

Making sense of online banking

So what should you do? Let me make a suggestion: If you use a bank that provides online banking, go ahead and try the service. It isn't very expensive — probably a few dollars a month. If, later on, you decide that you don't like the service, you can always go back to banking the old-fashioned way.

If you use a bank that doesn't provide online banking services and you're really bummed out about it, you can try the online bill payment component of online banking using Intuit's online bill payment service. (Online bill payment is the part where you send instructions—either to your bank, if it provides the service, or to Intuit—to write and mail checks for you.) You can use the online bill payment service with any account — in essence, you just give Intuit permission to automatically deduct money from your account so that they can make payments for you.

If you use a bank that doesn't provide online banking and you couldn't care less, don't try the online banking stuff, don't read any more of this chapter, and consider taking the rest of the afternoon off.

Signing Up for the Service

Signing up for the online banking service isn't difficult. All you need to do is choose the Online⇨Online Banking⇨Getting Started command. This command displays a dialog box that includes buttons you can click to learn more about, sign up for, and set up online banking (as shown in Figure 11-3).

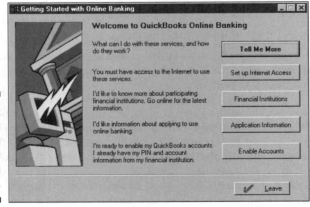

Figure 11-3: The Getting Started with Online Banking dialog box.

Click Tell Me More to learn more about online banking. Click Application Information to request an application for the online banking service, and click Enable Accounts once you've received, filled out, and sent in the online banking application and received the necessary information to set up an account for online banking.

Note: In order to actually begin transmitting online payments or making account inquiries, you need to complete the application from your bank or Intuit and have that application processed.

Making an Online Payment

Plan to create and send online payments a good week before they're due. It takes time for the online bill payment service to process your request, then print and send a check. And a check your bank sends doesn't go through the mail any faster than a check you send yourself. So don't expect online bill payment to win you any time over sending checks you print or hand-write yourself.

After you sign up for online banking, making payments is easy. Just follow these steps:

1. **Click the Checking and Credit Cards tab of the QuickBooks Navigator and click the Checks icon.**

   If you've written checks with QuickBooks before, you'll see your old familiar friend, the Write Checks window (see Figure 11-4).

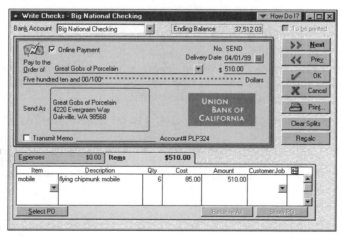

Figure 11-4: The Write Checks window.

2. **Click the Ban<u>k</u> Account drop-down list at the top of the window and choose the account from which you want to write this check.**

   Choosing the account is a really important step. Make sure that you're accessing the right account before you write a check.

3. **Check the Online Payment box.**

   (The box is in the upper-left corner of the check, by the way.)

   This one is another really important step. If you don't check this box, you're not making an online payment; you're just writing a regular check that you'll need to print or hand write.

4. **Fill in the check.**

   If you've written a check to this person or party before, the AutoFill feature fills in the name of the payee in the Pay to the Order Of line after you type a few letters. How QuickBooks can know who you're paying may seem akin to magic, but filling in the information really isn't that tough. QuickBooks just compares what you've typed so far with names on your lists of customers, employees, and other names. When it can match the letters you've typed so far with a name on one of these lists, it grabs the name and address. For online bill payment, it's important to have the correct address. If the address is incomplete, QuickBooks warns you and asks you to correct it. (If you haven't written a check to this person or party before, QuickBooks asks you to Quick Add or Set Up the payee name. Do that.)

   Enter the amount of the check next to the dollar sign and press Tab. QuickBooks writes out the amount for you on the Dollars line.

5. **Fill in the E<u>x</u>penses and Ite<u>m</u>s tabs, if necessary.**

   Don't know what these are? Chapter 6 explains them in minute detail. Start turning those pages.

6. **Click <u>N</u>ext or OK to finish writing the check.**

   Click Next if you want to write another check or click OK if you're done writing checks for the moment. There you have it. Your check is written, entered in the Checking register, and ready to be sent so that your bank or Intuit can print and mail it.

   And you thought this stuff was going to be tough, didn't you?

People who have grown accustomed to Quicken, a cousin product of QuickBooks, may want to use the register window to make online payments. You can use the register window in QuickBooks, too, although doing so isn't quite as slick. You just enter the payment in the usual way — except that you type the word SEND in the Check Number text box.

Transferring Money Electronically

You can electronically transfer money between bank accounts, too — as long as the accounts are at the same bank. (Both accounts, of course, also need to be set for online banking.) Here's what you need to do:

1. **Click the Checking and Credit Cards tab of the QuickBooks Navigator and click the Transfer Money icon.**

   You see the Transfer Funds Between Accounts window, shown in Figure 11-5.

Figure 11-5:
The
Transfer
Funds
Between
Accounts
window.

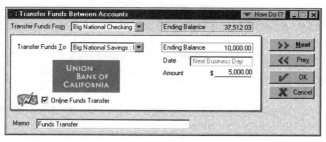

2. **Select the bank account that you're going to transfer the money from.**

   In the Transfer Funds From box at the top of the screen, choose the account from the drop-down list.

3. **Select the bank account to which you want to transfer the money.**

   In the Transfer Funds To drop-down list box, select the account that you want to receive the funds.

4. **Check the Online Funds Transfer box.**

   This action tells QuickBooks that you want to make this transfer electronically.

5. **Enter the amount that you want to transfer and fill in the Memo line.**

   Someday, you may go into the register for the account you're writing this check in and wonder where you transferred this money and why. Filling in the Memo line solves this little mystery beforehand.

6. **Click OK.**

   The transfer is recorded. After you transmit the transfer instructions (described a little later in this chapter), the transfer transaction is posted to your account. Maybe not immediately, but as fast as a telephone transfer or ATM machine transfer is posted.

Changing Instructions

QuickBooks doesn't actually send, or transmit, your payment and transfer instructions until you tell it to. This little fact means that you can change, or edit, your payment instructions (what you enter with the Write Checks window) and your transfer instructions (what you enter with the Transfer Funds Between Accounts window) until you actually transmit them. You edit online payments and account transfers in the same way that you edit regular payments and account transfers. Refer to Chapter 8 if you need more information.

Transmitting Instructions

After you describe the online payments and account transfers that you want QuickBooks to make, you transmit that information to the bank. To do so, follow these steps:

1. **Click the Checking and Credit Cards tab of the QuickBooks Navigator and click the Online Banking icon.**

   You see the Online Banking Center window, shown in Figure 11-6.

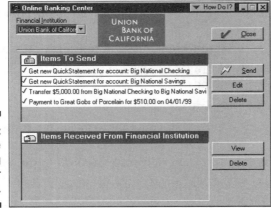

Figure 11-6:
The Online
Banking
Center
window.

2. **Select the bank to which you're transmitting payment and transfer instructions.**

   In the Financial Institution box at the top of the screen, choose the bank from the drop-down list.

3. **Review the payment and transfer instructions one last time.**

   Take one last peek at the Items To Send list box to make sure that the payment and transfer instructions you're sending are correct. If you have questions about a particular instruction, click it and then click the Edit button. If you know that a particular payment instruction is incorrect, click it and then click the Delete button.

4. **Transmit the payment and transfer instructions.**

   You can guess how this works, right? You just click the Send button. If this is the first time you've transmitted payment and transfer instructions, you're probably prompted to change your personal identification number, or PIN. If this isn't the first time you've transmitted payment and transfer instructions, QuickBooks prompts you to enter your existing PIN.

5. **Review any transactions that the bank tells you about.**

   Figure 11-6 doesn't show any transactions in the Items Received From Financial Institution list box, but do you see this box at the bottom of the dialog box? While you're transmitting payment and transfer instructions to your bank, your bank may be transmitting transaction information to QuickBooks. For example, the bank may transmit a service charge transaction. Any new transactions that the bank charges or records for your bank account appear in the Items Received From Financial Institution list box. You should review these new transactions in the same way that you review transactions that appear on your bank statement. If you have further questions about a particular transaction, click it and then click the View button.

6. **Click Close.**

   Hey, when you're done, you're done.

Message in a Bottle

Doing all your banking electronically can be a little unsettling when you're first starting out. What if, for example, you have a question? Fortunately, this situation is no problem. All you do is send an e-mail message to the bank asking the people there whatever question you would normally ask in a telephone call or at the drive-through window. To do this, follow these steps:

1. **Choose Online➪Online Banking➪Create Message➪ Online Banking Message.**

   QuickBooks displays the Home Banking Message dialog box shown in Figure 11-7 and fills in the bank name (as long as you only use online banking services with one bank). If you use online banking services with more than one bank, select the name of the bank to whom you want to send a message from the Message To drop-down list box.

Figure 11-7:
The Home
Banking
Message
dialog box.

2. **Describe the subject or purpose of your message.**

   Click the Subject box and then type a brief description of your message's subject. You may know this already, but most e-mail readers simply display a list of messages that includes the sender, the message subject, and the date. Therefore, the message subject that you use is one of the first bits of message information that the bank sees.

3. **Select the online account to which the message is in regard.**

4. **Type your message.**

   Click the Message box and then type your message. You're on your own here.

5. **Optionally, print a copy of your message.**

   To do so, just click the Print button.

6. **Click OK.**

   When you click OK, you add the message to the list of stuff that's ready to send the next time you go online with your bank. You can send the instructions immediately by following the steps under "Transmitting Instructions" earlier in this chapter.

If you have a question about a specific online payment, you can use a slightly more precise method for inquiring about the payment. First, display the bank account's check register and select the online payment. Then choose Online➪Online Banking➪Create Message➪Online Payment Inquiry and use the dialog box that QuickBooks displays to inquire about the payment instruction you selected.

Chapter 12
Payroll

. . . .

In This Chapter

▶ Creating payroll accounts

▶ Requesting an employer ID number

▶ Obtaining withholding information

▶ Computing an employee's gross wages, payroll deductions, and net wages

▶ Recording a payroll check in QuickBooks

▶ Making federal tax deposits

▶ Preparing quarterly and annual payroll tax returns

▶ Producing annual wage statements, such as W-2s

▶ Handling state payroll taxes

. . . .

*P*ayroll is one of the major headaches of running a small business. When I think of all the time I've wasted figuring out withholding amounts, writing checks, and trying to fill out wickedly ridiculous payroll tax returns, it just makes me want to scream. Fortunately, QuickBooks helps. And in a big way. In this chapter, I explain how.

Getting Ready to Do Payroll

To prepare payroll checks and summarize the payroll information that you need to prepare quarterly and annual returns, you need to set up some special accounts. You also need to do some paperwork. This section describes how to do both tasks.

Making sure that QuickBooks is ready

The very first thing you should do before starting this process is to choose
Help⇨About Tax Table from the QuickBooks menu. A dialog box that looks
incredibly similar to the one shown in Figure 12-1 appears. This box tells
you the tax information that QuickBooks is currently using. If, for any
reason, you think that your information may not be up-to-date, follow the
instructions and call the Intuit number listed in the dialog box to check it.

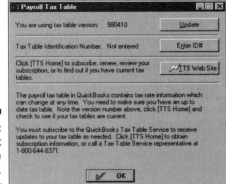

Figure 12-1:
The About
Tax Table
dialog box.

To do payroll in QuickBooks, you need several liability accounts, a payroll
expense account, and several payroll expense subaccounts. Fortunately,
none of these is particularly difficult to create. In fact, as long as you told
QuickBooks that you were going to use it for payroll and you specified all
the payroll information QuickBooks asked for in the EasyStep Interview,
QuickBooks has already set up most or all of the accounts you need. Your
Payroll Item List is probably ready or close to it.

Figure 12-2 shows the Payroll Item List window. It includes several employee
wage accounts, employee withholding accounts, and employer tax accounts.
To see whether your QuickBooks company has the needed payroll accounts
set up, click the Payroll and Time tab of the QuickBooks Navigator and click
the Payroll Items icon.

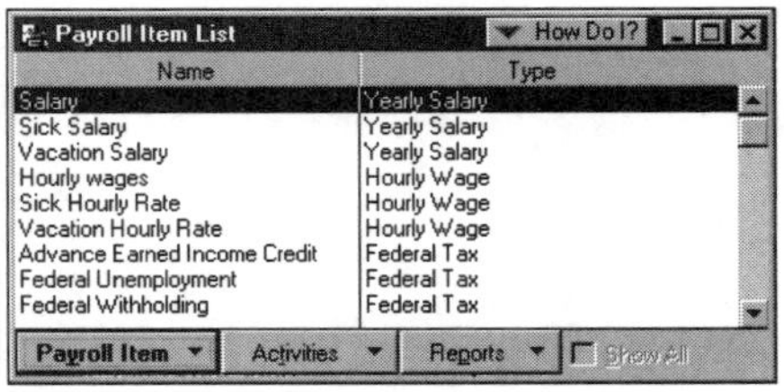

Figure 12-2:
The Payroll
Item List
window.

Note: How payroll works depends partly on which version of QuickBooks you have (QuickBooks, the regular version, or QuickBooks Pro, the Cadillac version) and how you've set up QuickBooks. Your payroll windows and dialog boxes, therefore, may look slightly different from what I show here. They should still all work in the same basic way, however.

You should have set up year-to-date payroll amounts for the period of time up to your QuickBooks start date during the EasyStep Interview (see Chapter 1). If you didn't do this, click the Payroll and Time tab of the QuickBooks Navigator and click the YTD Amounts icon. Then enter year-to-date amounts from paycheck stubs using the Set Up YTD Amounts wizard.

Adding payroll taxes and deductions

You may need to add payroll items to your Payroll Item list in QuickBooks if you add some new expense or benefit (such as an IRA deduction, an employee bonus, or a new state or local tax) after you set up your payroll items in the EasyStep Interview (as I explain in Chapter 1).

If you have a payroll expense, withholding, or employer tax account that you need to set up, and you understand the taxes shown in Figure 12-2 — and you will if you read a bit more — you'll have no trouble dealing with other employee withholding or other employer taxes. You treat local income taxes, for example, basically the same way that you treat federal or state income tax. And another employer payroll tax should be treated the same way that you treat the employer-paid portions of social security taxes.

To add a new account, open the Payroll Item list (if it isn't open already), click the Payroll Item button at the bottom of the window, and choose New. This starts a wizard that helps you set up payroll items (see Figure 12-3).

Figure 12-3: The first page of the Payroll Item Setup wizard.

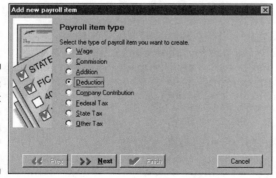

The steps in the wizard differ depending on the kind of item you're setting up, but here's how you set up a payroll item for a simple IRA deduction:

1. **Choose Deduction in the first dialog box and click Next.**

2. **Enter a name for the deduction.**

   In the example of a simple IRA, you might want to choose a name like "simple IRA." Click Next when you're done.

3. **Enter the name of the agency you're paying, your account number with that agency, and the liability account you want to use to track the liability.**

   Click Next after you complete the dialog box.

4. **Choose a tax item to track the deduction.**

   In the case of a simple IRA, you would choose SIMPLE Retirement Ded. Click Next once you've decided.

5. **Check which taxes are calculated after the deduction.**

   In the case of a simple IRA, you probably check only Federal Withholding. FUTA taxes are calculated based on gross pay. Click Next to proceed.

6. **If the deduction is based on performance (quantity of items sold), check the Based on Quantity box in the next dialog box. Then click Next.**

   For a simple IRA deduction, leave this box empty.

7. **Enter a percentage rate or amount for the deduction if it's the same for all or most employees.**

8. **Enter a limit for the deduction.**

   In the case of a simple IRA, the limit is $6,000 as of this writing.

9. **Click Finish.**

   You're done! The payroll item now shows up on your Payroll Item list.

If you have other payroll items to deal with (especially other deductions that affect an employee's gross pay for income tax purposes but not for FUTA) and you need help, just ask your accountant. (Providing general answers that will work for everyone who reads this book is just too difficult — and actually kind of dangerous, too. Sorry.)

Doing taxes the right way

You need a couple of other things if you want to do payroll the right way: an employer identification number and some W-4 tax forms. (If you want to do payroll the wrong way, you're reading the wrong book.)

Getting an employer ID number

First, you need to file an SS-4, or Request for Employer Identification Number form, with the Internal Revenue Service (IRS) so that you can get an employer identification number. You can get this form by calling the IRS and asking for one. Or if you have a friend who's an accountant, that person may have one of these forms. (See, there *is* a reason to invite people like me to your dinner parties.)

In one of its cooler moves, the IRS changed its ways regarding the process. Now you can apply for and receive an employer identification number over the telephone. You still need to fill out the SS-4 form, however, so that you can answer the questions that the IRS asks during the short telephone application process. (You also need to mail or fax the form to the IRS after you have your little telephone conversation.)

Having employees do their part

You also need to do something else before you can know how to handle all those taxes — you need to have each of your employees fill out a W-4 form to tell you what filing status they'll use and how many personal exemptions they'll claim. Guess where you get blank W-4 forms? That's right: from your friendly IRS agent.

Paying Your Employees

After you set up your payroll accounts and get an employer identification number, you're ready to pay someone. This section is going to blow your mind, especially if you've been doing payroll manually. It will make your whole decision to use QuickBooks Pro to do your payroll worthwhile.

1. **Start the payroll process.**

   Click the Payroll and Time tab of the QuickBooks Navigator and click the Create Paychecks icon. The Select Employees To Pay window appears, as you can see in Figure 12-4. If you don't see a name that you're looking for in this list, it means that you never added the employee to your Employee list. If you need help adding employees to your list, read Chapter 2.

2. **Change any settings that you want to.**

   Unless you're not going to print the checks — maybe you handwrite them and just use QuickBooks to keep the books — leave the To Be Printed check box checked.

   Indicate the bank account from which the employees are paid in the appropriate drop-down list box.

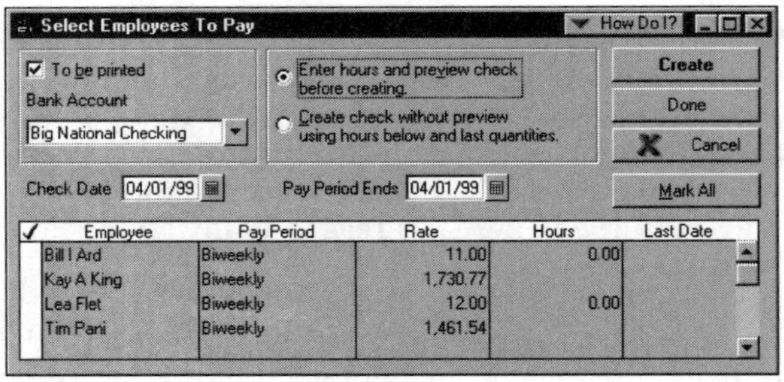

Figure 12-4:
The Select
Employees
To Pay
window.

I suggest leaving the Enter Hours and Preview Check Before Creating option marked, just in case.

Set the Check Date and the Pay Period Ends dates appropriately.

3. Select the employees whom you're paying.

If you're paying all the employees listed, just click the Mark All button on the right side of the screen. If you need to mark the employees individually, just click next to each one in the left column — the column with the check mark in the heading.

4. Fill out the payroll information and click the Create button.

Fill in the number of hours the person worked and apply these hours to a customer or job, if necessary. You also can change the payroll item or rate or add another payroll item, if you need to. Watch this. QuickBooks calculates the company and employee taxes and the amount of the net check, as you can see in Figure 12-5. If some information is inaccurate, simply click the amount and change it, either by deleting it or replacing it with the correct information.

You might also note that QuickBooks keeps totals both for the current check and for the year to date.

5. Click the Create button. (Yes, again.)

After you check all the employees' paychecks, QuickBooks returns to the Select Employees To Pay dialog box.

6. Click Done.

Just because you are.

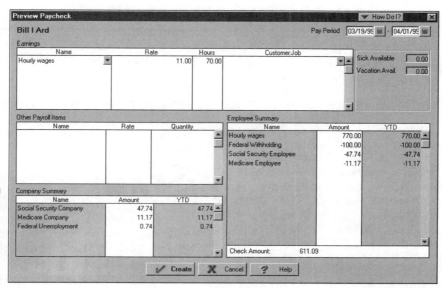

Figure 12-5:
The
Preview
Paycheck
dialog box.

To print the checks, just choose File⇨Print Forms⇨Print Paychecks, and the Select Paychecks To Print dialog box appears (see Figure 12-6). Choose the checks you want to print, make sure that the printer's loaded with the appropriate forms, and then click OK. From then on, it's like printing any other check — except the check pays an employee's wages and not a bill from some vendor. The same old Print Checks window appears, which you've seen many, many times by now, and so on, and so on.

Note: Got questions about printing employee payroll checks? Take a look at Chapter 10.

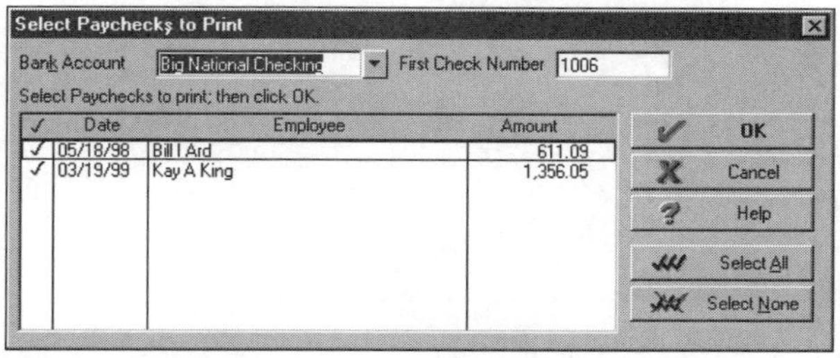

Figure 12-6:
The Select
Paychecks
To Print
dialog box.

The QuickBooks online payroll service

QuickBooks 6 now includes an online service you can sign up for to make processing payroll and payroll taxes quick and easy. The QuickBooks Online Payroll Service comes with two parts: Online Direct Deposit, which allows you to electronically deposit employee's paychecks directly in their bank accounts, and the Online Payroll Tax Service, which allows you to pay your liability taxes and prepare and file tax forms electronically. When you sign up for Online Payroll Tax Service, you also get automatic updates of the payroll tax tables sent directly to your computer. To sign up for one or both of QuickBooks' Online Payroll Services, you need to first call a customer service representative at 1-800-332-4844 and supply a whole bunch of information about your business (so it's wise to be sitting by your computer and have your QuickBooks file open when you make this call). The customer service representative gives you a number that you need to set up the online payroll service in QuickBooks. Once you have this number, choose Online⇨Payroll Service⇨ Payroll Service Sign-Up. Then follow the wizard shown in the figure below.

If you sign up for Online Direct Deposit, you also need to add your employee's direct deposit information to your employee list. To do this, open the Employee List by clicking the Payroll and Time tab of the QuickBooks Navigator. Then click the Employees icon. Double-click an employee to display that employee's information. Click the Payroll tab and then click the Direct Deposit button and fill out the name and routing number of the employee's bank, and the employee's account number(s). (Employees can split their paychecks between two accounts, such as a savings and a checking account, if they so desire.) To send direct deposit instructions, complete payroll as you usually do and then display the Online Banking Service window. The direct deposit paychecks show up in the Items To Send list. Click Send to send the instructions.

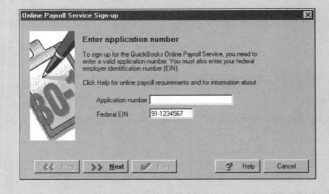

Making Deposits to Uncle Sam

Make no mistake. Big Brother wants the money you withhold from an employee's payroll check for federal income taxes, social security, and Medicare. Big Brother also wants the payroll taxes you owe — the matching social security and Medicare taxes, federal unemployment taxes, and so on. So every so often you need to pay Big Brother the amounts you owe.

Making this payment is actually simple. Just write a check equal to the account balances shown in the payroll tax liability accounts.

You do so by clicking the Payroll and Time tab of the QuickBooks Navigator and clicking the Pay Liabilities icon, whereupon the Pay Liabilities window appears, as shown in Figure 12-7.

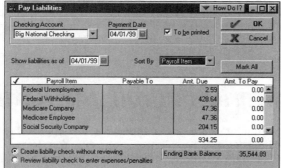

Figure 12-7:
The Pay
Liabilities
window.

All you have to do now is choose the liabilities or taxes that you want to pay by clicking in the left column and indicating the portion you want to pay of the amount due. Unless you've clicked the Review Liability Check To Enter Expenses/Penalties option at the bottom of the screen, QuickBooks automatically writes the check and puts it in your register. QuickBooks automatically gives the check the appropriate date and schedules it to pop up in your Reminders window at the right time.

When do you make payroll tax deposits? That's a question that frequently comes up. The general rule about United States federal tax deposits is this: If your accumulated payroll taxes are less than $500 for the quarter, you can just pay the taxes the following month with your quarterly return. This is called the De Minimis rule. (My understanding is that the law was named after Congresswoman Dee Minimis.) If you owe $500 or more, other special rules come into play that determine whether you pay deposits monthly, semimonthly, weekly, or even immediately. The IRS tells you, by the way, how often you're supposed to make payments.

If you owe a large amount of money, you're required to deposit it almost immediately. For example, if you owe $100,000 or more, you need to make the payroll tax deposit by the next banking day. Some nuances apply to these rules, so unless you don't owe very much and, therefore, can fall back on the De Minimis rule, you may want to consult a real, live tax adviser (or call the Internal Revenue Service).

Paying tax deposits in QuickBooks is easy, so a good rule of thumb when you write payroll checks is to make the last checks you write the ones that pay your federal and state tax deposits when they come due. You'll never get into late payment trouble if you follow this approach. It will also make your life a lot easier when it comes time to fill out Schedule B of Form 941, if this is something you have to do.

To make a payroll tax deposit, just deliver your check with a federal tax deposit coupon to a financial institution that's qualified as a depository for federal taxes, or to the Federal Reserve bank that serves your geographical area. The IRS should have already sent you a book of coupons as a result of your asking for an employer ID number. And one other thing: Make your check payable to the depository or to the Federal Reserve.

Preparing Quarterly Payroll Tax Returns

At the end of every quarter, you need to file a quarterly payroll tax return. (By quarters here, I'm referring to calendar quarters. You don't have to file these returns four times on a Sunday afternoon as you or your couch potato spouse watch football.)

If you're a business owner, for example, you must file a Form 941, which is just a form that you fill out to say how much you paid in gross wages, how much you withheld in federal taxes, and how much you owe for employer payroll taxes.

If you have to fill out Schedule B of Form 941, I hope that you heeded my earlier advice and just paid the liabilities as they came due. This makes filling out Schedule B a piece of cake: The date your liability check was due is the same as the date you wrote and deposited the check. You can use QuickBooks to create a list of all the dates on which you wrote liabilities checks in the quarter by finding just one liabilities check in your register and then clicking the Q-Report button. Then set the date for the correct quarter. QuickBooks produces a list of your liabilities checks in the blink of an eye. If, on the other hand, you didn't always pay your liabilities as they came due, you need to open your Payroll Liabilities account and scroll through the whole quarter finding the day your balance went over $500.

If you have household employees, such as a nanny, you must file a Form 942. Again, Form 942 is just a form you fill out to say how much you paid in gross wages, withheld in federal taxes, and owe in payroll taxes.

You'll find that QuickBooks makes filling out these forms darn simple. As a matter of fact, QuickBooks prepares the 941 for you. If you need to fill out the 942 or a state payroll tax form, QuickBooks can also be of great help. All you really need to know for these other forms is what the gross wages totals are.

To get the gross wages totals and the balances in each of the payroll tax liability accounts at the end of the quarter, print the payroll summary report. Choose Reports⇨Payroll Reports⇨Summary. QuickBooks displays the Payroll Summary report (see Figure 12-8). Specify the range of dates as the quarter for which you're preparing a quarterly report. Scroll across to the Total column, which shows the gross wages upon which your employer payroll taxes are calculated.

The withholding account amounts are the amounts you've recorded to date for the employee's federal income taxes withheld and the employee's social security and Medicare taxes, so you need to double these figures to get the actual social security and Medicare taxes owed. Choose Reports⇨Payroll Reports⇨ Liabilities. QuickBooks creates a report similar to Figure 12-9.

		Pine Lake Porcelain - QuickBooks Pro			
File	Edit	Lists	Activities	Reports	Online	Window	Help

Figure 12-8:
The Payroll
Summary
report.

Pine Lake Porcelain
Payroll Summary
January through March 1999

	Kay A King			TOTAL		
	Hours	Rate	Jan - Mar '99	Hours	Rate	Jan - Mar '99
Employee Wages, Taxes and Adjustments						
Gross Pay						
Salary	40		1,730.77	40		1,730.77
Hourly wages			0.00	72		792.00
Total Gross Pay			1,730.77			2,522.77
Adjusted Gross Pay			1,730.77			2,522.77
Taxes Withheld						
Federal Withholding			-242.31			-328.64
Medicare Employee			-25.10			-36.19
Social Security Employee			-107.31			-156.41
Total Taxes Withheld			-374.72			-521.24
Net Pay			**1,356.05**			**2,001.53**
Employer Taxes and Contributions						
Federal Unemployment			1.06			1.85
Medicare Company			25.10			36.19
Social Security Company			107.31			156.41
Total Employer Taxes and Contributions			**133.47**			**194.45**

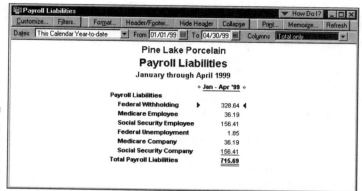

Figure 12-9:
The Payroll
Liabilities
report.

QuickBooks will create and print out a copy of Form 941 for you, so that you don't have to get out your calculator or mess around with lining up the red form in your typewriter. Just click the Payroll and Time tab of the QuickBooks Navigator and click the Process 941 icon. QuickBooks runs you through a wizard that asks you for the name of the state from which you're filing and the number of employees you had over the quarter. QuickBooks then summarizes each line of the form. When QuickBooks is all done, all you have to do is print out the form, and you're done.

By the way, if your accountant is the person who will fill out the 941 or 942 form, you don't even need to read this stuff. Your accountant won't have any problem completing the quarterly payroll tax return using the QuickBooks Payroll report, and in fact — I kid you not — your accountant will probably even enjoy it.

Filing Annual Returns and Wage Statements

At the end of the year, you need to file some annual returns — such as the 940 federal unemployment tax return — and the W-2 and W-3 wages statements.

As a practical matter, the only thing that's different about filling out these reports is that you need to use a Payroll report that covers the entire year, not just a single quarter. So you need to enter the range of dates in the report window as the year for which you're filing the return. Use the Employee Earnings Summary report as the basis for preparing your employees' W-2 statements. To produce this report, choose Reports⇨Payroll Reports⇨ Employee Earnings.

The 940 annual return is darn easy if you've been wrestling with the 941 quarterly returns. The 940 annual return works the same basic way as those more difficult quarterly tax returns. You print the Payroll report, enter a few numbers, and then write a check for the amount you owe.

Note that you need to prepare any state unemployment annual summary before you prepare the 940 because the 940 requires information from the state returns.

QuickBooks also creates and prints the 940 for you. All you have to do is click the Payroll and Time tab of the QuickBooks Navigator and click the Process 940 icon. QuickBooks asks you for a little information, and then it does the calculating for you. All you have to do is check QuickBooks' records against your own, and if everything matches, print that puppy out.

For the W-2 statements and the summary W-3 (which summarizes your W-2s), you just click the Payroll and Time tab of the QuickBooks Navigator and click the Process W-2 icon. Select the employees from the list and print away.

If you have a little trouble, call the IRS. If you have a great deal of trouble, splurge and have someone else fill out the forms for you. Filling out these forms doesn't take a rocket scientist, by the way. Any experienced book-keeper can do it for you.

Please don't construe my "rocket scientist" comment as personal criticism if this payroll taxes business seems terribly complicated. My experience is that some people — and you may very well be one of them — just don't have an interest in things such as payroll accounting. If, on the other hand, you're a "numbers are my friend" kind of person, you'll have no trouble at all after you learn the ropes.

The State Wants Some Money, Too

Yeah. I haven't talked about state payroll taxes — at least not in any great detail. I wish that I could provide this sort of detailed, state-specific help to you. Unfortunately, doing so would make this chapter about 150 pages long. It would also cause me to go stark, raving mad.

My sanity and laziness aside, however, you still need to deal with state payroll taxes. Let me say, however, that you apply to state payroll taxes the same basic mechanics that you apply to federal payroll taxes. For example, a state income tax works the same way as the federal income tax; employer-paid state unemployment taxes work like the employer-paid federal taxes; and employee-paid state taxes work like the employee-paid social security and Medicare taxes.

If you've tuned in to how federal payroll taxes work in QuickBooks, you really shouldn't have a problem with the state payroll taxes — at least, not in terms of mechanics.

Chapter 13

The Balancing Act

In This Chapter

▶ Selecting the account that you want to balance

▶ Telling QuickBooks to balance an account

▶ Giving QuickBooks the bank statement balance

▶ Entering monthly service charges and interest income

▶ Marking account transactions as cleared or uncleared

▶ Ten things to do if your account doesn't balance

I want to start this chapter with an important point: Balancing a bank account in QuickBooks is easy and quick.

I'm not just trying to get you pumped up about an otherwise painfully boring topic. I don't think that balancing a bank account is any more exciting than you do. (At the Nelson house, we never answer the question "What should we do tonight?" by saying, "Hey, let's balance an account.")

My point is this: Because bank account balancing can be tedious and boring, use QuickBooks to speed up the drudgery.

Selecting the Account You Want to Balance

This step is easy. And you probably already know how to do it, too.

To reconcile an account, click the Checking and Credit Cards tab of the QuickBooks Navigator and click the Reconcile icon. You see the Reconcile window, shown in Figure 13-1. Select the account that you want to balance from the Account To Reconcile drop-down list box. QuickBooks shows all outstanding checks or payments and all deposits to date.

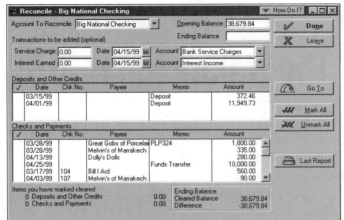

Figure 13-1:
The
Reconcile
window.

As Figure 13-1 shows, the Reconcile window is basically just two lists — one of account withdrawals and one of account deposits. While reconciling your account, the dialog box also displays some extra information at the bottom of the screen. It shows you how many deposits and withdrawals you've marked as cleared, along with a total amount for each. It also shows the Cleared Balance (the dollar amount of the cleared checks and deposits you click off in the dialog box) and the Difference (the difference, if any, between what your bank says your balance is and what you say your balance is when you click off deposits and withdrawals). (You fill in the Ending Balance box with the balance shown on your bank statement after you get started.)

Balancing a Bank Account

As I said, balancing a bank account is remarkably easy in QuickBooks. In fact, I'll go so far as to say that if you have any problems, they stem from . . . well, sloppy record keeping that preceded your use of QuickBooks.

Enough of this blather; I'll get started.

Giving QuickBooks the information from the bank statement

As you probably know, in a reconciliation, you compare your records of a bank account with the bank's records of the same account. You should be able to explain any difference between the two accounts — usually by pointing to checks that you've written but that haven't cleared. (Sometimes deposits fall into the same category; you've recorded a deposit and mailed it, but the bank hasn't yet credited your account.)

The first step, then, is to supply QuickBooks with the bank's account information. You get this information from your monthly statement. Supply QuickBooks with the figures it needs as follows:

1. **Verify the bank statement Opening Balance.**

   QuickBooks displays an amount in the Opening Balance text box (see Figure 13-1). If this amount isn't correct, replace it with the correct one. (You don't need to enter a dollar sign or any commas, just the dollars and cents with a decimal point in between.) You can replace this amount because the number you enter in this text box doesn't figure into any of the QuickBooks calculations. To change the Opening Balance amount, move the cursor to the text box and type over the given amount. (If this is the first time you've reconciled this account, QuickBooks gets this opening balance amount from your starting account balance. If you've reconciled this account before, QuickBooks uses the Ending Balance that you specified the last time you reconciled as the Opening Balance.)

   For more information, see the sidebar, "Why isn't my opening balance the same as the one in QuickBooks?" in this chapter.

2. **Enter the ending balance.**

   What is the ending, or closing, balance on your bank statement? Whatever it is, move the cursor to the Ending Balance text box and enter the ending balance.

3. **Enter the bank's service charge.**

   If the bank statement shows a service charge and you haven't already entered it, move the cursor to the Service Charge text box and enter the amount.

4. **Enter a transaction date for the service charge transaction.**

   QuickBooks supplies the current system date from your computer's internal clock as the default service charge date. If this date isn't correct, enter the correct one.

   Remember that you can adjust a date one day at a time by using the plus (+) and minus (–) keys. You can also click the calendar button on the right side of the text box to select a date from the calendar. See the cheat sheet at the front of this book for a list of other secret date-editing tricks.

5. **Assign the bank's service charge to an account.**

   Enter the expense account to which you assign bank service charges in the first Account text box — the one beside the Date text box. Activate the drop-down list by clicking the down arrow, highlight the category by using the arrow keys, and press Enter. I bet anything that you record these charges in the Bank Service Charges account that QuickBooks sets up by default.

6. Enter the account's interest income.

If the account earned interest for the month and you haven't already entered this figure, enter an amount in the Interest Earned text box (for example, type **9.17** for $9.17).

7. Enter a transaction date for the interest income transaction.

You already know how to enter dates. I won't bore you by explaining it again (but see Step 4 if you're having trouble).

8. Assign the interest to an account.

Enter the account to which this account's interest should be assigned in the second Account text box. I bet that you record this one under the Interest Income account, which is near the bottom of the Account drop-down list. To select a category from the Account list, activate the drop-down list by clicking the down arrow, highlight the category, and press Enter.

Why isn't my opening balance the same as the one in QuickBooks?

If your opening balance isn't the same as the one shown in the Opening Balance text box, it can mean a couple of things.

First, you may have mistakenly cleared a transaction the last time you reconciled. If you cleared a transaction last month that didn't go through until this month, your opening balance is wrong. Go back to the Checking register and start examining transactions. Each one that's cleared has a check mark next to it in the narrow column between the Payment and Deposit columns. If one of the checks that appears on this month's statement has a check mark, you made a boo-boo last month. From the Checking register, click the check mark to remove it. You're asked to confirm

your actions. The check now appears in the Reconcile window.

The other reason why the opening balance is different can be that a transaction that you cleared in the past got changed. If you deleted a transaction that occurred before this reconciliation period, for example, it threw your balance off. Why? Because the transaction that you deleted helped balance your account the last time around, but now that transaction is gone.

Whatever happens, don't fret. If worse comes to worst and you can't track down the faulty transaction, you can just have QuickBooks adjust the balance for you, as I explain later in this chapter.

Marking cleared checks and deposits

Now you need to tell QuickBooks which deposits and checks have cleared at the bank. (Refer to the bank statement for this information.)

1. **Identify the first deposit that has cleared.**

   You know how to do so, I'm sure. Just leaf through the bank statement and find the first deposit listed.

2. **Mark the first cleared deposit as cleared.**

   Scroll through the transactions listed in the Deposits and Other Credits section of the Reconcile window, find the deposit, and then click it. You also can highlight the deposit by using the Tab and arrow keys and then pressing Enter. QuickBooks places a check mark in front of the deposit to mark it as cleared and updates the cleared statement balance.

   If you have a large number of deposits to make and you can identify them quickly, click the Mark All button and then simply unmark the transactions that aren't on the bank statement. To unmark a transaction, click it. The check mark disappears.

3. **Record any cleared, but missing, deposits.**

   If you can't find a deposit, you haven't entered it into the Checking register yet. I can only guess why you haven't entered it. Maybe you just forgot. Click the Minimize button in the Reconcile window. (This is the little button third from the right in the upper-right corner of the Reconcile window.) The Reconcile window shrinks and drops down to the lower-left corner of your screen. Now open the Checking register and enter the deposit in the register in the usual way. To return to the Reconcile window, just click the button third from the right once more. (This button is now called the Restore button.)

4. **Repeat Steps 1, 2, and 3 for all deposits listed on the bank statement.**

   Make sure that the dates match and that the amounts of the deposits are also correct. If they're not, go back to the register and correct them. To get to the register, click the Go To button. You see the Write Checks or Make Deposits window where the transaction was originally recorded. Make the corrections there and click OK.

5. **Identify the first check that has cleared.**

   No sweat, right? Just find the first check or withdrawal listed on the bank statement.

6. **Mark the first cleared check as cleared.**

   Scroll through the transactions listed in the Checks and Payments section of the Reconcile window, find the first check, and then click it.

You also can highlight it by pressing Tab and an arrow key. Then press Enter. QuickBooks inserts a check mark to label this transaction as cleared and updates the cleared statement balance.

7. Record any missing, but cleared, checks.

If you can't find a check or withdrawal — guess what? — you haven't entered it in the register yet. Shrink the Reconcile window by clicking its Minimize button. Then display the Checking register and enter the check or withdrawal. To return to the Reconcile window, click the Restore button.

8. Repeat Steps 5, 6, and 7 for all withdrawals listed on the bank statement.

By the way, these steps don't take very long. Reconciling my account each month takes me about two minutes. And I'm not joking or exaggerating. By two minutes, I really mean two minutes.

If the difference equals zero

After you mark all the cleared checks and deposits, the difference between the Cleared Balance for the account and the bank statement's Ending Balance should equal zero. Notice that I said "should," not "will." Figure 13-2 shows a Reconcile window in which everything is hunky-dory, and life is grand.

Figure 13-2:
The Reconcile window filled in with the Ending Balance and Cleared Balance in agreement.

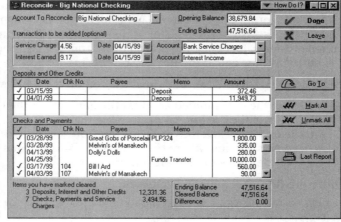

If the difference does equal zero, you're finished. Just click the Done button. QuickBooks displays a congratulatory message box telling you that the reconciliation is complete. As a reward for being such a good boy or girl, the message box asks you whether you want to print a free, all-expenses-paid Summary or Full reconciliation report. Click Summary or Full and click OK if you want to print the report. Otherwise, just click OK.

Can't decide whether to print the reconciliation report? Unless you're a business bookkeeper or an accountant who is reconciling a bank account for someone else — your employer or a client, for example — you don't need to print the reconciliation report. All printing does is prove that you reconciled the account. (Basically, this proof is the reason why you should print the report if you're a bookkeeper or an accountant. The person for whom you're reconciling the account will know that you did your job and has a piece of paper to come back to later with any questions.)

Now each deposit, withdrawal, and check that you just cleared is marked with a check mark in your register. If you don't believe me, open the register and find out.

If the difference doesn't equal zero

If the difference doesn't equal zero, you've got a problem. If you click Done, QuickBooks shows you the Reconcile Adjustment dialog box (see Figure 13-3). This dialog box tells you how unbalanced your account is and asks whether you want to adjust your maladjusted account.

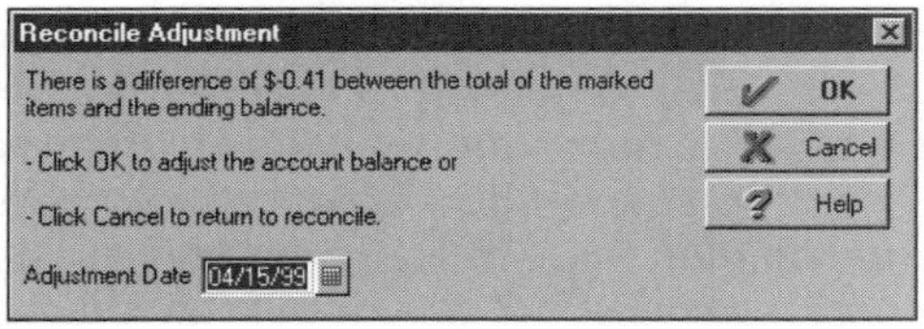

Figure 13-3: The Reconcile Adjustment dialog box.

Click Cancel if you want to go back to the Reconcile window and start the search for the missing or incorrectly entered transaction.

If you want to force the two amounts to agree, click OK. Forcing the two amounts to agree isn't a very good idea. To do so, QuickBooks adds a cleared transaction equal to the difference. (I talk about this transaction a little later in the chapter.)

Postponing a reconciliation and not choosing to adjust the bank account balance is usually the best approach because it enables you to locate and correct problems. (The next section contains some ideas that can help you determine what the problem is.) Then you can restart the reconciliation and finish your work. (You restart a reconciliation the same way that you originate one.)

Ten Things to Do If Your Account Doesn't Balance

I want to give you some suggestions for reconciling an account when you're having problems. If you're sitting in front of your computer wringing your hands, try the tips in this section.

✔ **Make sure that you're working with the right account.** Sounds dumb, doesn't it? If you have several different bank accounts, however, ending up in the wrong account is darn easy. So go ahead and confirm, for example, that you're trying to reconcile your checking account at Mammoth International Bank by using the Mammoth International Bank checking account statement.

✔ **Look for transactions that the bank has recorded but you haven't.** Go through the bank statement and make sure that you've recorded every transaction that your bank has recorded. You can easily overlook cash machine withdrawals, special fees, or service charges (such as charges for checks or your safe-deposit box), automatic withdrawals, direct deposits, and so on. If the difference is positive — that is, the bank thinks that you have less money than you think that you should have — you may be missing a withdrawal transaction. If the difference is negative, you may be missing a deposit transaction.

✔ **Look for reversed transactions.** Here's a tricky one: If you accidentally enter a transaction backward — a deposit as a withdrawal or a withdrawal as a deposit — your account doesn't balance. And the error can be difficult to find. The Reconcile window shows all the correct transactions, but a transaction amount appears in the wrong list. (It appears in the Deposits and Other Credits list if it belongs in the Checks and Payments list or vice versa.) The check that you wrote to Acme Housewreckers for the demolition of your carport appears in the Deposits and Other Credits list, for example.

✔ **Look for a transaction that's equal to half the difference.** One handy way to find the transaction that you entered backward — if there's only one — is to look for a transaction that's equal to half the irreconcilable difference. If the difference is $200, for example, you may have entered a $100 deposit as a withdrawal or a $100 withdrawal as a deposit.

✔ **Look for a transaction that's equal to the difference.** While I'm on the subject of explaining the difference by looking at individual transactions, I'll make an obvious point: If the difference between the bank's records and yours equals one of the transactions listed in your register, you may have incorrectly marked the transaction as cleared or incorrectly left the transaction unmarked (shown as uncleared). I don't know. Maybe that was too obvious. Naaaah.

✔ Check for transposed numbers. Transposed numbers occur when you flip-flop two digits in a number. For example, you enter $45.89 as $48.59. These turkeys always cause headaches for accountants and bookkeepers. If you look at the numbers, detecting an error is often difficult because the digits are the same. For example, when you compare a check amount of $45.89 in your register with a check for $48.59 shown on your bank statement, both check amounts show the same digits: 4, 5, 8, and 9. They just show them in different orders. Transposed numbers are tough to find, but here's a trick that you can try. Divide the difference shown in the Reconcile window by 9. If the result is an even number of dollars or cents, chances are good that you have a transposed number somewhere.

✔ Have someone else look over your work. This idea may seem pretty obvious, but it amazes me how often a second pair of eyes can find something that you've been overlooking. Ask one of your coworkers (preferably that one person who always seems to have way too much free time) to look over everything for you.

✔ Be on the lookout for multiple errors. By the way, if you find an error by using this laundry list and there's still a difference, start checking at the top of the list again. You may, for example, discover after you find a transposed number that you entered another transaction backward or incorrectly cleared or uncleared a transaction.

✔ Try again next month (and maybe the month after that). If the difference isn't huge in relation to the size of your bank account, you may want to wait until next month and attempt to reconcile your account again. Before my carefree attitude puts you in a panic, consider the following example: In January, you reconcile your account, and the difference is $24.02. Then you reconcile the account in February, and the difference is $24.02. You reconcile the account in March and, surprise, surprise, the difference is still $24.02. What's going on here? Well, your starting account balance was probably off by $24.02. (The more months you try to reconcile your account and find that you're always mysteriously $24.02 off, the more likely it is that this type of error is to blame.) After the second or third month, I think that it's pretty reasonable to have QuickBooks enter an adjusting transaction of $24.02 so that your account balances. (In my opinion, this is the only circumstance that merits your adjusting an account to match the bank's figure.) By the way, if you've successfully reconciled your account with QuickBooks before, your work may not be at fault. The mistake may be (drumroll, please) the bank's! And in this case, you should do something else. . . .

✔ Get in your car, drive to the bank, and beg for help. As an alternative to the preceding idea — which supposes that the bank's statement is correct and that your records are incorrect — I propose this idea: Ask the bank to help you reconcile the account. Hint that you think that the mistake is probably the bank's, but in a very nice, cordial way. Smile a lot. And one other thing — be sure to ask about whatever product the bank is currently advertising in the lobby. (This will encourage the staff to think that you're interested in that 180-month certificate of deposit, and they'll be extra nice to you.) In general, the bank's record keeping is usually pretty darn good. I've never had a problem as a business banking client or as an individual. (I've also been lucky enough to deal with big, well run banks.) Nevertheless, it's quite possible that your bank has made a mistake, so ask for help. Be sure to ask for an explanation of any transactions that you've learned about only by seeing them on your bank statement. By the way, you'll probably pay for this help.

Chapter 14

Reporting on the State of Affairs

. . . .

. . . .

*O*ne of the fastest ways to find out whether your business is thriving or diving is to use the QuickBooks Reports feature. The different kinds of reports in QuickBooks cover everything from invoices to missing checks, not to mention QuickReports. QuickReports are summary reports that you can get from the information on forms, account registers, or lists by merely clicking the mouse.

This chapter tells you how to prepare reports, how to print them, and how to customize reports for your special needs.

What Kinds of Reports Are There, Anyway?

If you run a small business, you don't need all the reports that QuickBooks offers, but many of these reports are extremely useful. Reports can show you how healthy or unhealthy your business is, where your profits are, and where you're wasting time and squandering resources.

To make sense of what may otherwise become mass confusion, QuickBooks organizes all of its reports in categories, with two additional reports at the end of the menu. You can see what the ten categories are by pulling down the Reports menu (see Figure 14-1). The names of the reports read a bit like public television documentary names, don't they? "Tonight, Joob Taylor explores the mazelike federal budget in 'Budget Reports.' " (The last two menu items, QuickReport and Memorized Reports, are explained later in this chapter.) You select a report category to see a list of actual report names.

Figure 14-1:
The Reports
menu.

You also can select a report category on the QuickBooks Navigator. See the list of report categories at the bottom of the Navigator? Click a category to see a list of actual report names. Figure 14-2 shows the Company tab of the QuickBooks Navigator with the Profit & Loss report category selected.

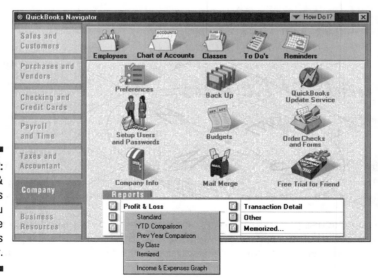

Figure 14-2:
The Profit &
Loss reports
submenu
on the
QuickBooks
Navigator.

Table 14-1 describes reports by category, along with a short description of the major reports in each category. To get a thorough description of a particular report, go to the Help feature. To find out what a standard Profit & Loss report does, for example, choose Help⇨Help Index. Type the letters **prof** in the text box and then double-click the profit and loss reports entry. This displays a list of topics relating to profit and loss reports. To read the details about a topic, double-click it in the list.

Table 14-1	QuickBooks Report Categories
Report Category	*Description*
Profit & Loss	These reports give you a bird's-eye view of the health of your company. They show income, expenses, and net profit or loss over time. You can group the expense and income data by job, class, item, or customer.
Balance Sheet	These reports give you a snapshot of your assets, liabilities, and equity. You can compare your present financial condition with your past financial condition and group information by account type.
A/R Reports	These Accounts Receivable reports are great for finding out where you stand in regard to your customer invoices. You can list unpaid invoices and group them in various ways, including by customer, job, and aging status.
Sales Reports	These reports show what you've sold and who your customers are. You can see your sales by item, by customer, or by sales representative.
Purchase Reports	These reports show from whom you bought, what you bought, and how much you paid. You can list purchases by item or by vendor. One handy report shows any outstanding purchase orders.
Inventory Reports	These reports help answer the all-important question, "What do I have in stock?" You can get an enormous amount of detail from these reports. For example, you can find out how much of an item you have on hand and how much you have on order. You can group inventory by vendor or by item. If you need price lists, you can print them using a special report from your QuickBooks file.
A/P Reports	These Accounts Payable reports tell you everything you need to know about your unpaid bills. You can list bills in a variety of ways, including by vendor and by aging status. This category also includes a report for determining sales tax liability.

(continued)

Table 14-1 _(continued)_	
Budget Reports	These reports show you once and for all whether your budgeting skills are realistic. You can view budgets by job, by month, or by balance sheet account. Then you can compare the budgets to actual income and expense totals. (You need to have a budget already set up to use this report — something I discuss in Chapter 15.)
Transaction Reports	These reports list individual transactions by date, vendor, or customer.
Transaction Detail Reports	These reports not only list the individual transactions but also add a column to give you the current balance of each entry. They can be listed by account, date, vendor, or customer.
Payroll Reports	These six reports (including three reports new to QuickBooks 6) offer ways to track payroll or check your payroll liability accounts. Believe me, these reports come in handy.
List Reports	These reports let you see your lists in detail. For example, you can see the contacts, phone numbers, and addresses on your Customer, Vendor, or Other Names lists. You also can create a detailed report of your inventory.
Project Reports	These eleven reports let you see job and item profitability, compare job estimates versus actual costs, and view time recorded on jobs and activities.
Other Reports	This catch-all category includes reports for estimating cash flow, listing missing checks, summarizing debits and credits, and showing transactions that were voided or modified. (If you're an accountant, you'll find all your favorites here.)

Creating and Printing a Report

After you decide what report you need, all you have to do is select it from the appropriate menu. To create a Standard report, for example, choose Reports➪Profit & Loss➪Standard.

Depending on how much data QuickBooks has to process, you may see a Building Report box before the report appears on the screen in all its glory. Figure 14-3 shows a Standard Profit & Loss report, also called an income statement. (If you see a Customize Report dialog box instead of a report, you can tell QuickBooks to change this option. To do this, click the

Company tab of the QuickBooks Navigator and click the Preferences icon. Then click Reports & Graphs from the list on the left. And click the My Preferences tab if you have one and it isn't already selected. Then remove the check in the Display Customize Report Window Automatically box.)

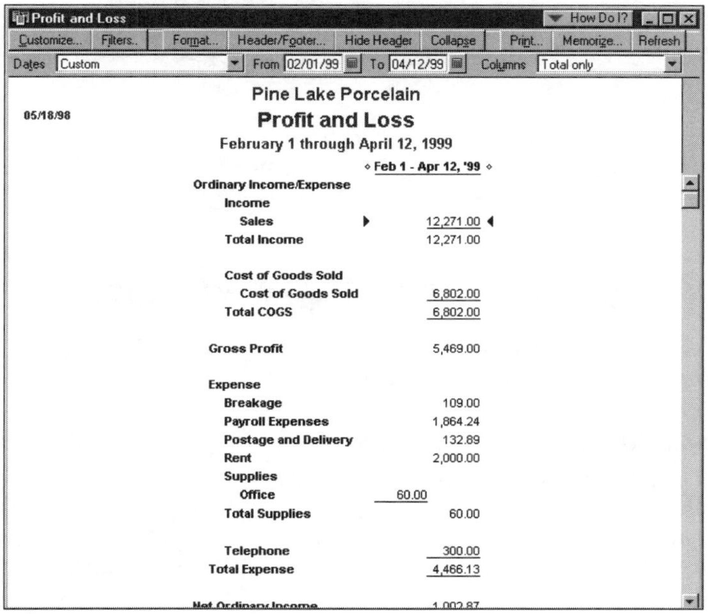

Figure 14-3:
A standard
Profit &
Loss report.

You can't see the entire on-screen version of a report unless your report is very small (or your screen is monstrously large). Use the Page Up and Page Down keys on your keyboard to scroll up and down, and the Tab and Shift+Tab keys to move left and right. Or, if you're a mouse lover, you can click and drag various pieces of the scrollbars.

To print a report, click the Print button at the top of the report. QuickBooks displays the Print Reports dialog box, shown in Figure 14-4. To accept the given specifications, which are almost always fine, just click the Print button. You'll never guess what happens next: QuickBooks prints the report!

Before I forget, you can use the Print To option buttons to tell QuickBooks where it should send the report it produces: to the printer or to an ASCII, Excel/Lotus 1-2-3 spreadsheet, or tab delimited disk file. The Orientation setting tells QuickBooks how the report is supposed to appear on the paper. The Page Range settings specify the pages you want to print. And the two check boxes are probably pretty self-evident.

You also can preview the report by clicking the Preview button. The next section of the chapter describes how some of the options for the preview work.

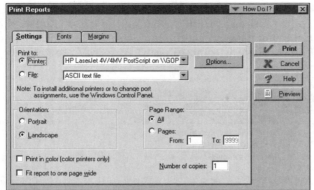

Figure 14-4:
The Print
Reports
dialog box.

Visiting the report dog-and-pony show

You can do some neat things with the reports you create. Here's a quick run-down of some of the most valuable tricks.

QuickZooming mysterious figures

If you don't understand where a number in a report comes from, point to it with the mouse. As you point to numbers, QuickBooks changes the mouse pointer to a magnifying glass marked with a Z. Double-click the mouse to have QuickBooks display a list of all the transactions that make up that number.

This feature, called QuickZoom, is extremely handy for understanding the figures that appear on reports. All you have to do is double-click any mysterious-looking figure in a report. QuickBooks immediately tells you exactly how it arrived at that figure.

Sharing report data with spreadsheets

If you use a Windows spreadsheet program, such as Microsoft Excel, Lotus 1-2-3, or Quattro Pro, you can print the report to a disk file by marking the File option button in the Print Reports dialog box, choosing the appropriate file type from the list, and then clicking Print (take a look at Figure 14-4). This dialog box is the one that QuickBooks displays when you click the Print button at the top of the report document window. When you select Tab Delimited File, QuickBooks displays the Create Disk File dialog box, shown in Figure 14-5.

If you want to export the report to a program not listed in the drop-down list box (such as a word processor), select the Tab Delimited File entry. A tab-delimited file is a common type of file used for reports and can be imported by most programs.

Use the Directories and Drives list boxes to specify where you want the file located. For example, to stick the file on another disk — such as a floppy disk — activate the Drives drop-down list box and click the disk you want.

You don't have to fiddle with the List Files of Type drop-down list box, by the way. QuickBooks automatically uses the file extension .TXT for tab-delimited disk files that you create.

To work with the new file from inside a spreadsheet program, start the spreadsheet program first. Then open or input the file. (In Excel, open the new disk file by using the File⇨Open command, and make sure that the Files of Type box is set to either Text File or All Files.)

Sharing report data with word-processing programs

You can share report data with a word-processing program, too. No sweat. Just follow these steps:

1. **Click the Print button at the top of the report document window.**

   The Print Reports dialog box, shown in Figure 14-4, appears from within the recesses of QuickBooks.

2. **Click the File button and choose ASCII Text File from the drop-down list.**

3. **Click Print.**

   QuickBooks needs a name for the ASCII file.

4. **Name that file.**

   Use the Create Disk File dialog box, shown in Figure 14-5, to name the file. You can name the file whatever you want, but don't name it after me. I don't want any more little Steve Nelsons running around this planet.

5. **To work with the new file from inside a word-processing program, start the word-processing program.**

6. **Choose File⇨Open.**

7. **Change the filename extension to .TXT, if necessary.**

   Watch the filename extensions. For example, Microsoft Word's default looks only for files ending with .DOC so unless the File Type is set properly, you won't find the report on the list of files.

8. **Find your QuickBooks file, click OK, and thar she be — your QuickBooks report ready for you to use.**

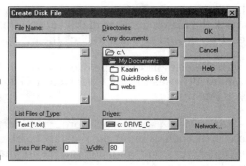

Figure 14-5:
The Create
Disk File
dialog box.

Editing and rearranging reports

You might have noticed that when QuickBooks displays the report document window, it also displays a row of buttons: Customize, Filters, Format, Header/Footer, Hide Header, Collapse, Print, Memorize, and Refresh (as you can see in Figure 14-6). Below this toolbar are some drop-down list boxes that have to do with dates and a drop-down list called Columns. (Not all these list boxes are available in every report document window. I don't know why, really. Maybe just to keep you guessing.)

Figure 14-6:
The Report
options
toolbar
buttons.

You don't need to worry about these buttons. Read through the discussion that follows only if you're feeling comfortable, relaxed, and truly mellow, okay?

Customizing

The Customize button works pretty much the same way no matter which report shows in the report document window.

When you click this button, QuickBooks displays the Customize Report dialog box (see Figure 14-7). From this dialog box, you change the time period that the report covers (in Report Dates), add extra columns in the report (in Columns), and choose between basing the report on expected payments (the Accrual option) or payments already made (the Cash option). I suggest marking the Accrual option so that you can use accrual-basis accounting. If you're curious as to why, take a look at Appendix B.

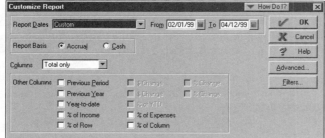

Figure 14-7:
The
Customize
Report
dialog box.

Filtering

You click the Filters button to filter a report. (I don't know how they came up with the term *filter*. Maybe the programmers had one of those aquarium screen savers.) Filtering is a little like sorting a database in that you use the Report Filters dialog box (see Figure 14-8) to tell QuickBooks what data to include and exclude in the report. You have a large number of choices here, and more power to you.

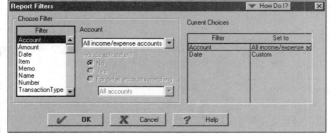

Figure 14-8:
The Report
Filters
dialog box.

Select a filter from the list along the left edge of the dialog box and then define the parameters for the filter in the boxes and buttons that QuickBooks provides. Maybe an example will help. If you want to filter by customer type, you select Customer Type from the Filter list and then select the customer type you want to see.

Memorizing

If you do play around with the remaining buttons, you can save any custom report specifications that you create. Just click the Memorize button. QuickBooks displays a dialog box that asks you to supply a name for the customized report (see Figure 14-9). After you name the customized report, QuickBooks lists it whenever you choose Reports⇨Memorized Reports. To use your report, select your customized report in the list and click the Report button.

QuickBooks 6 now memorizes the print orientation with the report, so if the print orientation is not the way you want it for the report, you should first change it by choosing File⇨Printer Setup. Select the orientation you want to memorize, click OK, and then memorize the report.

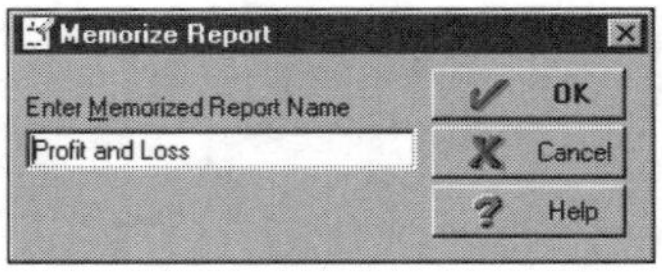

Figure 14-9:
The
Memorize
Report
dialog box.

Memorize Report	☒
Enter Memorized Report Name	✔ OK
Profit and Loss	✘ Cancel
	? Help

The other buttons and boxes

The Format button, between the Filters and Header/Footer buttons, gives you several options for displaying numbers and changing the fonts of the report text. If you want to see how the Header/Footer, Hide Header, Collapse, and Dates stuff works, just noodle around. You can't hurt anything.

If you change the report dates, click the Refresh button to update the report. (To set refresh options for reports, click the Company tab of the QuickBooks Navigator and click the Preferences icon. Then click the Reports & Graphs icon from the list on the left and click the My Preferences tab if necessary. Click one of the Reports and Graphs options and click OK.)

Reports Made to Order

If you intend to print a large number of reports, and more important, if you intend to print a large number of reports and show them to customers, investors, and other important people, you want your reports to look good and be easy to understand. I believe that beauty is in the eye of the be-holder, so I'm not going to get into the aesthetics of report layouts. What I am going to do is explain how you can make QuickBooks reports look exactly the way you want them to look.

Click the Company tab of the QuickBooks Navigator and click the Prefer-ences icon. Then click Reports & Graphs from the list on the left and the Company Preferences tab to see the Preferences dialog box for reports and graphs (see Figure 14-10).

Accrual is one of those cruel accounting terms that's hard to understand at first. If you choose Accrual in the Summary Reports Basis panel, you tell QuickBooks to date all your transactions, purchases, expenses, and so on from the moment they're recorded, not from the time you receive or pay cash for them. If you choose Cash, all the financial transactions in your reports are dated from the time payments are made.

Accountants follow the accrual method because it gives a more accurate picture of profits.

If you click Age from Due Date in the Aging Reports panel, QuickBooks counts your expenses and invoices from the day that they fall due. Otherwise, QuickBooks counts them from the day they're recorded.

Click the Format button if you want to improve the look of your reports. In the Report Format Preferences dialog box, shown in Figure 14-11, you can choose preferences for displaying numbers, decimal fractions, and negative numbers. You also can fool around with different fonts and point sizes for labels, column headings, titles, and other things in your reports.

You can even click the Header/Footer button and enter your company name or some other text that you want to appear on all your reports.

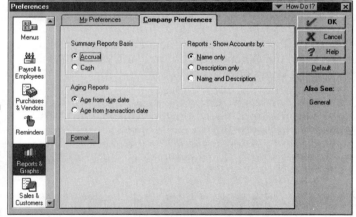

Figure 14-10:
The Preferences dialog box for reports and graphs.

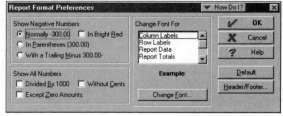

Figure 14-11:
The Report Format Preferences dialog box.

Click the Default buttons in the Report Format Preferences and Reporting Preferences dialog boxes after you're finished. Now the choices you just made affect all your reports. If you decide that you don't like your choices after all, you can redo everything or click Customize in the report document window and customize your reports as you make them.

Last but Not Least: The QuickReport

The last kind of report is the QuickReport, which is one of the best kinds of reports, so I've saved it for last. You can generate a QuickReport from a list, from invoices and bills with names of people or items on them, and from account registers. QuickReports are especially useful when you're studying a list and you see something that momentarily baffles you. Simply make sure that the item you're curious about is highlighted, and click the QuickReport button (sometimes called the Q-Report button). You see a payment history, expense transaction, a list of unpaid bills, or whatever's appropriate to the open window, to satisfy your curiosity.

You can also right-click an item and choose the shortcut menu's QuickReport option to create a QuickReport of the item.

Figure 14-12 shows a QuickReport produced from an Accounts Receivable register. I clicked the Q-Report button to display this Register QuickReport window with the complete invoice information for Coastal Collectibles.

The QuickReport option is also on the Reports menu. You can display a QuickReport from a form, even though no QuickReport button appears, by choosing the menu option. For example, if you're writing a check to Acme Co., you can enter the company name on the check and choose Reports⇨ QuickReport to see a report of transactions involving the Acme Co.

Figure 14-12:
A
QuickReport
made from
an entry in
the Accounts
Receivable
register.

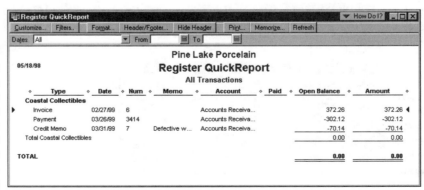

Chapter 15

QuickBooks Dirty Work

● ●

In This Chapter

▶ Formatting floppy disks

▶ Backing up QuickBooks data

▶ Deciding when and how often to back up your data

▶ Restoring your QuickBooks data (if you lose it)

▶ Using Accountant's Review

▶ Condensing your QuickBooks data

● ●

*O*kay, you don't need to worry about chasing dust bunnies in QuickBooks, but you do have little housekeeping tasks to take care of. This chapter describes these chores and how to do them correctly with minimal hassle.

Formatting Floppy Disks

You need a safe place to store the company information that you collect with QuickBooks — someplace in addition to your computer's hard disk. No, I'm not talking about under your mattress or that secret place in the attic. I'm talking about floppy disks. So, you, my friend, need to know how to format a floppy disk.

A floppy disk needs to be formatted before you can store information on it. If you buy pre-formatted floppy disks of a density your floppy drive can read (double or high) and for the right operating system (such as for Windows and not the Mac), you're all set. You also want to make sure that you buy the right size, but it's hard to go wrong here. Even though it's still possible to get your hands on the old larger $5^1/_4$-inch disks, you want to buy the small, hard-plastic $3^1/_2$-inch variety.

Density is a little trickier because you can use both low- and high-density disks in a high-density drive, but you can only use low-density disks in a low-density drive. If you don't know the density of your drive, find the paperwork that came with the computer. The paperwork should tell you whether the drive is high-density (designated by the code HD), allowing 1.44MB (megabytes) of storage space per disk; or low-density (designated by the code DS/DD, for Double-Sided/Double-Density), allowing 720K (kilobytes) of storage space per disk. You also can scrounge around to see whether you've been using low-density or high-density floppy disks — disk labels usually tell storage capacities and often feature either the HD or the DS/DD code. Mystery solved.

Anyway, after you figure out the density and size thing (and you only need to know enough to be able to find the right kind of disk for your computer; you won't be tested on megabytes, kilobytes, or even mosquito bites at the end of this book), you can format the disk. Just follow these steps:

1. **Slip the unformatted floppy in the appropriate drive.**

   In other words, if the disk doesn't fit, don't force it — a good, general rule to follow in life.

2. **Double-click the My Computer icon.**

   It's usually the first icon in the upper-left corner of the desktop, providing that no windows are covering it. You also can right-click the Start button and choose Explore from the shortcut menu if you prefer to work with Windows Explorer instead of My Computer.

3. **Right-click the icon for the appropriate floppy drive.**

   Be sure that you right-click the correct icon! When you format a disk, you're also erasing any existing information on it. You can imagine what would happen if you clicked the wrong icon. (I'm getting chills just thinking about such a catastrophe. Guess why I can relate to this so well. A hint: I wasn't always this apprehensive.)

4. **Choose Format.**

   The Format dialog box opens (see Figure 15-1).

5. **For Format type, click Full if the disk hasn't been formatted before or if it's in another format.**

   You also can recycle used PC disks by formatting them to quickly erase their contents. To do this, click the Quick (Erase) option.

   Make sure that the Display Summary When Finished box is checked. This allows you to verify that the formatting went okay and that the disk doesn't have any errors. If the message box that Windows displays after formatting the disk tells you that the disk has errors (bad sectors), throw away the disk and use a different one.

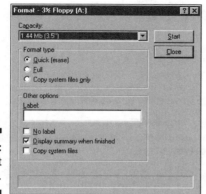

Figure 15-1:
The Format
dialog box.

6. **Click Start.**

   (If you want to know about the other options in the Format dialog box, feel free to look at your Windows documentation.)

7. **Celebrate.**

   You're finished!

Close the window and live it up. Measure your life with coffee spoons. Have your cake and eat it, too. Spit in the eye of death. Dance in the disco of life. Whatever metaphor makes you happy.

More is involved in this formatting business than I've described here. If you want more information and you're adventurous, flip open the user's guide that came with your computer and look up the Format command in the index. Or better yet, buy the appropriate *...For Dummies* book, which will undoubtedly be more fun to read.

If you're not adventurous, you should probably just buy preformatted floppy disks.

Backing Up Is (Not That) Hard to Do

You should back up the files that QuickBooks uses to store your financial records. But you need to know how to back up before you can back up. Got it? So get to it. . . .

Backing up the quick-and-dirty way

You're busy. You don't have time to fool around. You just want to do a passable job of backing up. Sound like your situation? Then follow these steps:

1. **Insert a blank, formatted floppy disk in your floppy drive.**

   If you have two floppy drives, one is drive A, and one is drive B. I'm going out on a limb here and assuming that you're using the ol' drive A. (If not, just substitute the drive letters accordingly.)

2. **If you store data for more than one company, make sure that the company whose data you want to back up is the active company.**

   Yes, I know that all your companies are active — I'm hoping they're not dead in the water. My point is that you want to back up the right company. To find out whether the right company is active, just look at the QuickBooks application window's title bar, which names the active company. (If you don't remember setting up multiple files, don't worry. You probably have only one file — the usual case.)

3. **Click the Company tab of the QuickBooks Navigator and click the Back Up icon to begin the backup operation.**

   QuickBooks displays the Back Up Company To dialog box, shown in Figure 15-2.

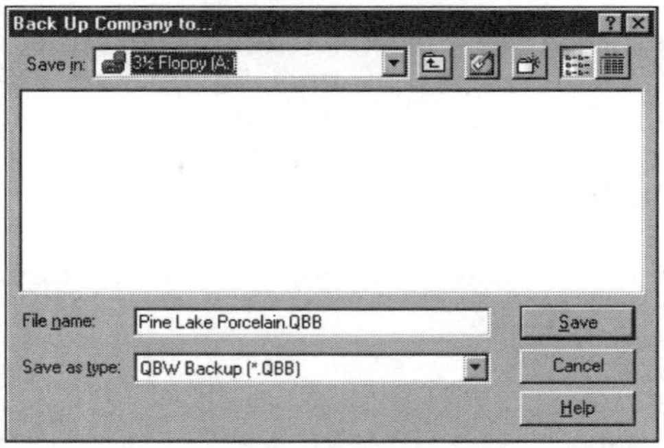

Figure 15-2:
The Back Up Company To dialog box.

4. **Identify the backup floppy drive.**

   Click the Save In drop-down list and select the letter of the floppy drive that you stuffed the disk into.

5. **Click Save.**

   You see a message box on-screen that says, "Aye, Cap'n, I'm working just as fast as I can" (or something to that effect). Then you see a message box saying that the backup procedure is complete.

Don't worry. You never see a message that says, "She's starting to break up, Cap'n. She can't take warp 9 much longer." You may see a warning message if the file you want to back up is too large. In that case, you need to shrink it. (Later in the chapter, I describe how to shrink files in the section "Shrinking files that are too big for their own good.")

6. **Click OK.**

Knowing when to back up

Sure, I can give you some tricky, technical examples of fancy backup strategies, but they have no point here. You want to know the basics, right?

The guiding rule is that you back up anytime you work on something that you wouldn't want to redo. Some people think that a week's worth of work is negligible, and others think that a month's worth of work is negligible.

So here's what I do to back up my files. I back up every month after I reconcile my accounts at work. Then I stick the floppy disk in my briefcase so that if something terrible happens, I don't lose both my computer and the backup disk with the data. (I carry my briefcase around with me — a sort of middle-age security blanket — so that it won't get destroyed in some after-hours disaster.) I also keep all the paperwork in a file folder through the month and do all the reconciling at one time.

I admit that my strategy has its problems, however. Because I'm backing up monthly, for example, I may have to re-enter as much as a month's worth of data if the computer crashes toward the end of the month. In my case, I wouldn't lose all that much work. However, if you're someone with heavy transaction volumes — if you prepare hundreds of invoices or write hundreds of checks each month, for example — you probably want to back up more frequently, perhaps once a week.

A second problem with my strategy is only remotely possible but still worth mentioning. If something bad does happen to the QuickBooks files stored on my computer's hard disk *and* the files stored on the backup floppy disk, I'll be up the proverbial creek without a paddle. (I should also note that a floppy disk is far more likely to fail than a hard drive.) If this worst-case scenario actually occurs, I'll need to start over from scratch from the beginning of the year.

To prevent this scenario from happening, some people who are religiously careful circulate three sets of backup disks to reduce the chance of this mishap. They also regularly move one copy off-site, such as to a safe deposit box. In this scenario, whenever you back up your data, you use the oldest set of backup disks. Say you back up your data every week, and your hard disk not only crashes, but bursts into a ball of flames rising high into the night. To restore your files, you use the most recent set of backups — one week old, max. If something is wrong with those, you use the next recent set — two weeks old. If something is wrong with those, you use the last set — three weeks old. This way, you have three chances to get a set that works — a nice bit of security for the cost of a few extra floppy disks. I should also add that, generally, one company account's backup file doesn't take more than one floppy disk.

You know what else? All backup files are condensed to save on disk space. If you're so inclined (I'm not), open Windows Explorer or My Computer and look in the Qbooksw folder for your company's file. (The backup file is, of course, on the disk you specified in the previous procedure.) If you set Windows Explorer to show file size — click the Views button and choose Details from the drop-down menu to do this — you'll notice that your backup file (the one with the .QBB extension) is a fraction of the size of its regular company file counterpart (the one with the .QBW extension). QuickBooks shrinks the backup file in order to keep the disk from getting too crowded.

Getting back QuickBooks data if you've backed up

What happens if you lose all your QuickBooks data? First of all, I encourage you to feel smug. Get a cup of coffee. Lean back in your chair. Gloat for a couple of minutes. You, my friend, will have no problem. You have followed instructions.

After you've gloated sufficiently, carefully do the following to reinstate your QuickBooks data on the computer:

1. **Get your backup floppy disk.**

   Find the backup disk you created and carefully insert it into one of the disk drives. (If you can't find the backup disk, forget what I said about feeling smug — stop gloating and skip to the next section, "Trying to get back QuickBooks data if you haven't backed up.")

2. **Start QuickBooks.**

   You already know how to do this, right? By the way, if the disaster that caused you to lose your data also trashed other parts of your computer, you may need to reinstall QuickBooks. You also may need to reinstall all your other software.

3. **Choose File⇨Restore.**

   QuickBooks closes whatever company file you have open. Guess what happens then? QuickBooks displays the Restore From dialog box. Figure 15-3 shows you what this box looks like.

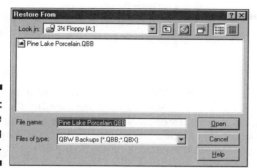

Figure 15-3:
The Restore
From dialog
box.

4. **In the Look In box, click the name of the drive that contains the backup file. (This is your floppy disk drive, if you've been following along here. If you haven't, take a look at the earlier section, "Backing up the quick-and-dirty way.")**

   QuickBooks looks at the floppy disk in this drive and displays a list of the files stored on the floppy disk in the box under the section headed "File Name," — see Figure 15-3. (If you have only one QuickBooks file on the disk — the usual case — only one file is listed.)

5. **Select the file that you want to restore and click Open.**

   Use the arrow keys or the mouse to highlight the file you want to restore and click OK or double-click the filename.

   You see the Restore To dialog box, shown in Figure 15-4. In the File Name box, you should see the .QBW name of the .QBB file that you want to restore. QuickBooks lists the .QBW name to let you know the name that the restored file will have and, if necessary, offers you an opportunity to give it a different name.

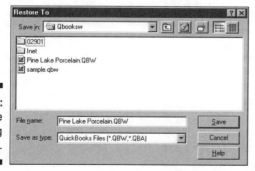

Figure 15-4:
The Restore
To dialog
box.

6. **Change folders and drives in the Save In drop-down list box.**

   Make sure that you place the restored file in the Qbooksw folder on the correct drive.

7. **Click Save.**

   If the file you're trying to restore already exists, you see a message box telling you so. Either click Yes to overwrite or replace the file with the one stored on the floppy disk, or click No to keep the original copy. (If you click Yes, a message box similar to the one in Figure 15-5 appears — the QuickBooks way of saying, "Just checking, boss.")

Figure 15-5:
Just
checking,
boss.

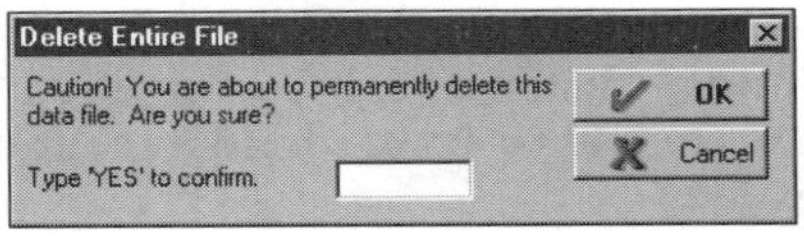

QuickBooks may ask you for your password so that it can verify that you have administrative permission to restore the file. Then, if everything goes okay, you see a message box that says so. Breathe a deep sigh of relief and give thanks.

When you restore a file, you replace the current version of the file with the backup version stored on the floppy disk. Don't restore a file for fun. Restore a file only if the current version is trashed and you want to start over by using the version stored on the backup floppy disk.

Just to be on the safe side, you should back up the file after you complete this process. I've heard that lightning never strikes the same place twice, but I'm not sure that the old saying is true. If you have hard disk problems or another recurring problem, whatever fouled up your file this time may rear its ugly head again — and soon.

I almost forgot: You need to complete one last step to finish restoring your data. You need to re-enter everything you entered since you made the backup copy. I know. You're bummed out. Hopefully, it hasn't been all that long since you backed up.

Trying to get back QuickBooks data if you haven't backed up

What do you do if you haven't backed up your files in a while and you lose all the data in your QuickBooks files? Okay. Stay calm. All may not be lost.

Try restoring from the backup file on the hard drive. To restore from this file, you follow the same file-restoration steps I cover earlier in the chapter, with one minor exception. (See "Getting back QuickBooks data if you've backed up.") When you get to the Restore From dialog box (refer to Figure 15-13), you use the Look In list boxes to indicate that you want to see the backup files in the QuickBooks folder on the hard drive. You'll probably choose drive C from the Drives list box and open the Qbooksw folder. At this point, you may see a file with a name similar to the name of the file that you lost. If the file you lost had the name Pine Lake Porcelain.QBW, for example, you may see a file named Pine Lake Porcelain.QBB. Select it. QuickBooks uses the file to restore the current file. This method may just work. And if this method does, you should feel very lucky. Very lucky indeed.

Okay, suppose that you've tried the approach described in the preceding paragraph. Suppose that it didn't work. What next?

All you have to do is re-enter all the transactions for the entire year. Yeah. I know — what a bummer. This method isn't quick, and it isn't pretty, but it works. (Besides, I bring this up in the interest of showing you the alternative of not backing up your files.)

If you have hard copies (printed copies) of the invoices, checks, purchase orders, and so on, you can, of course, use these sources for the information that you need to re-enter. If you don't have copies of these kinds of things, you need to use bank statements and any other paper financial records that you have.

Accountant's Review

Hey. While I'm on the subject of stuff you can do with your QuickBooks files, let me mention the Accountant's Review feature.

Accountant's Review allows your accountant to make adjustments in a special copy of your QuickBooks data file while you continue to enter your daily transactions in the master file. When your accountant returns the updated file, you can then merge the changes back into the master file.

To use Accountant's Review, click the Taxes and Accountant tab of the QuickBooks Navigator and click the Accountant's Review icon. Use the Accountant's Review Activities dialog box to create the accountant's copy (this is a special kind of copy with the file extension .QBX) and import the accountant's changes. If you need help with this feature, you should talk to your accountant.

Shrinking Files That Are Too Big for Their Own Good

You can enter a large number of transactions in a QuickBooks company file. Even so, you may want to shrink or condense the .QBW or working set of your data file. Working with files of a manageable size means that QuickBooks runs faster because your computer has more memory and disk space available.

Condensing defined

If your company file has gotten too big for its own good, you can knock it down to size by condensing it. As part of condensing the file, QuickBooks lets you decide which parts should be condensed and which parts should be readily accessible. You make this decision based on a cutoff date of your choice. In other words, if you have two or three years' worth of data records and the stuff from three years ago doesn't pertain to you for the most part, you can condense it. You also can condense unused accounts, information on inactive customers and vendors, old invoices, and Audit Trail information.

Condensed information isn't lost — it's merely summarized. QuickBooks retains numeric totals and dates of the transactions but deletes other details, such as the names. In other words, if you wrote a check to Tuggey's Hardware on July 31, 1996, QuickBooks retains the amount of the check and the date it was written but loses the name of the hardware store.

Don't despair, however, about losing crucial data. In all its wisdom, QuickBooks can tell if a data item that you want to condense still bears on transactions that you enter in the future, and QuickBooks won't condense these transactions. If you choose to condense all information from before January 1, 1998, and you just so happen to have skipped a monthly rent payment in December 1997, for example, QuickBooks still retains all accounts payable information pertaining to your missed payment. And quit trying to pull a fast one, you rascal.

Unpaid invoices, bills, and credit memos; undeposited customer payments that have been applied to invoices; unreconciled transactions in credit card and checking accounts; and anything whatsoever that has been checked To Be Printed are not condensed.

For the purposes of tax liability, QuickBooks doesn't condense any of your tax data. QuickBooks retains all information about taxable items and tax vendors. If you get audited, you won't be able to point to your computer and say, "There you are. Just uncondense that, Mr. Taxman."

Condensing means that you get to work with a smaller file. And that, in turn, means QuickBooks runs faster. (The memory thing comes into play again.) And a smaller file should make backing up easier because you can probably keep your file small enough to fit on a single floppy disk.

Call me a Nervous Nellie — or a Nervous Nelson — but because shrinking a file involves wholesale change, I'd really feel more comfortable about helping you through this process if you backed up the file you're about to shrink before you start. I don't think that you need to get anxious about anything, but just in case something does go wrong during the shrinking process, I know that you'd like to have a backup copy of the file to fall back on.

I tell you what happens to your company file when you shrink it in the following section.

Condensing made simple

To condense a QuickBooks file, follow these steps:

1. **Start from a blank QuickBooks screen.**

   Close registers, reports, or anything else on-screen.

2. **Choose File➪Utilities➪Condense Data.**

   QuickBooks displays a portrait of Barry Nelson, the first actor to portray James Bond. No, not really — I just wanted to see whether you were awake. Actually, QuickBooks displays the Condense Data dialog box, as shown in Figure 15-6.

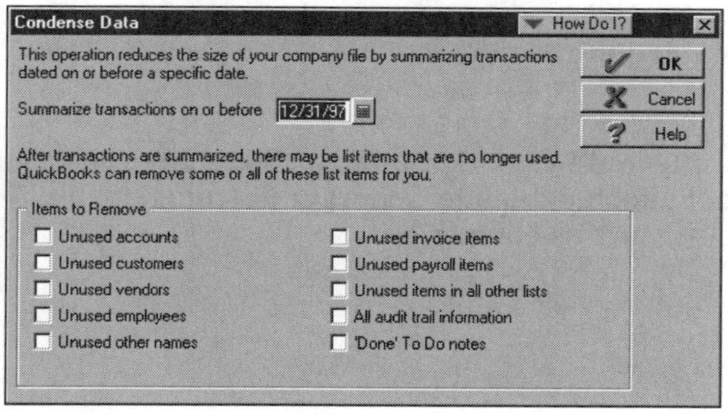

Figure 15-6:
The
Condense
Data dialog
box.

3. **Specify a cutoff date.**

   In the Summarize Transactions On Or Before line, enter a cutoff date. QuickBooks keeps all transactions with dates that fall after this cutoff date. But all transactions with dates that fall before this cutoff date are condensed (with the exceptions noted earlier in this chapter).

4. **(Optional) Select other items in the Items to Remove list.**

   Take a look at the Items to Remove list. You may see something that you can condense. Prime candidates are employees you have nothing to do with (and whose tax information you no longer need) and inactive vendors.

5. **Click OK.**

   A message box appears, telling you that transactions exist before the date you entered in Step 4. You knew that, but QuickBooks is an exceptionally courteous program, and it wants to know whether you really want to condense this stuff.

6. **Click OK (again).**

   Or click Cancel if you get nervous.

   At this point, QuickBooks gives you another chance to create a backup file. Why not? Create yet another backup to be on the safe side. (I explain how to create a backup earlier in this chapter.) Condensing your file may take a while, depending on how large it is. So expect a little whirring and humming from the computer. After QuickBooks condenses the file, you see a message box confirming the process.

7. **Click OK in the QuickBooks Information message box.**

How condensing is summarized on registers

QuickBooks summarizes data on registers into the generic GENJRNL entry. So if you condense all data from 1997, your Accounts Payable register for May 1997 shows a GENJRNL entry totaling all accounts payable transactions from that month. You don't see the individual transactions that have been condensed.

Some reports are affected by condensed data. Summary reports about your total equity are not affected, but any report concerning details — classes, items, and so on — aren't as complete.

Chapter 16

Building the Perfect Budget

In This Chapter

▶ Powerful tips for business budgets

▶ Setting up a budget manually

▶ Setting up a budget automatically

I don't think that a budget amounts to financial handcuffs, and neither should you. A budget is just a plan that outlines the way you should spend your money and organize your financial affairs.

Is This a Game You Want to Play?

If you've created a good, workable chart of accounts, you're halfway to a good, solid budget. (In fact, for 99 out of 100 businesses, the only step left is to specify how much you earn in each income account and how much you spend in each expense account.)

Does everybody need a budget? No, of course not. Maybe you've got a simple financial plan that you can monitor some other way. Maybe in your business, you make money so effortlessly that you don't need to plan your income and outgo. Maybe Elvis Presley really is still alive and living somewhere in the Midwest.

For everyone else, though, a budget improves your chances of getting to wherever you want to go financially. It gives you a way to "plan your work and work your plan." In fact, I'll stop calling it a budget. The word has such negative connotations. I know — I'll call it *The Secret Plan*.

All Joking Aside

Before I walk you through the mechanics of outlining your secret plan, I want to give you a few tips. After that, I want to tell you a secret. A very special secret.

Some basic budgeting tips

Following are four ways to increase the chances that your secret plan works:

- **Plan your income and expenses as a team, if that's possible.** For this sort of planning, two heads are invariably better than one. What's more, although I don't really want to get into marriage counseling or partnership counseling here, a business's budget — oops, I mean secret plan — needs to reflect the priorities and feelings of everyone who has to live within the plan: partners, partners' spouses, key employees, and so on. So don't use a secret plan as a way to minimize what your partner spends on marketing or on long-distance telephone charges talking to pseudocustomers and relatives in the old country. You need to resolve such issues before you finalize your secret plan.

- **Include some cushion in your plan.** In other words, don't budget to spend every last dollar. If you plan from the start to spend every dollar you make, you'll undoubtedly have to fight the mother of all financial battles: paying for unexpected expenses when you don't have any money. (You know the sort of things I mean: the repair bill when the delivery truck breaks down, a new piece of essential equipment, or that cocktail dress or tuxedo you absolutely must have for a special party.)

- **Regularly compare your actual income and outgo to your planned income and outgo.** This comparison is probably the most important part of budgeting, and it's what QuickBooks can help you with the most. As long as you use QuickBooks to record what you receive and spend and to describe your budget, you can print reports that show what you planned and what actually occurred.

- **Make adjustments as necessary.** When you encounter problems with your secret plan — and you will — you'll know that part of your plan isn't working. You can then make adjustments (by spending a little less on calling the old country, for example).

All these tips also apply to a family's secret plan. And that brings up another important subject. If you're a small-business owner or partner who relies on the profits of the business to buy things such as groceries for your family or to pay the rent, you need to also have a solid family budget. In fact, in my opinion, planning your family finances is as important as planning your business finances. If your business is like most businesses, your profits probably bounce up and down like a yo-yo. You need to have enough slack in your personal finances so that a bad (or a so-so) business year doesn't cause all sorts of trouble at home.

The QuickBooks cousin product, Quicken, is a great personal finance program. It includes record-keeping tools that you can use to track all your personal financial information. It also has some nifty planning tools that enable you to intelligently think about and plan for things such as retirement, your children's college expenses, and your income taxes.

Can I say one more thing about the relationship between your family's finances and the business's finances? If you let me say this one more thing, I'll get off my soapbox. I promise. Okay. Here's my other point. Please, please, please: Don't gear up your living and lifestyle when you have a great year in the business. When you have a good year or even a few good years, keep your living expenses modest. Stash the extra cash. Build up some financial wealth that's independent and apart from your business assets. (One great way to do this, for example, is by contributing to an IRA or by setting up a SEP/IRA.) For more information about IRAs or help with personal financial planning, you might want to check out a copy of *Personal Finance For Dummies,* 2nd Edition, or *Investing For Dummies,* both by Eric Tyson (IDG Books Worldwide). You might also want to read *The Millionaire Kit* (Random House/Times Books), a soon-to-be-published book that provides a step-by-step plan for creating real wealth and the software tools to implement the plan.

A budgeting secret

I also have a secret tip for business budgeting. (I'm going to write very quietly now so that no one else hears. . . .)

Here's the secret tip: Go to the library, ask for the Robert Morris & Associates Survey, and look up the ways that other businesses like yours spend money.

This survey is really cool. Robert Morris & Associates surveys bank lending officers, creates a summary of the information that these bankers receive from their customers, and publishes the results. For example, you can look up what percentage of sales the average tavern spends on beer and peanuts.

Plan to spend an hour or so at the library. Getting used to the way that the Robert Morris & Associates information is displayed takes a while. The taverns page doesn't actually have a line for beer and peanuts, for example. Instead, you see the words *cost of goods sold* or some similarly vague accounting term.

Remember to make a few notes so that you can use the information you glean to better plan your own business financial affairs.

Two things that really goof up secret plans

Because I'm talking about you-know-whats, I want to touch on a couple of things that really goof up your financial plans: windfalls and monster changes. (This stuff applies to both businesses and to families, but because this book's about business accounting, I talk about all this stuff from a business perspective.)

The problem with windfalls

Your big customer calls and asks you to come to his office for a meeting. When the time arrives, he calls you into his office, smiles, and then gives you the good news: He's buying a huge order of your [insert name of your product or service here], and you'll make about $50,000 on the deal. You read right — $50,000. Yippee, you think to yourself. On the outside, of course, you maintain your dignity. You act grateful, but not gushy. Then you call your husband, Bob.

Here's what happens next: Bob gets excited, congratulates you, and tells you he'll pick up a bottle of wine on the way home to celebrate. (If you don't drink, tell Bob to pick up something else. Geez. . . .)

On your drive home, you mull over the possibilities and conclude that you can use the $50,000 as a big down payment for some new machinery that you can use to make even more of [insert name of your product or service here]. Say that with the trade-in of your old machinery and the $50,000, your payments will be a manageable $2,000 a month.

Bob, on his way home, stops at a travel agency and books an eight-week tour through Europe for the two of you. (Apparently, at one point in the discussion, he tells the travel agent, "If you don't spend the big money, there's no sense in making it, right?") A few minutes later, your loving husband has charged $18,000 on his credit card.

You may laugh at this scenario, but suppose that these events really happened. Furthermore, pretend that you really do buy that new machinery. At this point, you've spent $68,000 on a combination of business and personal expenditures, and you've signed up for what you're guessing will be another $2,000-a-month payment.

The scenario doesn't sound all that bad now, does it?

Here's the problem: When you finish the accounting and you take out the business and personal taxes, your net profit on the deal isn't going to be $50,000. No way. You may pay as much as $7,500 in social security and Medicare taxes, maybe around $15,000 in federal income taxes, and then probably some state income taxes.

Other business expense or personal expenditure money may be taken out, too, for forced savings plans (such as a 401K plan) or for charitable giving. After all is said and done, you'll get maybe half the profit in cash — perhaps $25,000.

Now you see the problem, of course. You've got $25,000 in cold, hard cash, but, with knucklehead Bob's help, you've already spent $68,000 and signed up for $2,000-a-month payments.

In a nutshell, the two big problems with windfalls are these:

- ✔ You never get the entire windfall — but spending money as if you will get the entire amount is easy.

- ✔ Windfalls, by their very nature, tend to be used for big business and personal purchases (often as down payments) that ratchet up your operating or living expenses. Boats. New houses. Cars.

My advice regarding windfalls is simple:

- ✔ Don't spend the money until you've paid all the expenses, made all the estimated tax payments, and actually hold the check in your hot little hand. (Waiting six months or so is even better. That way Bob can really think about whether he needs the super-luxurious "Grand Continental" tour.)

- ✔ Don't spend a windfall on something that increases your monthly business (or family) expenses without redoing your budget.

About monster income changes

I have some special business-family pointers for any business owners or partners reading this book. If your business and, therefore, your personal income changes radically, planning becomes really hard.

Suppose, for example, that your income doubles. One day you're cruising along making $35,000, and the next day you're suddenly making $70,000. (Congratulations, by the way.)

I'll tell you what you'll discover, however, should you find yourself in this position. You'll find that $70,000 a year isn't as much money as you may think.

Go ahead. Laugh. But for one thing, if your income doubles, your income taxes almost certainly more than quadruple.

One of the great myths about income taxes is that the rich don't pay very much or that they pay the same percentage. Poppycock. If you make $30,000 a year and you're an average family, you probably pay about $1,500 in federal income taxes. If you make $200,000 a year, you pay about $45,000 a year.

So if your salary increases by roughly 7 times, your income taxes increase by about 30 times. I don't bring this point up to get you agitated about whether making the rich pay more is right or fair. I bring it up so that you can better plan for any monster income changes you experience.

Another thing — and I know it sounds crazy — but you'll find that wisely spending $70,000, for example, is hard when you're used to making half that much. And if you start making some big purchases, such as houses, cars, and motorboats, you'll not only burn through a lot of cash, but you'll also ratchet up your monthly living expenses. This happens because a couple of funny phenomena tend to occur when it comes to raising your standard of living. First is that just one or two relatively small, innocent purchases quickly lead to more and more purchases like a domino effect — you buy a stereo, then you need an entertainment system to put it on, then more new furniture and new carpeting, and so forth. The second thing that happens is that major purchases are typically not just one-time deals, but instead come with long-term expense commitments, ones that are often not taken into consideration at the time of purchase. Take for example the purchase of a motorboat: Not only does it probably require the initial purchase of various pieces of nautical gear, but it also comes with monthly moorage expenses, as well as regular maintenance and license expenses.

Monster income changes that go the other way are even more difficult. If you've been making, say, $70,000 a year and then see your salary drop to a darn respectable $35,000, that drop is going to hurt, probably more than you think. (This factor, by the way, is the main reason that I suggest earlier in this chapter that you not ratchet up your living expenses to what your business makes in a good year.)

That old living expenses ratcheting effect comes into play here, of course. Presumably, if you've been making $70,000 a year, you've been spending it — or most of it.

But, at least initially, some other reasons make having a monster salary drop very difficult. You've probably chosen friends (nice people, like the Joneses), clothing stores, and hobbies that are in line with your income.

Another thing is sort of subtle. You probably denominate your purchases in amounts related to your income. Make $35,000, and you think in terms of $5 or $10 purchases. But make $70,000 a year, and you think in terms of $10 or $20 purchases. This way of thinking makes perfect sense. But if your income drops from $70,000 to $35,000, you'll probably still find yourself thinking of those old $20 purchases.

So what to do? If you experience a monster income change, redo your secret plan. Be particularly careful and thoughtful, though.

The Nelson philosophy

I keep weaving between issues related to a business's budget and issues related to a business owner's family budget. I'm sorry if this flip-flopping is confusing, but I've found the two budgets to be closely connected in small businesses. So, because of that closeness, I want to make a short philosophical digression about your family budget.

At the point that you've provided yourself and your family with the creature comforts — a cozy home, adequate food, and comfortable clothes — more stuff won't make the difference that you think it will.

I don't mean to minimize the challenges of raising a family of four on, say, $14,000 a year. But, hey, I work with a fair number of small-business people who've been very successful. What continually surprises me is that when you get right down to it, someone who makes $300,000 or $600,000 a year doesn't live a better life than someone who makes $30,000.

Sure, they spend more money. They buy more stuff. They buy more expensive stuff. But they don't live better. They don't have better marriages. Their kids don't love them more. They don't have better friends or more considerate neighbors.

But you already know all this stuff. I know you do.

Setting Up a Secret Plan

Okay, enough metaphysical stuff. The time has come to set up your budget — er, your secret plan. Follow these steps:

1. **Click the Company tab of the QuickBooks Navigator, and then click the Budgets icon.**

   QuickBooks displays the Set Up Budgets window (see Figure 16-1).

2. **Select the fiscal year that you want to budget.**

   Use the Budget for Fiscal Year line to specify the fiscal year. You use the up and down arrows at the end of the box to adjust the year number incrementally.

3. **Choose the account that you want to budget.**

   See the Account drop-down list box? You use it to specify which account you're budgeting. Normally, you'll probably limit yourself to budgeting just income and expense accounts. You can, however, budget balance sheet accounts, too.

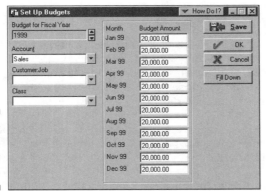

Figure 16-1:
The Set Up
Budgets
window.

Note that I said that you can budget balance sheet accounts. I don't recommend doing so. Here's why:

Many line items are fairly easy to anticipate. If you own a freelance writing business, for example, anticipating your sales for the month is fairly easy. Balance sheet accounts — frequently referred to as "real" accounts — are infinitely more complicated, which makes them much harder to forecast. For example, take your "cash" account. In order to come up with a figure for this account properly, you probably need at least to consider income, expenses, loans taken out, loans paid off, and more. Moreover, having figures from the previous year to use in calculating the potential amounts would be helpful — but why would you want to spend all that time putting last year's figures into QuickBooks just for a budget?

Look at it this way: Assembling a budget for balance sheet accounts is usually not tackled in undergraduate accounting degree programs until the third year of studies, and even then, they use big spreadsheets.

4. (Optional) Specify the customer or job.

If you want to budget an account by customer or job, activate the Customer:Job drop-down list. Then click the customer or job. (If you're just starting out in your budgeting, one way to make things easier is to not budget by customer or job.)

5. (Optional) Specify the class.

If you want to budget an account by class, activate the Class drop-down list. Then click the class. (Again, if you're just starting out in your budgeting, you may want to make things easier by not budgeting by class.)

6. **Enter the first month's budget amount.**

   To enter the budget, type the budgeted amount for the account into the first month's text box. You need to remember just two things:

   - If you're budgeting an income or expense account, you need to enter the amount of income you'll earn or the expense you'll incur over the month.

   - If you're budgeting an amount for a balance sheet account, you need to enter the account balance that you expect at the end of the month you're budgeting.

7. **Enter the budget amounts for subsequent months.**

   You can enter the budget amounts for subsequent months into the other text boxes manually.

   If monthly budgeted amounts are the same over the year or the monthly amounts grow by a constant percentage or amount, you can use the Fill Down button. When you click Fill Down, QuickBooks displays the Fill Down dialog box (see Figure 16-2). Enter the percentage change (followed by a percent symbol) or the dollar change you want from one month to the next. If you don't want the monthly amount to change, leave the percentage change as 0.0%.

Figure 16-2:
The Fill
Down
dialog box.

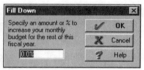

To create a complete budget, you need to repeat Steps 6 and 7 for each of the accounts you want to budget. I know that I said this stuff earlier, but let me repeat a couple of things: If you're budgeting some income or expense amount, enter the amount of income you'll earn or the expense you'll incur over the month; if you're budgeting some balance sheet account — an asset, liability, or owner's equity amount — enter the account balance that you expect at the end of the month you're budgeting.

After you enter your secret plan, click Save to save your work and leave the Set Up Budgets window open. Or click OK to save your work but close the Set Up Budgets window.

I should mention, too, that you can just click Cancel if you don't want to save your work (in case you've just been noodling around).

Using business-planning and budgeting software

You can usually create a family budget on a few sheets of paper and without too many hours of work. You put down your salary. You estimate your expenses. You're done.

Unfortunately, budgeting a business is more complicated. More specifically, budgeting any of your balance sheet accounts — assets, liabilities, and owner's equity — is really tough. (Remember that cash is a balance sheet account.) To do this sort of budgeting with any degree of accuracy, you need either budgeting or business-planning software or a spreadsheet program (such as Microsoft Excel) and a fair amount of accounting knowledge. How you do this kind of budgeting is way, way beyond this book. But I did want to mention that several good packages are available.

Are you interested in more information? You can call the Planet Corp. at 800-366-5111 to order one of the company's stand-alone packages such as Business Foundation. If you want more information about the products Planet Corp. offers, you can check out its Web site at www.planet-corp.com. If you want a business planning tool that works with your spreadsheet program, you can call Palo Alto Software at 800-229-7526 and order Business Plan Pro, or you can check out the company's Web site at www.pasware.com.

Part IV
The Part of Tens

The 5th Wave   By Rich Tennant

With QuickBooks, Tonto was finally able to calculate his billable hours as "friend and trusted scout."

In this part . . .

As a writing tool, laundry lists aren't something high school English teachers encourage. But you know what? The old laundry list format is pretty handy for certain types of information.

With this in mind (and, of course, with deepest apologies to my high school English teacher, Mrs. O'Rourke), this part simply provides you with almost-ten-item lists of information about QuickBooks.

Chapter 17

Ten Things You Should Do
If You're Audited

*B*ecause you probably use QuickBooks to produce the reports that you or your accountant uses to prepare your annual income tax returns, I want to mention some things that you should do if your business gets audited.

Leave QuickBooks at Home

Don't bring QuickBooks with you to an IRS audit — even if you're really proud of that new laptop.

Here's the problem: The QuickBooks reporting capabilities are incredibly powerful. If you've been using QuickBooks diligently, you own a rich database that describes almost all of your financial affairs. When you bring QuickBooks (and your QuickBooks file) to the IRS, you spill your financial guts.

Now I'm not one who recommends sneaking stuff by the IRS. But giving an IRS agent the opportunity to go on a fishing expedition is dumb. Remember, the agent isn't going to be looking for additional deductions.

I know of a young, inexperienced CPA who took Quicken, the younger sibling of QuickBooks, to an audit. The IRS agent would ask a question, and the CPA would proudly tap a few keys on the laptop, smile broadly, and then, for example, show the agent all the individual entertainment expenses claimed by the taxpayer in question.

Funny thing, though; the IRS agent also saw some other stuff on-screen — such as money that should have been claimed as income, reporting requirements that the taxpayer failed to meet, and obvious out-of-line deductions.

Print Transaction Reports for Questionable Accounts

Ol' QuickBooks can be your friend, though, if you're audited.

Before you go to the audit, find out what the IRS is questioning. Print a transaction report of every questioned income or expense account: supplies, travel and entertainment, yachting expenses, and so on. You will have an easy-to-understand report that explains how you came up with every number that the IRS wants to examine.

Collect All Source Documents

After you print a transaction report of every questioned deduction, collect all the source documents — usually canceled checks, invoices, and bills — that prove or indicate a transaction in question.

If you claim $600 in postage expenses, for example, the report summarizing this deduction may show twelve $50 checks written to the local postmaster. To verify this report, find the twelve canceled checks. Even better, find the twelve $50 receipts supplied by the postal clerk who sold you the stamps.

Call a Tax Attorney If the Agent Is Special

An IRS special agent isn't an agent endorsed by Mr. Rogers. Internal Revenue Service special agents investigate criminal tax code violations. If a special agent is auditing your return, you're in a heap of trouble. So get a tax attorney.

In my mind, being audited by a special agent is like being arrested for murder. Call me a scaredy-cat, but I'd want legal representation even if I were innocent.

Don't Volunteer Information

Loose lips sink ships. Don't volunteer any information — even if it seems innocuous. Just answer the questions you're asked.

Again, I'm not suggesting that you lie. The agent, however, is looking for income that you forgot or deductions that you overstated. The more information you provide, the more likely you'll reveal something damaging.

For example, if you offhandedly tell the agent about your other business — where you knit socks for golf clubs — you may wind up debating whether that cute little business is really a business (and not a hobby) and whether knitting golf socks entitles you to deduct those country club dues and greens fees.

Consider Using a Pinch Hitter

I don't think that an audit should terrify you. And I'm someone who's scared of everything: dinner parties where I don't know anyone, stormy nights when the neighborhood seems particularly deserted, driving on bald tires. You get the idea. Nonetheless, if you used a paid preparer and you're horrified at the notion of coming face to face with the IRS, think about sending the preparer in your place and staying at home and making yourself some tea.

You pay for this service, of course. But you may benefit from having the person who prepared your return do the talking.

Understand Everything on Your Return

Be sure that you understand everything on your return. You won't help yourself if you tell an agent that you don't have a clue about some number on the return.

Be Friendly

Be nice to the IRS. Remember, the agents actually work for you. In fact, the more taxes that the agents collect from people who owe the federal government, the less the rest of us have to pay. (An article in *Money* a few years ago suggested that everyone ends up paying several hundred dollars more a year in income taxes because so many people cheat.)

Don't Worry

If you've been honest and careful, you have nothing to worry about. Sure, maybe you made a mistake. Maybe the agent will find the mistake. And maybe you'll have to pay additional taxes.

If you haven't been honest and careful, I offer my condolences. Sorry.

Don't Lie

Don't lie; it may be perjury. You could go to jail and share a cell with someone named Skullcrusher. And develop a close relationship.

You get the picture. And it's not pretty. So don't lie.

Chapter 18

(Almost) Ten Secret Business Formulas

In This Chapter

▶ The first "most expensive money you can borrow" formula

▶ The second "most expensive money you can borrow" formula

▶ The "How do I break even?" formula

▶ The "You can grow too fast" formula

▶ The first "What happens if . . ." formula

▶ The second "What happens if . . ." formula

▶ The economic order quantity formula

▶ The Rule of 72

I have some good news and some bad news for you. The good news is that you can use some powerful formulas to better your chances of business success and increase your profits. No, I'm not joking. Formulas such as these do exist. You can and should use them. And in the pages that follow, I explain the formulas and how to use them.

Now for the bad news: To use these formulas, you need to feel comfortable with a bit of arithmetic. You don't need to be a serious mathematician or anything. But you do need to feel comfortable with percentages and calculators.

Even if you're not particularly fond of (or all that good at) math, I want to encourage you to skim through this chapter. You can pick up some weird insights into the world of finance.

You can use the standard Windows Calculator accessory, available from within QuickBooks, to calculate any of the secret formulas.

The First "Most Expensive Money You Can Borrow" Formula

Here's something you may not know: The most expensive money that you borrow is from vendors who offer cash or early payment discounts that you don't take. For example, perhaps your friendly office supply store offers a 2 percent discount if you pay cash at the time of purchase instead of paying within the usual 30 days. You don't pay cash, so you pay the full amount (which is 2 percent more than the cash amount) 30 days later. In effect, you pay a 2 percent monthly interest charge. A 2 percent monthly interest charge works out to a 24 percent annual interest charge. And that's a great deal of money.

Here's another example that is only slightly more complicated. Many, many vendors offer a 2 percent discount if you pay within the first 10 days an invoice is due instead of 30 days later. (These payment terms are often described and printed at the bottom of the invoice as "2/10, Net 30.")

In this case, you pay 2 percent more by paying 20 days later. (The 20 days later is the difference between 10 days and 30 days.) Two percent for 20 days is roughly equivalent to 3 percent for 30 days, or a month. So, a 2 percent 20-day interest charge works out to a 36 percent annual interest charge. And now you're talking serious money.

Table 18-1 shows how some common early payment discounts (including cash discounts) translate into annual interest rates. By the way, I've been a bit more precise in my calculations for this table, so these numbers vary slightly from (and are larger than) those given in the preceding paragraph.

Table 18-1	Annual Interest Rates for Early Payment Discounts	
Early Payment Discount	*For Paying 20 Days Early*	*For Paying 30 Days Early*
1%	18.43%	12.29%
2%	37.24%	24.83%
3%	56.44%	37.63%
4%	76.04%	50.69%
5%	96.05%	64.04%

Is it just me, or do those numbers blow you away? The 2 percent for 20 days early payment discount that you often see works out (if you do the math precisely) to more than 37 percent annual interest. Man, that hurts. And if you don't take a 5 percent for 20 days early payment discount when it's offered, you're effectively borrowing money at an annual rate of 96 percent. You didn't read that last number wrong. Yes, a 5 percent for 20 days early payment discount works out to an annual interest rate of almost 100 percent.

I want to make a couple more observations, too. Turning down a 1 percent discount for paying 30 days early isn't actually a bad deal in many cases. Look at Table 18-1. It shows that the 1 percent discount for paying 30 days early as 12.29 percent. Sure, that rate is pretty high. But that interest rate is less than for many credit cards. And it's less than for many small-business credit lines. So if you would have to borrow money in some other way in order to pay 30 days early, making an early payment may not be cost-effective.

The bottom line on all this ranting is that early payment discounts, if not taken, represent one of the truly expensive ways to borrow money. I'm not saying that you won't need to borrow money this way at times. I can guess that your cash flow gets pretty tight sometimes. (This circumstance is true in most businesses, as you probably know.) I am saying that you should never skip taking an early payment discount unless borrowing money at outrageous interest rates makes sense.

Oh, yes. The secret formula. To figure out the effective annual interest rate that you pay by not taking an early payment discount, use this formula:

Discount % / (1 – Discount %) * (365 / Number of Days of Early Payment)

So, to calculate the effective annual interest rate that you pay by not taking a 2 percent discount for paying 20 days early, calculate this formula:

.02 / (1 – .02) * (365 / 20)

Work out the mathematics and you get .3724, which is the same thing as a 37.24 percent interest rate. (Note that the discount percents are entered as their equivalent decimal values.)

The Scientific view of the Windows calculator includes parenthesis keys that you can use to calculate this formula and the others described in the chapter. Choose View⇨Scientific to switch to the Scientific view of the calculator.

What about cash payment discounts?

Good question. Cash discounts for your customers are different than early payment discounts. My doctor, for example, offers me a 2 percent discount if I pay him in cash at the end of my visit rather than 30 days later. Is my doctor stupid or desperate? No. Here's the reason: First, if I pay him on the spot, he doesn't have to bill me or the insurance company, which saves his bookkeeper time. If the $12/hour bookkeeper needs a quarter hour to prepare the invoice, send it out to both me and the insurance company, and then record and deposit the payment, my doctor has to pay $3 in real money to invoice me. So he saves $3 if he gets the cash up front.

The good doctor is too polite to bring up a more subtle reason for offering this discount. If the discount encourages patients to pay the fees up front, he'll probably have fewer uncollectible accounts receivable later on. This equation is tricky; I can't give you any formula for it. But the logic is that he'll collect at least some of the fees — 98 percent of the fees, to be precise — from deadbeats from whom he would otherwise collect nothing. And the potential deadbeats who pay 98 percent up front instead of stiffing him more than make up for the 2 percent discount that the nondeadbeats enjoy.

The Second "Most Expensive Money You Can Borrow" Formula

You know that "most expensive money you can borrow" stuff that I talk about in the preceding section? The very tragic flip side to that story is when you offer your customers early payment discounts and they take the discount. In effect, you borrow money from your customers, at the same outrageous interest rates. For example, if customer Joe Schmoe gets a 2 percent early payment discount for paying 20 days early, you, in effect, pay ol' Joe roughly 2 percent interest for a 20-day loan. Using the same formula I give for the first "most expensive money you can borrow" formula, the rate works out to 37.24 percent.

In some industries, customers expect early payment discounts. You may have to offer them. But you should never offer them willingly. You should never offer them just for fun. Borrowing money this way is just too expensive. A rate of 37.24 percent? Yikes!

Let me also offer a rather dour observation. In my experience, any time someone offers big early payment discounts — I've seen them as big as 5 percent — they're either stupid or desperate, and probably both.

The "How Do I Break Even?" Formula

I know that you're not interested in just breaking even. I know that you want to make money in your business. But, that said, knowing what quantities you need to sell just to cover your expenses is often super-helpful. If you're a one-person accounting firm (or some other service business), for example, how many hours do you need to work to pay your expenses and perhaps pay yourself a small salary? Or, if you're a retailer of, say, toys, how many toys do you need to sell to pay your overhead, the rent, and sales clerks?

You see my point, right? Knowing how much revenue you need to generate just to stay in the game is essential. Knowing your break-even point enables you to establish a benchmark for your performance. (Anytime you don't break even, you know that you have a serious problem you need to resolve quickly to stay in business.) And considering break-even points is invaluable when you think about new businesses or new ventures. As you ponder any new opportunity and its potential income and expenses, you need to know how much income you need to generate just to pay those expenses.

To calculate a break-even point, you need to know just three pieces of information: your *fixed costs* (the expenses you have to pay regardless of the business's revenue, or income), the revenue you generate for each sale, and the *variable costs* that you incur in each sale. (These variable costs, which also are called direct expenses, in case you care, aren't the same thing as the fixed costs.)

- Whatever you sell — be it thingamajigs, corporate jets, or hours of consulting services — has a *price*. That price is your revenue per item input.

- Most of the time, what you sell has a cost, too. If you buy and resell thingamajigs, those thingamajigs cost you some amount of money. The total of your thingamajigs costs varies depending on how many thingamajigs you buy and sell, which is why these costs are referred to as variable costs. A couple of examples of variables costs include hourly or contract labor and shipping. Sometimes the variable cost per item is zero, however. (If you're a consultant, for example, you sell hours of your time. But you may not pay an hourly cost just because you consult for an hour.)

- Your fixed costs are all those costs that you pay regardless of whether you sell your product or service. For example, if you have to pay an employee a salary regardless of whether you sell anything, that salary is a fixed cost. Your rent is probably a fixed cost. Things such as insurance and legal and accounting expenses are probably also fixed costs because they don't vary with fluctuations in your revenue.

✔ Fixed costs, by the way, may change a bit from year to year or may bounce around a bit during a year. So maybe fixed isn't a very good adjective. People use the term fixed costs, however, to differentiate these costs from variable costs, which are those costs that do vary with the number of goods you sell.

Take the book-writing business as an example. Suppose that as you read this book, you think, "Man, that guy is having too much fun. Writing about accounting programs . . . working day in and day out with buggy beta software . . . yeah, that would be the life."

Further suppose that for every book you write, you think that you can make $5,000, but that you'll probably end up paying about $1,000 a book for things such as long-distance telephone charges, overnight courier charges, and extra hardware and software. And suppose that you need to pay yourself a salary of $20,000 a year. (In this scenario, your salary is your only fixed cost because you plan to write at home at a small desk in your bedroom.)

Table 18-2 shows how the situation breaks down:

Table 18-2		Costs and Revenue
Variable	*Amount*	*Explanation*
Revenue	$5,000	What you can squeeze out of the publisher
Variable costs	$1,000	All the little things that add up
Fixed costs	$20,000	You need someplace to live and food to eat

With these three bits of data, you can easily calculate how many books you need to write to break even. Here's the formula:

Fixed Costs / (Revenue – Variable Costs)

If you plug in the writing business example data, the formula looks like this:

$20,000 / ($5,000 – $1,000)

Work through the math and you get five. So you need to write (and get paid for) five books a year to pay the $1,000 per book variable costs and your $20,000 salary. Just to prove that I didn't make up this formula and that it really works, Table 18-3 shows how things look if you write five books:

Table 18-3		The Break-Even Point
Description	*Amount*	*Explanation*
Revenue	$25,000	Five books at $5,000 each
Variable costs	($ 5,000)	Five books at $1,000 each
Fixed costs	($20,000)	A little food money, a little rent money, a little beer money
Profits	$0	Subtract the costs from the revenue, and nothing is left

Accountants, by the way, use parentheses to show negative numbers. That's why the $5,000 and the $20,000 are in parentheses.

But back to the game. To break even in a book-writing business such as the one described here, you need to sell and write five books a year. If you don't think that you can write and sell five books in a year, getting into the book-writing business makes no sense.

Your business is probably more complicated than book writing, but the same formula and logic apply. You need just three pieces of information: the revenue you receive from the sale of a single item, the variable costs of selling (and possibly making) the item, and the fixed costs that you pay just to be in business.

QuickBooks doesn't collect or present information in a way that enables you to easily pull the revenue per item and variable costs per item off some report. Nor does it provide a fixed costs total on some report. But if you understand the logic of the preceding discussion, you can easily massage the QuickBooks data to get the information you need.

The "You Can Grow Too Fast" Formula

Here's a weird little paradox: One of the easiest ways for a small business to fail is by being too successful. I know. It sounds crazy. But it's true. In fact, I'll even go out on a limb and say that business success is by far the most common reason that I see for business failure.

"Oh, geez," you say. "This nut is talking in circles."

Let me explain. Whether you realize it, you need a certain amount of financial horsepower, or *net worth,* to do business. (Your net worth is just the difference between your assets and your liabilities.) You have to have some cash in the bank to tide you over the rough times that everybody has at least occasionally. You probably have to have some office furniture and computers so that you can take care of the business end of the business. And if you make anything at all, you have to have adequate tools and machinery. This part all makes sense, right?

Okay, now on to the next reality. If your business grows and continues to grow, you need to increase your financial horsepower, or net worth. A bigger business, for example, needs more cash to make it through the tough times, more office furniture and computers, and more tools and machinery. Oh sure, you may be able to have one growth spurt because you started off with more financial horsepower (more net worth) than you needed. But — and this is the key part — you can't grow and continue to grow without increasing your net worth at some point. In other words, you can't sustain business growth without increasing your net worth.

Some of you are now saying things like, "No way, man. That doesn't apply to me." I assure you, my new friend, that it does. The reality is this: Growing a business means more than just growing your sales and growing your expenses. You need to grow your financial net worth, too.

Before I give you the actual formula, I want to tell you one more thing. The most important thing that you can take away from this discussion is this bit of knowledge: The growth rate that a business can sustain has a limit.

But back to the chase. As long as your creditors will extend you additional credit as you grow your business — and they should, as long as the business is profitable and you don't have cash flow problems — you can grow your business as fast as you can grow your net worth. If you can grow your net worth by 5 percent a year, your business can grow at an easily sustained rate of only 5 percent a year. If you can grow your net worth by 50 percent a year, your business can grow at an easily sustained rate of only (only?) 50 percent a year.

You grow your business's net worth in only two ways: One way is by reinvesting profits in the business, and the other way is by getting people to invest money in the business. If you're not in a position to continually raise money from new investors — and most small businesses aren't — the only practical way to grow is by reinvesting profits in the business. (Note that any profits that you leave in the business instead of drawing them out — such as through dividends or draws — are reinvested.) So you can calculate the growth rate that your business can sustain by using this formula:

Reinvested Profits / Net Worth

I should say, just for the record, that this formula is a very simple "sustainable growth" formula. But even so, it offers some amazingly interesting insights. For example, perhaps you are a commercial printer doing $500,000 in revenues a year with a business net worth of $100,000; your business earns $50,000 a year, but you leave only $10,000 a year in the business. In other words, your reinvested profits are $10,000. In this case, your sustainable growth is calculated as follows:

$10,000 / $100,000

Work out the numbers and you get .1, or 10 percent. In other words, you can grow your business by 10 percent a year (as long as you grow the net worth by 10 percent a year by reinvesting profits). For example, you can easily go from $500,000 to $550,000 to $605,000, and continue growing annually at this 10 percent rate. But your business can't grow any faster than 10 percent a year. For example, you'll get into serious trouble if you try to go from $500,000 to $600,000 to $720,000, and continue growing at 20 percent a year.

You can convert a decimal value to a percentage by multiplying the value by 100. For example, .1 x 100 equals 10, so .1 equals 10 percent. You can convert a percentage to a decimal value by dividing the value by 100. For example, 25 (as in 25 percent) divided by 100 equals .25.

By the way, the sustainable growth formula inputs are pretty easy to get after you have QuickBooks up and running. You can get the net worth figure off the balance sheet. You can calculate the reinvested profits by looking at the net income and deducting any amounts that you pulled out of the business.

Note: I'm not going to go through the mathematical proof of why this sustainable growth formula is true. My experience is that the formula makes intuitive sense to people who think about it for a few minutes. If you aren't into the intuition thing or you don't believe me, get a college finance textbook and look up its discussion of the sustainable growth formula.

I don't want to beat this sustainable growth thing to death, but let me close with a true and mercifully short story.

I just saw another entrepreneur fail because he was successful. At first, he ignored the symptoms of fast growth. He needed another computer, so he bought it. He had to hire another person, so he just did it. Cash flow was tight and getting tighter, but he ignored the problems. After all, he was making a large number of sales, and the business was growing. Sure, things were getting awkward, but he didn't need to worry, right?

Unfortunately, vendors were getting paid later and later. This situation went on for a few weeks until some vendors started insisting on cash payments.

One Friday, he couldn't make his payroll. He then committed the unpardonable sin of borrowing payroll tax money — something you should never, ever do.

Finally, he had a large number of bills to pay and not only no cash to pay the bills but no cash in sight. Employees quit. Vendors said, "No more." This lack of cash is what ultimately killed the business. When the telephone company cuts off your telephone service, you're in serious trouble. When your landlord locks you out of your business location, you're pretty much out of luck.

The paradox in this story is that the guy had a successful business. He just spread his financial resources too thin by growing too fast.

The First "What Happens If . . ." Formula

One curiosity about small businesses is that small changes in revenue or income can have huge impacts on profits. A retailer who cruises along at $200,000 in revenue and struggles to live on $30,000 a year never realizes that boosting the sales volume by 20 percent to $250,000 may increase profits by 200 percent to $60,000.

In fact, if you take only one point away from this discussion, it should be this curious little truth: If fixed costs don't change, small changes in revenue can produce big changes in profits.

The following example shows how this point works and provides a secret formula. For starters, say that you currently generate $100,000 a year in revenue and make $20,000 a year in profits. The revenue per item sold is $100, and the variable cost per item sold is $35. (In this case, the fixed costs happen to be $45,000 a year, but that figure isn't all that important to the analysis.)

Accountants like to whip up little tables that describe these sorts of things, so Table 18-4 gives the current story on your imaginary business.

Table 18-4		Your Business Profits
Description	*Amount*	*Explanation*
Revenue	$100,000	You sell 1,000 doohickeys at $100 a pop
Variable costs	($35,000)	You buy 1,000 doohickeys at $35 a pop
Fixed costs	($45,000)	All the little things: rent, your salary, and so on
Profits	$20,000	What's left over

Okay, Table 18-4 shows the current situation. But suppose that you want to know what will happen to your profits if revenue increases by 20 percent but your fixed costs don't change. Mere mortals, not knowing what you and I know, might assume that a 20 percent increase in revenue would produce an approximate 20 percent increase in profits. But you know that small changes in revenue can produce big changes in profits, right?

To estimate exactly how a change in revenue affects profits, you use the following secret formula:

Percentage * Revenue * (1 – Variable Cost per Item / Revenue per Item)

Using the example data provided in Table 18-4 (I'm sorry this example is starting to resemble those story problems from eighth-grade math), you make the following calculation:

.20 * $100,000 * (1 – 35 / 100)

Work out the numbers, and you get 13,000. What does this figure mean? It means that a 20 percent increase in revenue produces a $13,000 increase in profits. As a percentage of profits, this $13,000 increase is 65 percent ($13,000 / $20,000 = 65 percent).

To summarize, in this case, a 20 percent increase in revenues results in a 65 percent increase in profits.

Let me stop here and make a quick observation. In my experience, entrepreneurs always seem to think that they need to grow big to make big money. They concentrate on doing things that will double or triple or quadruple their sales. Their logic, though, isn't always correct. If you can grow your business without having to increase your fixed costs, small changes in revenues can produce big changes in profits.

Before I stop talking about this first "What happens if . . ." formula, I want to quickly describe where you get the inputs you need for the formula:

- ✔ The percentage change input is just a number that you pick. If you want to see what happens to your profits with a 25 percent increase in sales, for example, you use .25.

- ✔ The revenue input is your total revenue. You can get it from your Profit & Loss Statement. (Chapter 14 describes how you can create a Profit & Loss Statement using QuickBooks.)

- ✔ The revenue per item sold and variable costs per item sold figures work the same way as described for the break-even formula earlier in this chapter.

The Second "What Happens If . . ." Formula

Maybe I shouldn't tell you this. But people in finance, like me, usually have a prejudice against people in sales. And it's not just because people who are good at sales usually make more money than people who are good at finance. It's really not. Honest to goodness.

Here's the prejudice: People in finance think that people in sales always want to reduce prices.

People in sales see things a bit differently. They say, in effect, "Hey, you worry too much. We'll make up the difference in additional sales volume."

The argument is appealing: You just undercut your competitor's prices by a healthy chunk and make less on each sale. But because you sell your stuff so cheaply, your customers will beat a path to your door.

Just for the record, I love people who are good at sales. I think that someone who is good at sales is more important than someone who is good at finance.

But, that painful admission aside, I have to tell you that a problem exists with the "Cut the prices; we'll make it up with volume" strategy. If you cut prices by a given percentage — perhaps by 10 percent — you usually need a much bigger percentage gain in revenue to break even.

The following example shows what I mean and how this strategy works. Suppose that you have a business that sells some doohickey or thingamajig. You generate $100,000 a year in revenue and make $20,000 a year in profits. Your revenue per item, or doohickey, sold is $100, and your variable cost per item, or doohickey, sold is $35. Your fixed costs happen to be $45,000 a year; but, again, the fixed costs aren't all that important to the analysis. Table 18-5 summarizes the current situation.

Table 18-5		Your Current Situation
Description	*Amount*	*Explanation*
Revenue	$100,000	You sell 1,000 doohickeys at $100 a pop
Variable costs	($35,000)	You buy 1,000 doohickeys at $35 a pop
Fixed costs	($45,000)	All the little things: rent, your salary, and so on
Profits	$20,000	What's left over

Then business is particularly bad for one month. Joe-Bob, your sales guy, comes to you and says, "Boss, I've got an idea. I think that we can cut prices by 15 percent to $85 a doohickey and get a truly massive boost in sales."

You're a good boss. You're a polite boss. Plus, you're intrigued. So you think a bit. The idea has a certain appeal. You start wondering how much of an increase in sales you need to break even on the price reduction.

You're probably not surprised to read this, but I have another secret formula that can help. You can use the following formula to calculate how many items (doohickeys, in the example) you need to sell just to break even on the new, discounted price. Here's the formula:

(Current Profits + Fixed Costs) / (Revenue per Item – Variable Cost per Item)

Using the example data provided earlier, you make the following calculation:

($20,000 + $45,000) / ($85 – $35)

Work out the numbers, and you get 1,300. What does this figure mean? It means that just to break even on the $85 doohickey price — just to break even — Joe-Bob needs to sell 1,300 doohickeys. Currently, per Table 18-3, Joe-Bob sells 1,000 doohickeys a year. As a percentage, then, this jump from 1,000 doohickeys to 1,300 doohickeys is exactly a 30 percent increase. (Remember that Joe-Bob proposes a 15 percent price cut.)

Okay, I don't know Joe-Bob. He may be a great guy. He may be a wonderful salesperson. But here's my guess: Joe-Bob isn't thinking about a 30 percent increase in sales volume. (Remember, with a 15 percent price reduction, you need a 30 percent increase just to break even!) And Joe-Bob almost certainly isn't thinking about a 50 percent or 75 percent increase in sales volume — which is what you need to make money on the whole deal, as shown in Table 18-6.

Table 18-6 How Profits Look at Various Sales Levels

Description	1,300 Units Sold	1,500 Units Sold	1,750 Units Sold
Revenue	$110,500	$127,500	$148,750
Variable costs	($45,500)	($52,500)	($61,250)
Fixed costs	($45,000)	($45,000)	($45,000)
Profits	$20,000	$30,000	$42,500

In summary, you can't reduce prices by, say, 15 percent and then go for some penny-ante increase. You need huge increases in the sales volume to get big increases in profits. If you look at Table 18-6, you can see that if you can increase the sales from 1,000 doohickeys to 1,750 doohickeys — a 75 percent increase — you can more than double the profits. This increase assumes that the fixed costs stay level, as the table shows.

I want to describe quickly where you get the inputs you need for the formula:

- ✔ The profit figure can come right off the QuickBooks Profit & Loss Statement.

- ✔ The fixed costs figure just tallies all your fixed costs. (I talk about fixed costs earlier in this chapter in the paragraphs that describe how to estimate your break-even point.)

- ✔ The revenue per item is just the new price that you're considering.

- ✔ Finally, the variable cost per item is the cost of the thing you sell. (I discuss this cost earlier in the chapter, too.)

Please don't construe the preceding discussion as proof that you should never listen to the Joe-Bobs of the world. The "cut prices to increase volume" strategy can work wonderfully well. The trick, however, is to increase the sales volume massively. Sam Walton, the late founder of Wal-Mart, used the strategy and became, at one point, the richest man in the world.

The Economic Order Quantity (a.k.a. Isaac Newton) Formula

Isaac Newton invented differential calculus. This fact is truly amazing to me. I can't imagine how someone could just figure out calculus. I could never, in a hundred years, figure it out. But I'm getting off the track.

The neat thing about calculus — and no, I'm not going to do any calculus here — is that it enables you to create optimal values equations. One of the coolest such equations is called the economic order quantity, or EOQ, model. I know that this stuff all sounds terribly confusing and totally boring, but stay with me for just another paragraph. (If you're not satisfied in another paragraph or so, skip ahead to the next secret formula.)

Perhaps you buy and then resell — oh, I don't know — 2,000 cases of vintage French wine every year. The EOQ model enables you to decide whether you should order all 2,000 cases at one time, order 1 case at a time, or order some number of cases in between 1 case and 2,000 cases.

Another way to say the same thing is that the EOQ model enables you to choose the best, or optimal, reorder quantity for items that you buy and then resell.

If you're still with me at this point, I figure that you want to know how this formula works. You need to know just three pieces of data to calculate the optimal order quantity: the annual sales volume, the cost of placing an order, and the annual cost of holding one unit in inventory. You plug this information into the following formula:

$$\sqrt{(2 * \text{Sales Volume} * \text{Order Cost})} / \text{Annual Holding Cost per Item}$$

You buy and resell 2,000 cases a year, so that amount is the sales volume. Every time you place an order for the wine, you need to buy an $800 round-trip ticket to Paris (just to sample the inventory) and pay $200 for a couple of nights at a hotel. So your cost per order is $1,000. Finally, with insurance, interest on a bank loan, and the cost of maintaining your hermetically sealed, temperature-controlled wine cellar, the cost of storing a case of wine is about $100 a year. In this example, then, you can calculate the optimal order quantity as follows:

$$\sqrt{(2 * 2000 * \$1000)} / \$100$$

Work through the numbers, and you get 200. Therefore, the order quantity that minimizes the total cost of your trips to Paris and of holding your expensive wine inventory is 200 cases. You could, of course, make only one trip to Paris a year and buy 2,000 cases of wine at once, thereby saving travel money; but you would spend more money on holding your expensive wine inventory than you would save on travel costs. And, although you could reduce your wine inventory carrying costs by going to Paris every week and picking up a few cases, your travel costs would go way, way up. (Of course, you would get about a billion frequent flyer miles a year.)

You can use the Standard view of the calculator to compute economic order quantities. The trick is to click the $\sqrt{}$ (square root) key last. For example, to calculate the economic order quantity in the preceding example, you enter the following numbers and operators:

2 * 2000 * 1000 / 100 $\sqrt{}$

Part IV: The Part of Tens

The Rule of 72

The Rule of 72 isn't exactly a secret formula. It's more like a rule of thumb. Usually, people use it to figure out how long it will take for some investment or savings account to double in value. The Rule of 72 is a cool little trick, however, and it has several useful applications for businesspeople.

What the rule says is that if you divide the value 72 by an interest rate percentage, your result is approximately the number of years it will take to double your money. For example, if you can stick money into some investment that pays 12 percent interest, it will take roughly six years to double your money because 72 / 12 = 6.

The Rule of 72 isn't exact, but it's usually close enough for government work. For example, if you invest $1,000 for six years at 12 percent interest, what you really get after six years isn't $2,000 but $1,973.92.

If you're in business, you can use the Rule of 72 in a couple other ways, too. If you want to forecast how long it will take inflation to double the price of an item, you can just divide 72 by the inflation rate. For example, if you own a building that you figure will at least keep up with inflation, and you wonder how long it will take to double in value if inflation runs at 4 percent, you just divide 72 by 4. The result is 18, meaning that it will take roughly 18 years for the building to double in value. Again, the Rule of 72 isn't exactly on the money, but it's dang close. A $100,000 building increases in value to $202,581.65 over 18 years if the annual inflation rate is 4 percent.

Another way that business owners can use the Rule of 72 is to forecast how long it will take to double sales volume, given some annual growth rate. For example, if you can grow your business by, say, 9 percent a year, you will roughly double the size of the business in eight years because 72 / 9 = 8. (I'm becoming kind of compulsive about this point, I know, but let me say again that the rule isn't exact, but it's very close. If a $1,000,000-a-year business grows 9 percent annually, its sales equal $1,992,562.64 after eight years of 9 percent growth. This figure really means that the business will generate roughly $2,000,000 of sales in the ninth year.)

Chapter 19
Ten Tips for Business Owners

· ·

In This Chapter
▶ Sign all your own checks

▶ Don't sign a check the wrong way

▶ Review canceled checks before your bookkeeper does

▶ How to choose a bookkeeper if you use QuickBooks

▶ Cash-basis accounting doesn't work for all businesses

▶ What to do if QuickBooks doesn't work for your business

▶ Keep things simple

· ·

*I*f you run a business and you use QuickBooks, you need to know the information in this chapter. You can find out this stuff by sitting down with your certified public accountant over a cup of coffee at $100 an hour. Or you can read this chapter.

Sign All Your Own Checks

I have nothing against your bookkeeper. In a small business, however, it's just too darn easy for people — especially full-charge bookkeepers — to bamboozle you. By signing all the checks yourself, you keep your fingers on the pulse of your cash outflow.

Yeah, I know this can be a hassle. I know this means you can't easily spend three months in Hawaii. I know this means you have to wade through paperwork every time you sign a stack of checks.

By the way, if you're in a partnership, I think that you should have at least a couple of the partners cosign checks.

Don't Sign a Check the Wrong Way

If you sign many checks, you may be tempted to use a John Hancock-like signature. Although scrawling your name illegibly makes great sense when you're autographing baseballs, don't do it when you're signing checks. A clear signature, especially one with a sense of personal style, is distinctive. A wavy line with a cross and a couple of dots is really easy to forge.

Which leads me to my next tip. . . .

Review Canceled Checks before Your Bookkeeper Does

Be sure that you review your canceled checks before anybody else sees the monthly bank statement.

This chapter isn't about browbeating bookkeepers. But a business owner can discover whether someone is forging signatures on checks only by being the first to open the bank statement and by reviewing each of the canceled check signatures.

If you don't examine the checks, unscrupulous employees — especially bookkeepers who can update the bank account records — can forge your signature with impunity. And they won't get caught if they never overdraw the account.

Another point: If you don't follow these procedures, *you* will probably eat the losses, not the bank.

Choose a Bookkeeper Who Is Familiar with Computers and Knows How to Do Payroll

Don't worry. You don't need to request an FBI background check.

In fact, if you use QuickBooks, you don't need to hire people who are familiar with small-business accounting systems. Just find people who know how to keep a checkbook and work with a computer. They shouldn't have a problem understanding QuickBooks.

Of course, you don't want someone who just fell off the turnip truck. But even if you do hire someone who rode into town on one, you're not going to have much trouble getting that person up to speed with QuickBooks.

A bookkeeper who knows double-entry bookkeeping would be super-helpful. But, to be fair, such knowledge probably isn't essential. I will say this, however: When you hire someone, find someone who knows how to do payroll — not just the federal payroll tax stuff (see Chapter 12) but also the state payroll tax monkey business.

Choose an Appropriate Accounting System

When you use QuickBooks, you use either cash-basis accounting or accrual-basis accounting. (I describe the difference between these two methods in Appendix B.)

Cash-basis accounting is fine when a business's cash inflow mirrors its sales and its cash outflow mirrors its expenses. This situation isn't the case, however, in many businesses. A contractor of single-family homes, for example, may have cash coming in (by borrowing from banks) but may not make any money. A pawnshop owner who loans money at 22 percent may make scads of money even if cash pours out of the business daily. As a general rule, when you're buying and selling inventory, accrual-basis accounting works better than cash-basis accounting.

This news may not be earthshaking, but making the switch is something that you should think about doing. Note that you can easily switch to accrual-basis accounting simply by telling QuickBooks that you want reports prepared on an accrual basis and by promptly recording customer invoices and vendor bills.

If QuickBooks Doesn't Work for Your Business

QuickBooks is a great small-business accounting program. In fact, I'd even go so far as to say that QuickBooks is probably the best small-business accounting program.

However, if QuickBooks doesn't seem to fit your needs — if, for example, you need a program that works better for a manufacturer or that includes some special industry-specific feature — you may want one of the more complicated but also more powerful small-business accounting packages.

One possibility is another popular (and more powerful) full-featured Windows accounting program: Peachtree Accounting for Windows from Peachtree. If that program doesn't work, you may want to talk to your accountant about industry-specific packages. (For example, if you're a commercial printer, some vendor might have developed a special account-ing package just for commercial printers.)

I'm amazed that PC accounting software remains so affordable. You can buy a great accounting package — one that you can use to manage a $5 million or a $25 million business — for a few hundred bucks. Accounting software is truly one of the great bargains in life.

Keep Things Simple

Let me share one last comment about managing small-business financial affairs: Keep things as simple as possible. In fact, keep your business affairs simple enough that you can easily tell whether you're making money and whether the business is healthy.

This advice may sound strange, but as a CPA, I've worked for some very bright people who have built monstrously complex financial structures for their businesses, including complicated leasing arrangements, labyrinth-like partnership and corporate structures, and sophisticated profit-sharing and cost-sharing arrangements with other businesses.

I can only offer anecdotal evidence, of course, but I strongly believe that these super-sophisticated financial arrangements don't produce a profit when you consider all the costs. What's more, these super-sophisticated arrangements almost always turn into management and record-keeping headaches.

Chapter 20

Ten Tips for All QuickBooks Users

An amazing number of people use QuickBooks for small-business accounting: dentists, contractors, lawyers, and so on. And, not surprisingly, a great number of small-business bookkeepers use QuickBooks.

If you're jumping up and down, waving your hands, saying, "I do, I do, I do," this chapter is for you. I tell you here what you need to know to make your use of QuickBooks smooth and sure.

Tricks for Learning QuickBooks If You're New on the Job

First of all, let me congratulate you on your new job. Let me also remind you of how thankful you should be that you'll be using QuickBooks and not one of the super-powerful-but-frightening, complex accounting packages.

If you're new to computers, you need to know a thing or two about them. Don't worry. Using a computer isn't as difficult as you may think. (Remember that a bunch of anxious folks have gone before you.) For a good introduction to using a computer, you can also check out a copy of *PCs For Dummies,* 5th Edition, by Dan Gookin (IDG Books Worldwide, Inc.).

Getting Started

Before you use the computer, you need to do the following:

1. **Turn on the power on the computer by either flipping the power switch or pushing the power button.**

   (The switch or button is usually either labeled "Power" or marked by a circle with a vertical line inside.)

2. **Flip a switch or push a button to turn on the monitor (the televisionlike screen).**

3. **Flip a switch to turn on the printer.**

Even if you're a little timid, go ahead and ask your boss how to turn on the computer and its peripherals. This question won't be considered stupid. You turn on different computers in different ways. For example, the switches on the computer and its peripherals may already be turned on, and the equipment may be plugged into a power strip that may be turned off. (By the way, the word peripherals refers to pieces of equipment that work with the computer, such as the printer.)

Starting QuickBooks

You use Windows to start QuickBooks. (QuickBooks 6 works on Windows 95 or later and Windows NT Version 4.0 or higher; it no longer works on Windows 3.x.) If you don't "do" Windows, refer to your *Windows User's Guide* or to one of the *Windows For Dummies* or *Small Business Windows For Dummies* books (published by IDG Books Worldwide, Inc.) for your flavor of Windows.

Windows starts on its own when you turn on the computer. After the computer finishes booting up, click the Start button and then choose Programs⇨QuickBooks⇨QuickBooks (or Programs⇨QuickBooks Pro⇨ QuickBooks Pro if you purchased the Pro version of QuickBooks), and the program starts.

Using QuickBooks

When you know how to turn on the computer and how to start QuickBooks, you're ready to rock. Give Part II of this book a quick read. Then carefully read those chapters in Part III that apply to your work, too.

One last point: Using QuickBooks is much easier than you think. Remember when you learned how to drive a car? Sure, driving was confusing at first: all those gauges and meters . . . the tremendous power at your fingertips . . . traffic. After you gained some experience, though, you loosened your death grip on the wheel. Heck, you even started driving in the left lane.

Give yourself a little time. Before long, you'll be zipping around QuickBooks, changing lanes three at a time.

Cross-Referencing Source Documents and Filing Them

Be sure to cross-reference and file (neatly!) the source documents (checks, deposit slips, and so on) that you use when you enter transactions. I won't tell you how to set up a document filing system. Chances are pretty good that you can do this better than I can — in fact, I usually use a crude, alphabetical scheme.

Invoice forms, sales receipts, and checks are all numbered, so you can cross-reference these items simply by entering form numbers when recording a check transaction.

Cross-referencing enables you to answer any questions about a transaction that appears in your QuickBooks system. All you have to do is find the source document that you used to enter the transaction.

Reconciling Bank Accounts Promptly

This one is a pet peeve, so bear with me if I get a little huffy.

I think that you should always reconcile, or balance, a business's bank accounts within a day or two after you get the bank statement. You'll catch any errors that you and the bank have made.

You also minimize the chance that you'll suffer financial losses from check forgery. If a business or individual promptly alerts a bank about a check forgery, the bank, rather than the business, suffers the loss in most cases.

Reconciling in QuickBooks is fast and easy, leaving you with no good excuse not to reconcile promptly. Chapter 13 describes how to reconcile accounts in QuickBooks.

Things You Should Do Every Month

In a business, everyone has some routine tasks: Go through the In basket. Return phone messages. Clean the coffee machine. Make macaroni and cheese for the potluck. You know.

Here are six bookkeeping chores that you should probably do at the end of every month:

1. **If the business uses a petty cash system, replenish the petty cash fund. Make sure that you have receipts for all withdrawals.**

2. **Reconcile the bank and credit card accounts.**

3. **If you're preparing payroll, be sure to remit any payroll tax deposit money owed.**

   The Internal Revenue Service can give you information about how this works for businesses in the United States.

   You may need to remit payroll tax money more frequently than monthly.

4. **Print one copy of the trial balance.**

   Set this copy aside with permanent financial records. This report enables you to answer any questions that the IRS may have about the activities in your accounts. Chapter 14 describes how to print reports.

5. **Print two copies of the monthly cash flow statement, the Profit & Loss Statement, and the balance sheet.**

   Give one copy to the business's owner or manager. Put the other copy with the permanent financial records.

6. **If you haven't done so already during the month, back up the file containing the QuickBooks accounts to a floppy disk.**

   You can reuse the floppy disk every other month. Chapter 15 describes how to back up files.

Don't view the preceding list as all-inclusive. You may need to do other tasks, too. I'd hate for people to say, "Well, it doesn't appear on Nelson's list, so I don't have to do it." Yikes!

Things You Should Do Every Year

Here are the things that I think you should do at the end of every year:

1. **Do all the usual end-of-month chores for the last month in the year.**

    See the list in the preceding section.

2. **Prepare and file any state and federal end-of-year payroll tax returns.**

    Businesses in the United States, for example, need to prepare the annual federal unemployment tax return (Form 940).

3. **Print two copies of the annual cash flow statement, the annual Profit & Loss Statement, and the year-end balance sheet.**

    Give one copy to the business's owner or manager. Put the other copy with the permanent financial records.

4. **Print a copy of the year-end trial balance.**

    This report helps whoever prepares the corporate tax return.

5. **Back up the file containing the QuickBooks accounts to a floppy disk.**

    Store the floppy disk as a permanent archive copy.

6. **Be sure to prepare and distribute any of the informational returns that the tax people want: W-2s, 1099s, and so on.**

If you need help or have questions about these tax forms, call the local Internal Revenue Service office or check out *Taxes For Dummies* by Eric Tyson (IDG Books Worldwide, Inc.). If you're nervous and don't want the IRS tracing the call, telephone them from a phone booth.

Again, don't view the preceding list as all-inclusive. If you think of other tasks, do them.

Using Debits and Credits

If you've worked with a regular small-business accounting system, you may miss your old friends, debit and credit. (Is it just me, or do debit and credit sound like the neighbor kid's pet frogs to you, too?)

QuickBooks is a double-entry accounting system, but it doesn't require you to work with debits and credits. If you want to work with debits and credits — maybe you enjoy creating journal entries — you can use the General Journal Entry window, where you can make journal entries till the cows come home. To display this window, click the Taxes and Accountant tab of the QuickBooks Navigator and then click the Make Journal Entry icon.

Converting to QuickBooks

If you're converting to QuickBooks from a manual system or from another more complicated small-business accounting system, here are two important tips:

✔ Start using QuickBooks at the beginning of a year. The year's financial records are then in one place — in the QuickBooks system.

✔ If it's not the beginning of the year, go back and enter the year's transactions. Again, the year's financial records are then in one place — in the QuickBooks system. (Entering the transactions takes quite a bit of time if you have many transactions to enter. In fact, you may want to postpone your conversion to QuickBooks to the beginning of the following year.)

Income Tax Evasion

A nice fellow wandered into my office the other day and told me that he had inadvertently gotten entangled in his employer's income tax evasion. He didn't know what to do.

He had (unwittingly, he said) helped his employer file fraudulent income tax returns. Then, already sucked into the tar pit, he had lied to the IRS during an audit.

I didn't have anything good to tell him.

I never did get the fellow's name, so I'll just call him Chump.

Helping his employer steal really didn't make any financial sense for Chump. Chump didn't get a share of the loot; he just helped his employer commit a felony. For free.

Although Chump didn't receive (supposedly) any of the booty, he's probably still in serious trouble with the IRS. The criminal penalties can be enormous, and prison, I understand, is not fun.

I'm not going to spend any more time talking about this. But I do have a piece of advice for you: Don't be a Chump.

Segregating Payroll Tax Money

While I'm on the subject of terrible things that the IRS can do to you, let me touch on the problem of payroll tax deposits — the money you withhold from employee checks for federal income taxes, social security, and Medicare.

If you have the authority to spend the money you withhold, don't — even if the company will go out of business if you don't. If you can't repay the payroll tax money, the IRS will go after the business owners and also after you.

It doesn't matter that you're just the bookkeeper, it doesn't matter whether you regularly attend church, and it doesn't matter whether you remember your spouse's birthday (which, if you don't, is a whole different kind of trouble). The IRS doesn't take kindly to people who take what belongs to the federal government.

By the way, I should mention that the IRS is more lenient in cases in which you don't have any authority to dip into the payroll tax money and the business owner or your boss uses the tax money. If you see that someone else is using the tax money, however, be darn careful not to get involved. And start looking for a new job.

Chapter 21

Tips for Handling Ten Tricky Situations

● ●

In This Chapter

▶ Selling an asset

▶ Tracking owner's equity

▶ Doing multiple-state accounting

▶ Obtaining and repaying loans

● ●

*A*s your business grows and becomes more complex, your accounting does, too. I can't describe and discuss all the complexities you'll encounter, but I can give you some tips on handling (just about) ten tricky situations.

In QuickBooks, you make journal entries by using the General Journal Entry window. If you don't understand double-entry bookkeeping but you'd like to, or if you want help with using the General Journal Entry window, take a gander at Appendix B.

To track the depreciation of an asset that you've already purchased (and added to the chart of accounts), you need two new accounts: an asset account called something like Accumulated Depreciation and an expense account called something like Depreciation Expense.

After you set up these two accounts, you can record the asset depreciation with a journal entry such as the following one that records $500 of depreciation expense:

	Debit	*Credit*
Depreciation expense	$500	
Accumulated depreciation		$500

The federal tax laws provide a special form of depreciation called Section 179 depreciation. Section 179 depreciation enables you to depreciate the entire cost of some assets, which is a big break for small businesses. You can't, however, use more than $18,500 of Section 179 depreciation in a year. You also need to know about some other nitty-gritty details, so confer with your tax adviser if you have questions.

Selling an Asset

When you sell an asset, you need to back out (get rid of) the asset's account balance, record the payment of the cash (or whatever) that somebody pays you for the asset, and record any difference between what you sell the asset for and its value as a gain or loss.

If you purchase a piece of land for $5,000 but later resell it for $4,000, for example, you use the following journal entry to record the sale of this asset:

	Debit	*Credit*
Cash	$4,000	
Loss	$1,000	
Asset		$5,000

Note: You may need to set up another income account for the gain or another expense account for the loss. Refer to Chapter 1 for information on setting up new accounts.

Selling a Depreciable Asset

Selling a depreciable asset works almost identically to selling an asset that you haven't been depreciating. When you sell the asset, you need to back out (or get rid of) the asset's account balance. You need to back out (or get rid of) the asset's accumulated depreciation. (This part of selling a depreciable asset is the only thing that's different from selling an asset that you haven't been depreciating.) You need to record the payment of the cash (or whatever) that somebody pays you for the asset. Finally, any difference between what you sell the asset for and what its net-of-accumulated-depreciation value is gets counted as a gain or loss.

This process sounds terribly complicated, but an example will help. Suppose that you purchased a $5,000 piece of machinery and have accumulated $500 of depreciation thus far. This means that the asset account shows a $5,000 debit balance and that the asset's accumulated depreciation account shows a $500 credit balance. Suppose also that you sell the machinery for $4,750 in cash.

To record the sale of this depreciable asset, you would use the following journal entry:

	Debit	*Credit*
Cash	$4,750	
Accumulated depreciation	$500	
Asset		$5,000
Gain		$250

Owner's Equity in a Sole Proprietorship

Actually, tracking owner's equity in a sole proprietorship is easy. You can use the single account that QuickBooks sets up for you, called Opening Bal Equity, to track what you've invested in the business. (You may want to rename this account something like Contributed Capital.)

To track the money you withdraw from the business, you can set up and use a new owner's equity account called something like Owner's Draws. Table 21-1 gives an example of owner's equity accounts in a sole proprietorship.

Table 21-1	An Example of Owner's Equity Accounts in a Sole Proprietorship
Account	*Amount*
Contributed capital	$5,000
Retained earnings	$8,000
Owner's draws	($2,000)
Owner's equity (total)	$11,000

Owner's Equity in a Partnership

To track the equity for each partner in a partnership, you need to create three accounts for each partner: one for the partner's contributed capital, one for the partner's draws, and one for the partner's share of the distributed income.

Amounts that a partner withdraws, of course, get tracked with the partner's draws account.

The partner's share of the partnership's profits gets allocated to the partner's profit share account. (Your partnership agreement, by the way, should say how the partnership income is distributed among the partners.) Table 21-2 gives an example of owner's equity accounts in a partnership.

Table 21-2   An Example of Owners Equity Accounts in a Partnership

Account	Partner A's Amount	Partner B's Amount
Contributed capital	$5,000	$7,000
Profit share	$6,000	$6,000
Draws	($3,000)	($4,000)
Equity (total)	$8,000	$9,000

Owner's Equity in a Corporation

Yikes! Accounting for the owner's equity in a corporation can get mighty tricky mighty fast. In fact, I don't mind telling you that college accounting textbooks often use several chapters to describe all the ins and outs of corporation owner's equity accounting.

As long as you keep things simple, however, you can probably use three or four accounts for your owner's equity:

- A *par value* account. You get the par value amount by multiplying the par value per share by the number of shares issued.

- A *paid-in capital in excess of par value* account for the amount investors paid for shares of stock in excess of par value. You get this amount by multiplying the price paid per share less the par value per share by the number of shares issued.

- A *retained earnings* account to track the business profits left invested in the business.

- A *dividends paid* account to track the amounts distributed to shareholders.

Table 21-3 is an example of owner's equity accounts in a corporation.

Table 21-3	An Example of Owner's Equity in a Corporation
Account	**Amount**
Par value	$500
Paid-in capital in excess of par value	$4,500
Retained earnings	$8,000
Dividends paid	($3,000)
Shareholder's equity	$10,000

Multiple-State Accounting

For multiple-state accounting, the best approach is to set up a chart of accounts that includes a complete set of income and expense accounts (and, if necessary, a complete set of asset and liability accounts) for each state. After you set up this chart of accounts, all you have to do is use the correct state's income and expense accounts to record transactions.

If you do business in both Washington and Oregon, for example, sales in Oregon would be recorded as Oregon sales, and sales in Washington would be recorded as Washington sales. You would treat other income accounts and all your expense accounts in the same way.

Getting a Loan

Getting a loan is the hard part. After you get the money, recording it in QuickBooks is easy. All you do is record a journal entry that increases cash and that recognizes the new loan liability. For example, if you get a $5,000 loan, you record the following journal entry:

	Debit	*Credit*
Cash	$5,000	
Loan payable		$5,000

Note: You'll already have a cash account set up, but you may need to set up a new liability account to track the loan.

Repaying a Loan

To record loan payments, you need to split each payment between two accounts: the interest expense account and the loan payable account. For example, suppose that you're making $75-a-month payments on a $5,000 loan. Also, suppose that the lender charges 1 percent interest each month. The following journal entry records the first month's loan payment:

	Debit	*Credit*	*Explanation*
Interest expense	$50		Calculated as 1 percent of $5,000
Loan payable	$25		The amount leftover and applied to principal
Cash		$75	The total payment amount

The next month, of course, the loan balance is slightly less (because you've made a $25 dent in the loan payment, as shown in the preceding loan payment journal entry). The following journal entry records the second month's loan payment:

	Debit	*Credit*	*Explanation*
Interest expense	$49.75		Calculated as 1 percent of $4,975, the new loan balance
Loan payable	$25.25		The amount leftover and applied to principal
Cash		$75.00	The total payment amount

Get the lender to provide you with an amortization schedule that shows the breakdown of each payment into interest expense and loan principal reduction.

Note: You can record loan payments by using either the Write Checks window or the Enter Bills window. Just use the Expenses tab to specify the interest expense account and the loan liability account.

Part V

Appendixes

The 5th Wave   By Rich Tennant

With this accounting program, I understand the "accrual-basis accounting" and the "accounts payable" part pretty well. It's that darn "2% 10 Net 30" payment term that stumps me.

In this part . . .

Appendixes are like basements. Why? You use them to store stuff that you want to keep but don't know where else to put. The appendixes that follow provide instructions for installing QuickBooks, an overview of accounting, help with project estimating, and a description of the QuickBooks Timer program.

Appendix A

How to Install QuickBooks in Eleven Easy Steps

• •

1 f you haven't already installed QuickBooks, get it over with right now.

1. **Turn on the PC.**

   Find and flip on the computer's power switch. (Depending on whether you're using Windows 95, 98, or NT, your screen may look a little different than the figures here.)

2. **Get the QuickBooks CD or disks.**

   Rip open the QuickBooks package and get out the CD (which looks exactly like the ones that play music) or the disks (those plastic $3^1/_2$ - inch squares).

   QuickBooks, like most other programs nowadays, is sold in stores only on CD. If you don't have a CD-ROM drive, you can order a copy of QuickBooks on floppy disks from Intuit (call 1-800-446-8848) or visit the Intuit Web site at www.intuit.com.

3. **Insert the CD in your CD-ROM drive or the first disk in your floppy disk drive.**

   If you're installing from a CD and have any amount of luck, Windows recognizes that you've inserted the QuickBooks CD and displays a dialog box (see Figure A-1) that asks if you want to install QuickBooks from the CD. Click the Install button and skip to Step 7.

   Click the button next to Other Installation Options to install QuickBooks, Internet Explorer, or Timer individually.

4. **If nothing happened when you inserted the QuickBooks CD or if you're installing from floppy disks, open the Control Panel window.**

   Click the Start button and then choose Settings⇨Control Panel from the Start menu. Figure A-2 shows the Control Panel window that appears.

Figure A-1:
The
QuickBooks
CD dialog
box on the
Windows
desktop.

Figure A-2:
The Control
Panel —
sort of
like the
bridge of
Star Trek.

5. Start the Windows Install program.

Double-click the Add/Remove Programs icon. When the dialog box in
Figure A-3 appears, click Install.

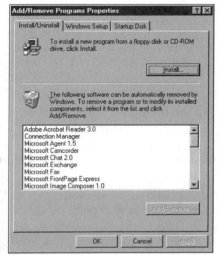

Figure A-3:
Ready to
install the
program,
Captain.

6. **Click Next.**

   The program searches through your drives, looking for Intuit's Install
   program. When it finds it, it stops and asks you if it has found the right
   one (see Figure A-4).The installation program is usually right, so go
   ahead and click Finish.

Figure A-4:
You're
almost
done!

If you're installing QuickBooks from a CD, Windows may not notice the
CD when you first click the Next button. That's because CD-ROM drives
are like your car when it's freezing outside — slow, slow, slow; the disk
drive may not have been ready when you clicked the Next button. If
Windows tells you that it can't find the installation program, click the
Back button to return to the first Add/Remove Programs window and
then click the Next button again. By this time, Windows has probably
noticed that you really do have a CD in your computer's drive.

7. **Tell QuickBooks how you want it to install itself.**

   The QuickBooks setup appears. Click Next to begin the installation process. Then follow the on-screen instructions. If you have a question about an installation option, just accept the QuickBooks suggestion by pressing Enter. (The suggested, or default, installation options are fine for 999 out of 1,000 users.)

8. **Click Next to begin copying the files.**

   QuickBooks gives you a summary of your installation choices and then tells you to click Next to begin copying the files. Do so. As the installation program runs, you should see a little bar that shows your progress.

   If you need to cancel the installation at any time, click Cancel. QuickBooks warns you that the setup is incomplete. That's okay — you just start the setup from scratch next time around.

   If you're installing QuickBooks from disks, QuickBooks asks you to remove one disk, insert another disk, and then press Enter. You'd better do what it says, or QuickBooks won't do what you want — that's Intuit's Golden Rule.

9. **Take 30 seconds or so to contemplate the meaning of life or get a drink of water.**

10. **After the Install program finishes, click Finish and restart Windows (if necessary).**

    Congratulations. You're finished with the installation. You have a new item on the Programs menu: QuickBooks (or QuickBooks Pro).

11. **(Optional) Celebrate.**

    Stand up at your desk, click your heels together three times, and repeat the phrase, "There's no place like home, Toto; there's no place like home." And watch out for flying houses.

As soon as you're done celebrating, you may want to flip to Chapter 1 and find out how to register the program. You'll probably want to register QuickBooks before you begin using it.

If you work on a network and want to be able to share a QuickBooks file using more than one computer on the network, you need to install QuickBooks on all of the other computers that you want to use to work with the file. (Note that you need a separate copy of QuickBooks — such as from the 5-pack version — for each computer on which you want to install QuickBooks.)

If Numbers Are Your Friends

• •

*Y*ou don't need to know much about accounting or about double-entry bookkeeping to use QuickBooks, which, as you know, is most of its appeal. But if you're serious about this accounting business or serious about your business, consider finding out a bit more; setting up QuickBooks and understanding all the QuickBooks reports will be easier, and you'll be more sophisticated in your accounting, too.

Keying In on Profit

Start with the big picture. The key purpose of an accounting system is to enable you to answer the burning question, "Am I making any money?"

Accounting is that simple. Really. So the rest of this appendix just talks about how to calculate a business's profits in a reasonably accurate but still practical manner.

Let me introduce you to the new you

To make this whole discussion more concrete, I'm going to use an example. You just moved to Montana for the laid-back living and fresh air. You live in a cute log cabin on Flathead Lake. To support yourself, you plan to purchase several rowboats and rent them to visiting fly fishermen. Of course, you'll probably need to do quite a bit of fly-fishing, too. But just consider that burden part of the price of being your own boss.

The first day in business

It's your first day in business. About 5 a.m., ol' Peter Gruntpaw shows up to deliver your three rowboats. He made them for you in his barn, but even so, they aren't cheap. He charges $1,500 apiece, so you write him a check for $4,500.

Peter's timing, as usual, is impeccable. About 5:15 a.m., your first customers arrive. Mr. and Mrs. Hamster (pronounced ohm-stair) are visiting from Phoenix. They want to catch the big fish. You're a bit unsure of your pricing, but you suggest $25 an hour for the boat. They agree and pay $200 in cash for eight hours.

A few minutes later, another couple arrives. The Gerbils (pronounced go-bells) are very agitated. They were supposed to meet the Hamsters and fish together, but the Hamsters are rowing farther and farther away from the dock. To speed the Gerbils' departure, you let them leave without paying. But you're not worried. As the Gerbils leave the dock, Ms. Gerbil shouts, "We'll pay you the $200 when we get back!"

Although you don't rent the third boat, you do enjoy a sleepy summer morning.

About 2 p.m., the Hamsters and Gerbils come rowing back into view. Obviously, though, a problem has occurred. You find out what it is when the first boat arrives. "Gerbil fell into the lake," laughs Mr. Hamster. "Lost his wallet, too." Everybody else seems to think that the lost wallet is funny. You secretly wonder how you're going to get paid. No wallet, no money.

You ask Mr. Gerbil if he would like to come out to the lake tomorrow to pay you. He says he'll just write you a check when he gets home to Phoenix. Reluctantly, you agree.

Look at your cash flow first

I have just described a fairly simple situation. But even so, answering the question, "Did I make any money?" is not going to be easy. You start by looking at your cash flow: You wrote a check for $4,500, and you collected $200 in cash. Table B-1 shows your cash flow.

Table B-1	The First Day's Cash Flow
Cash In and Out	*Amount*
Add the cash in:	
Rent money from Hamsters (pronounced ohm-stairs)	$200
Rent money from Gerbils (pronounced go-bells)	$0
Subtract the cash out:	
Money to purchase rowboats	($4,500)
Equals your cash flow:	($4,300)

To summarize, you had $200 come in but $4,500 go out. So your cash flow was -$4,300 (that's why the $4,300 is in parentheses). From a strictly cash-flow perspective, the first day doesn't look all that good, right? But does the cash flow calculation show you whether you're making money? Can you look at it and gauge whether your little business is on the right track?

The answer to both questions is *no*. Your cash flow is important. You can't, for example, write a $4,500 check unless you have at least $4,500 in your checking account. But your cash flow doesn't tell you whether you're making money. In fact, you may see a couple of problems with looking just at the cash flow of the rowboat rental business.

Depreciation is an accounting gimmick

Here's the first problem: If you take good care of the rowboats, you can use them every summer for the next few years. In fact, say that the rowboat rental season, which runs from early spring to late autumn, is 150 days long and that your well-made rowboats will last ten years. In this case, you can rent the rowboats for 1,500 days (150 days a year times 10 years equals 1,500 days). If your rowboats each cost $1,500 and you can rent them 1,500 times, counting only $1 per day of a rowboat's cost is more accurate in a profit calculation.

Do you see what I'm saying? If you have something that costs a great deal of money but lasts for a long time, spreading out the cost makes sense. This spreading out is usually called *depreciation*. The little $1 chunks that are allocated to a day are called the *depreciation expense*.

Note: Accountants use the terms cost and expense differently. A *cost* is the price you pay for something. If you pay Peter Gruntpaw $1,500 for a rowboat, the rowboat's cost is $1,500. An *expense,* on the other hand, is what you use in a profit calculation. The little $1 chunks of the rowboat's $1,500 cost (that are allocated to individual days) are expenses.

If this depreciation stuff seems wacky, remember that what you're really trying to do is figure out whether you made any money your first day of business. And all I'm really saying is that you shouldn't include the whole cost of the rowboats as an expense in the first day's profit calculation. Some of the cost should be included as an expense in calculating the profit in future days. That's fair, right?

Accrual-basis accounting is cool

You don't want to forget about the $200 that the Gerbils owe you either. Although Mr. Gerbil (remember that the name's pronounced go-bell) may not send you the check for several days, or even for several weeks, he will pay you. You've earned the money.

Different names, same logic

I don't see any point in hiding this nasty little accounting secret from you: Accountants call this cost-allocation process by different names, depending on what sort of cost is being spread out.

Most of the time, the cost allocation is called *depreciation*. You depreciate buildings, machinery, furniture, and many other items as well. But allocating the cost of a natural resource — such as crude oil that you pump, coal that you dig up, or minerals that you extract — is called *depletion*. And allocating the cost of things that aren't tangible — copyrights and patents, for example — is *amortization*.

This circumstance brings up another very important point. The principles of accounting say that you should include sales in your profit calculations when you earn the money and not when you actually collect it. The logic behind this "include sales when they're earned" rule is that it produces a better estimate of the business you're doing.

I want to show you how this rule works. Say that the day after the Gerbils and Hamsters rent the rowboats, you have no customers, but Mr. Gerbil comes out and pays you $200. If you use the "include sales when they're earned" rule — or what's called *accrual-basis accounting* — your daily sales look like this:

	Day 1	Day 2
Sales	$400	$0

If you instead use what's called *cash-basis accounting* (in which you count sales when you collect the cash), your daily sales look like this:

	Day 1	Day 2
Sales	$200	$200

Please, please, please notice that the traditional accounting method shows that you have a good day when you rent two boats and a terrible day when you don't rent any boats. In comparison, when you use cash-basis accounting, both days look the same. Your sales record looks as if you rented a boat each day. Now you know why accrual-basis accounting is a better way to measure profit.

By the way, accrual-basis accounting also works for expenses. The idea is that you should count an expense when you make it, not when you pay it.

For example, you call the local radio station and ask the people there to announce your new boat rental business a couple of times for a fee of $25. Although you do not have to pay the radio station the day you make the arrangements for your announcement, you should still count the $25 as an expense for that day.

Now you know how to measure profits

With what you now know, you're ready to measure the first day's profits. Table B-2 is a Profit & Loss Statement for the first day.

Table B-2	A Profit & Loss Statement for the First Day	
Description	*Amount*	*Explanation*
Sales	$400	Rental money from the Hamsters and the Gerbils
Expenses		
Depreciation	$3	3 rowboats x $1/day depreciation
Advertising	$25	Radio advertising
Total expenses	$28	Depreciation expense plus the advertising
Profit	$372	Sales minus the total expenses

Please notice that although the first day's cash flow was terrible, your little business is quite profitable. In fact, if you really do make about $370 a day, you'll recoup your entire $4,500 investment in less than three weeks. That's pretty darn good.

Some financial brain food

Now that you know how to measure profits, I can fill you in on some important conceptual stuff.

Here's the first concept (and it's so simple, too): You measure profits for a specific period of time. In the rowboat business example, you measured the profits for a day. Some people actually do measure profits (or they try to measure profits) on a daily basis. But most times, people use bigger chunks of time. Monthly chunks of time are common, for example. And so are three-month chunks of time. Everybody measures profits annually — if only because the government makes you do so for income tax accounting.

When people start talking about how often and for what chunks of time you measure profits, they use a couple of terms. The year you calculate profits for is called the *fiscal year*. The smaller chunks of time for which you measure profits over the year are called *accounting periods* or *interim accounting periods.* (You don't need to memorize the two new terms. But now that you've read them, you'll probably remember them.)

One other thing that I want to say may be obvious, but it's important nonetheless. The length of your accounting periods involves an awkward trade-off. Daily profit and loss calculations show you how well you did at the end of every day, but you have to collect the data and do the work every day. And preparing a Profit & Loss Statement is a great deal of work. (I made the example purposefully easy by including only a few transactions, but in real life, you have many more transactions to worry about and fiddle with.)

If you use a quarterly interim accounting period, you don't have to collect the raw data and do the arithmetic very often, but you know how you're doing only every once in a while. In my mind, checking your profits only four times a year isn't enough. A great deal can happen in three months.

In the Old Days, Things Were Different

If you're new to the arithmetic and logic of profit calculation — which is mostly what modern accounting is all about — you won't be surprised to hear that not all that long ago, most people couldn't and didn't do much profit calculating.

What they did instead was monitor a business's financial condition. They used — well, actually, they still use — a balance sheet to monitor the financial condition. A balance sheet just lists a business's assets and its liabilities at a particular point in time.

For example, say that at the start of your first day in the rowboat rental business — before you pay Peter Gruntpaw — you have $5,000 in your checking account. To make the situation interesting, $4,000 of this money is a loan from your mother-in-law, and $1,000 is cash that you have invested in your business. Your balance sheet at the beginning of the day looks like the one in Table B-3.

Table B-3	The Balance Sheet at the Beginning of the Day	
Description	*Amount*	*Explanation*
Assets		
Cash	$5,000	The checking account balance
Total assets	$5,000	Your only asset is cash, so it's your total, too

Description	Amount	Explanation
Liabilities and owner's equity		
Loan payable	$4,000	The loan from your mother-in-law
Total liabilities	$4,000	Your only liability is that crazy loan
Owner's equity	$1,000	The $1,000 you put in
Total liabilities and owner's equity	$5,000	The total liabilities plus the owner's equity

If you construct a balance sheet at the end of the first day, the financial picture is only slightly more complicated. Some of these explanations are too complicated to give in a sentence, so the paragraphs that follow describe how I got each number.

Note: Even if you don't pay all that much attention, I recommend that you quickly read through the explanations. Mostly, I want you to understand that if you try to monitor a business's financial condition by using a balance sheet, as I've done here, the picture gets messy. Later in this appendix, I talk about how QuickBooks makes all this stuff easier.

Table B-4 shows the balance sheet at the end of the first day.

Table B-4	The Balance Sheet at the End of the Day
Description	Amount
Assets	
Cash	$700
Receivable	$200
Rowboats	$4,497
Total assets	$5,397
Liabilities and owner's equity	
Payable	$25
Loan payable	$4,000
Total liabilities	$4,025
Owner's equity	$1,000
Retained earnings	$372
Total liabilities and owner's equity	$5,397

Cash is the most complicated line item to prove. If you were really in the rowboat rental business, of course, you could just look at your checkbook. But if you were writing an appendix about being in the rowboat rental business — as I am — you would need to be able to calculate the cash balance. Table B-5 shows the calculation of the cash balance for your rowboat rental business. The $200 receivable is just the money the Gerbils owe you.

Table B-5	The First Day's Cash Flow		
Description	*Payment*	*Deposit*	*Balance*
Initial investment		$1,000	$1,000
Loan from mother-in-law		$4,000	$5,000
Rowboat purchase	$4,500		$500
Cash from Hamsters		$200	$700

The Rowboats balance sheet value is $4,497 — which is weird, I'll grant you. But here's how you figure it: You take the original cost of the asset and deduct all the depreciation expense that you've charged to date. The original cost of the three rowboats was $4,500. You've charged only $3 of depreciation for the first day, so the balance sheet value, or net book value, is $4,497.

The only liabilities are the $25 you owe the radio station for those new business announcements and that $4,000 you borrowed from your mother-in-law. I won't even ask why you opened that can of worms.

Finally, the owner's equity section of the balance sheet shows the $1,000 you originally contributed and also the $372 of money you earned.

It's not a coincidence that the total assets value equals the total liabilities and total owner's equity value. If you correctly calculate each of the numbers that go on the balance sheet, the two totals are always equal.

Here's another point to remember: A balance sheet lists asset, liability, and owner's equity balances on a specific date. It gives you a financial snapshot at a point in time. Normally, you prepare a balance sheet whenever you prepare a Profit & Loss Statement. The balance sheet shows account balances for the last day of the fiscal year and interim accounting period. (I think it's kind of neat that after only a few pages of this appendix you're reading and understanding terms such as fiscal year and interim accounting period.)

What Does an Italian Monk Have to Do with Anything?

So far, I've provided narrative descriptions of all the financial events that affect the balance sheet and the income statement. For example, I described how you started the business with $5,000 of cash (a $4,000 loan from your mother-in-law and $1,000 of cash you yourself invested). At an even earlier point in this appendix, I noted how you rented a boat to the Hamsters for $200, and they paid you in cash.

Although the narrative descriptions of financial events — such as starting the business or renting to the Hamsters — make for just-bearable reading, they are unwieldy for accountants to use in practice. Partly, this awkwardness is because accountants are usually (or maybe always?) terrible writers. But an even bigger problem is that using the lots-and-lots-of-words approach makes describing all the little bits and pieces of information that you need difficult and downright tedious.

Fortunately, about 500 years ago an Italian monk named Lucia Pacioli thought the same thing. No, I'm not making this up. Five hundred years after the fact, what this monk did is a little unclear. But according to one group, Pacioli developed the double-entry bookkeeping system. (According to the other group, by the way, Pacioli just described the system the Venetian merchants were already using. But I'm not one to cast stones at a dead accounting hero.)

In either case, however, what Pacioli really said was, "Hey, guys. Hello? Is anybody in there? You have to get more efficient in the way that you describe your financial transactions. You have to create a financial shorthand system that works when you have a large number of transactions to record." Pacioli then proceeded to describe a financial shorthand system that made it easy to collect all the little bits and pieces of information needed to prepare income statements and balance sheets. The shorthand system he described? Double-entry bookkeeping.

His system is simplicity itself. Really. All he said was that rather than using a wordy explanation for every financial transaction, people should name the income statement or balance sheet line items or accounts that are affected and then give the dollar amount of the effect. The Profit & Loss Statement and the balance sheet line items are called *accounts.* You need to remember this term. (Just for your information, a list of Profit & Loss Statement and balance sheet line items is called a *chart of accounts.* You may already know this term from using QuickBooks.)

Pacioli also did one wacky thing. He used a couple of new terms — debit and credit — to describe the increases and decreases in accounts. Increases in asset accounts and in expense accounts are *debits,* and decreases in asset and expense accounts are *credits.* Increases in liability, owner's equity, and income accounts are credits, and decreases in liability, owner's equity, and income accounts are debits. Keeping these terms straight is a bit confusing, so Table B-6 may help you.

I'm sorry to have to tell you this, but if you want to use double-entry book-keeping, you need to memorize the information in Table B-6. If it's any consolation, this information is the only chunk of data in the entire book that I ask you to memorize. Or, failing that, mark this page — with a dog ear, for example — so that you can flip here quickly, or just refer to the Cheat Sheet.

Table B-6 The Only Stuff in This Book That I Ask You to Memorize

Account Type	Debits	Credits
Assets	Increase asset accounts	Decrease asset accounts
Liabilities	Decrease liability accounts	Increase liability accounts
Owner's equity	Decrease owner's accounts	Increase owner's equity accounts
Income	Decrease income accounts	Increase income accounts
Expenses	Increase expense accounts	Decrease expense accounts

And now for the blow-by-blow

The best way to learn this double-entry bookkeeping stuff is to show you how to use it to record all the financial events discussed thus far in this appendix. Start with the money that you have invested in the business and the money that you foolishly borrowed from your mother-in-law. You invested $1,000 in cash, and you borrowed $4,000 in cash. Here are the double-entry bookkeeping transactions — called journal entries, in case you care — that describe these financial events.

Journal entry 1: To record your $1,000 investment

	Debit	Credit
Cash	$1,000	
Owner's equity		$1,000

Journal entry 2: To record the $4,000 loan from your mother-in-law

	Debit	Credit
Cash	$4,000	
Loan payable to mother-in-law		$4,000

Journal entries are very cool for a simple reason. If you add up all the debits and credits, you get something called a trial balance. A *trial balance* isn't all that special — it's just a list of accounts and their debit or credit balance. But with a trial balance, you can easily prepare Profit & Loss Statements and balance sheets. For example, if you add up the debits and credits shown in journal entries 1 and 2, you get the trial balance shown in Table B-7.

Table B-7	Your First Trial Balance	
	Debit	Credit
Cash	$5,000	
Loan payable to mother-in-law		$4,000
Owner's equity		$1,000

This trial balance provides the raw data needed to construct the rowboat business balance sheet at the start of the first day. If you don't believe me, take a peek at Table B-3. Oh sure, the information shown in Table B-7 isn't as polished. Table B-7 doesn't provide labels, for example, that tell you that cash is an asset. And Table B-7 doesn't provide subtotals showing the total assets (equal to $5,000) and the total liabilities and owner's equity (also equal to $5,000). But it does provide the raw data.

Take a look at the journal entries you would make to record the rest of the first day's financial events:

Journal entry 3: To record the purchase of the three $1,500 rowboats

	Debit	Credit
Rowboats	$4,500	
Cash		$4,500

Journal entry 4: To record the rental to the Hamsters

	Debit	Credit
Cash	$200	
Sales		$200

Journal entry 5: To record the rental to the Gerbils

	Debit	Credit
Receivable	$200	
Sales		$200

Journal entry 6: To record the $25 radio advertisement

	Debit	Credit
Advertising expense	$25	
Payable		$25

Journal entry 7: To record the $3 of rowboat depreciation

	Debit	Credit
Depreciation expense	$3	
Accumulated depreciation		$3

To build a trial balance for the end of the first day, you add all the first day journal entries to the trial balance shown in Table B-7. The result is the trial balance shown in Table B-8.

Table B-8   The Trial Balance at the End of the First Day

	Debit	Credit
Balance sheet accounts		
Cash	$700	
Receivable	$200	
Rowboats — cost	$4,500	
Accumulated depreciation		$3
Payable		$25
Loan payable		$4,000
Owner's equity		$1,000
Profit & Loss Statement accounts		
Sales		$400
Depreciation expense	$3	
Advertising expense	$25	

The trial balance shown in Table B-8 provides the raw data used to prepare the balance sheet and Profit & Loss Statement for the first day.

If you look at the accounts labeled "Balance sheet accounts" in Table B-8 and compare these to the balance sheet shown in Table B-4, you see that this trial balance provides all the raw numbers needed for the balance sheet. The only numbers in Table B-4 that aren't directly from Table B-8 are the subtotals you get by adding up other numbers.

If you look at the accounts labeled as "Profit & Loss Statement accounts" in Table B-8 and compare them to the Profit & Loss Statement shown in Table B-2, you see that this trial balance also provides all the raw numbers needed for the Profit & Loss Statement. Again, the only numbers in Table B-2 that aren't directly from Table B-8 are the subtotals you get by adding up other numbers.

Blow-by-blow, part II

If you understand what I've discussed so far, you grasp how accounting and double-entry bookkeeping work. I want to show you about a half dozen more example transactions, however, to plug a few minor holes in your knowledge.

When you collect money you've previously billed, you record the transaction by debiting cash and crediting *receivables* (or accounts receivable). In the rowboat business, for example, you make this basic entry when Mr. Gerbil later pays you the $200 he owes you for the first day's rental.

Journal entry 8: To record a payment by a customer

	Debit	*Credit*
Cash	$200	
Receivable		$200

Notice that you don't record a sale when you collect the cash. The sale has already been recorded in journal entry 5.

When you pay the radio station for the advertising, you record the transaction by debiting accounts payable and crediting cash.

Journal entry 9: To record your payment of $25 to the radio station

	Debit	*Credit*
Payable	$25	
Cash		$25

The one other thing I want to cover — ever so briefly — is inventory accounting. Accounting for items you buy and resell or the items you make and resell is a bit trickier. And I don't have room to go into a great deal of detail.

When you buy items to resell, you debit an asset account, often named Inventory. If you purchase 300 of the $10 thingamajigs you hope to resell for $25 each, you record the following journal entry:

Journal entry 10: To record the cash purchase of thingamajigs

	Debit	Credit
Inventory	$3,000	
Cash		$3,000

When you sell a thingamajig, you need to do two tasks: record the sale and record the cost of the sale. If you need to record the sale of 100 thingamajigs for $25, for example, you record the following journal entry:

Journal entry 11: To record the sale of 100 thingamajigs for $25 apiece

	Debit	Credit
Receivable	$2,500	
Sales		$2,500

You also need to record the cost of the thingamajigs that you've sold as an expense and record the reduction in the value of your thingamajig inventory. If you reduce your inventory count from 300 items to 200 items, for example, you need to adjust your inventory's dollar value. You record the following journal entry:

Journal entry 12: To record the cost of the 100 thingamajigs sold

	Debit	Credit
Cost of goods sold	$1,000	
Inventory		$1,000

The cost of goods sold account, by the way, is just another expense. It appears on your Profit & Loss Statement.

How Does QuickBooks Help?

If you (or someone else) keep the books for your business manually, you have to actually make these journal entries. But if you use QuickBooks to keep the books, all this debiting and crediting business usually goes on behind the scenes. When you invoice a customer, QuickBooks debits accounts receivable and credits sales. When you write a check to pay some bill, QuickBooks debits the expense (or the accounts payable account) and credits cash.

In the few cases in which a financial transaction isn't recorded automatically when you fill in some on-screen form, you need to use the General Journal Entry window. To display the General Journal Entry window, shown in Figure B-1, click the Taxes and Accountant tab of the QuickBooks Navigator and click the Make Journal Entry icon. You use the General Journal Entry window to create journal entries — to record depreciation expense, for example.

QuickBooks automatically builds a trial balance, using journal entries it constructs automatically and any journal entries that you enter by using the General Journal Entry window. If you want to see the trial balance, just choose Reports➪Other Reports➪Trial Balance. QuickBooks prepares balance sheets, Profit & Loss Statements, and several other reports as well, using the trial balance.

Figure B-1:
The General
Journal
Entry
window.

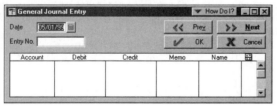

Two Dark Shadows in the World of Accounting

The real purpose of accounting systems such as QuickBooks is simple: Accounting systems are supposed to make succeeding in your business easier for you. You may think, therefore, that the world of accounting is a friendly place. Unfortunately, this scenario isn't quite true. I'm sorry to report that two dark shadows hang over the world of accounting: financial accounting standards and income tax laws.

The first dark shadow

"Financial accounting standards," you say. "What the heck are those?"

Here's the quick-and-dirty explanation: *Financial accounting standards* are accounting rules created by certified public accountants. These rules are supposed to make reading financial statements and understanding what's going on easier for people. (I happen to believe that just the opposite is true, by the way.) But because of what financial accounting standards purport to do, some people — such as bank loan officers — want to see Profit & Loss Statements and balance sheets that follow the rules. The exact catchphrase is one that you might have heard before: "Prepared in accordance with generally accepted accounting principles."

Unfortunately, the rules are very complicated. The rules are inconsistently interpreted. And actually applying the rules would soon run most small businesses into the ground. (And as you were running your business into the ground — you'll be happy to know — your certified public accountant would make a great deal of money helping you figure out what you were supposed to be doing.) So what should you do about this first dark shadow?

- ✔ Well, first of all, know that it exists. Know that people like your banker honestly think that you should follow a super-complicated set of accounting rules.

- ✔ And here's my second tip: Don't get sucked into the financial accounting standards tar pit. Tell people — your banker included — that you do your accounting in the way that you think enables you to best manage your business. Tell people a small business such as yours can't afford to have an in-house staff of full-time CPAs. And finally, tell people that you don't necessarily prepare your financial statements "in accordance with generally accepted accounting principles."

Do attempt to fully and fairly disclose your financial affairs to people who need to know about them. Lying to a creditor or an investor about your financial affairs or getting sneaky with one of these people is a good way to end up in jail.

The second dark shadow

And now here's the second dark shadow: income tax accounting laws. You know that Congress enacts tax legislation to raise revenue. And you know that it does so in a political environment strewn with all sorts of partisan, voodoo economic, and social overtones. So you won't be surprised to find out that the accounting rules that come out of the nation's capital and your state capital don't make much sense for running a business.

You need to apply the rules when you prepare your tax return, of course. But you don't have to use them the rest of the year. A far better approach is to do your accounting in a way that enables you to best run your business. That way, you don't use accounting tricks and gambits that make sense for income tax accounting but foul up your accounting system. At the end of the year when you're preparing your tax return, have your tax preparer adjust your trial balance so that it conforms to income tax accounting laws.

The Danger of Shell Games

This appendix is longer than I initially intended. I'm sorry about that. I want to share one more thought with you, however. And I think it's an important thought, so please stay with me just a little longer.

You could use the accounting knowledge that this appendix imparts to do the bookkeeping for a very large business. As crazy as it sounds, if you had 3,000 rowboats for rent — perhaps you have rental outlets at dozens of lakes scattered all over the Rockies — you might actually be able to keep the books for a $200,000,000-a-year business. You would have to enter many more transactions, and the numbers would all be bigger; but you wouldn't necessarily be doing anything more complicated than the transactions in this appendix.

Unfortunately, the temptation is great — especially on the part of financial advisers — to let the money stuff get more complicated as a business grows. People start talking about sophisticated leasing arrangements that make sense because of the tax laws. Some customer or vendor suggests some complicated profit-sharing or cost-reimbursement agreement. Then your attorney talks you into setting up a couple new subsidiaries for legal reasons.

All these schemes make accounting for your business terribly complicated. If you choose to ignore this complexity and go on your merry way, very soon you won't know whether you're making money. (I've seen plenty of people go this route — and it isn't pretty.) On the other hand, if you truly want to do accurate accounting in a complex environment, you need to spend a great deal of cash for really smart accountants. (This tactic, of course, supposes that you can find, hire, and afford these really smart accountants.)

If you're unsure about how to tell whether something is just too complicated, here's a general rule you can use: If you can't easily create the journal entries that quantify the financial essence of some event, you're in trouble.

So, what should you do? I suggest that you don't complicate your business's finances — not even if you think that the newfangled, tax-incentivized, sale-leaseback profit plan is a sure winner. Keep things simple, my friend. To win the game, you have to keep score.

Appendix C
Project Estimating

. . . .

*O*ne feature QuickBooks Pro has that the regular QuickBooks program doesn't is the capability to produce project estimates. This feature is particularly handy if you're in a business such as construction. The customer must know potential costs, and you must estimate construction materials and employee hours. Some items that you need to consider will count as overhead and won't be billed back to the customer.

You want to add a markup to some materials that you use for the project. And, if you complete the project, you'll want to be able to turn the estimate into an actual invoice without jumping through a couple of million hoops or, worse yet, having to jump through hoops that you've already jumped through before. It's a lot to demand from a program, but what the heck — weren't computers supposed to make your life easier? This is one area where QuickBooks Pro really comes through and delivers on the promise.

The Birth of an Estimate

I have to make a few assumptions before I begin:

- ✔ You should have a general knowledge of QuickBooks — an overall view of how the basic procedures work.

- ✔ Your lists should be up-to-date — your Item list, your Customer:Job list, and so on. If they're not, you should know how to update your lists as you go along. For example, if QuickBooks shows that an item you need to include on an estimate is not on the Item list, you should already have some idea of how to add the item.

A caveat before I begin: You can only produce one estimate per job. If you need more than one estimate for a job, list the estimates under different jobs. You can number them under the same customer, like Rec Room 1, Rec Room 2, and so on. You really should create a new job for any new work you do for a customer anyway, just to keep the records for each project straight.

On your mark, get set, go:

1. Get the form.

Click the Sales and Customers tab of the QuickBooks Navigator and click the Estimates icon. QuickBooks opens a Create Estimates form, which bears an uncanny resemblance to Figure C-1.

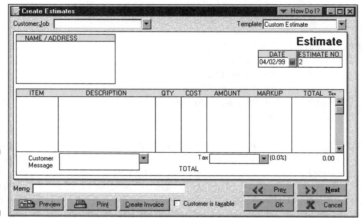

Figure C-1: Estimates, anyone?

2. Start filling in the blanks.

Choose the appropriate Customer:Job from the drop-down list box at the top of the form. QuickBooks Pro automatically fills in as much information as it can — usually at least the Name/Address box — on the form. If the customer is on the Customer:Job list but you're estimating a new job, choose the customer, click at the end of the customer's name in the Customer:Job drop-down list box, and then type a colon and the name of the new job. QuickBooks Pro gives you the opportunity to either Quick Add the job or set it up completely.

If you've configured QuickBooks Pro to track classes, the appropriate drop-down list box shows up in the upper-right corner of the form. Go ahead and use it, if appropriate.

Feel free to change the default settings — the Date and Estimate No., for example. The Date Setting tricks in Chapter 4 and on the Cheat Sheet in the front of this book may come in handy here.

3. Add the line items — details, details, details.

Ah, yes. This step is where I separate the wheat from the chaff. Click the first line of the Item column and begin typing the name of the first item in your estimate. QuickBooks Pro tries to anticipate the item name, automatically filling in the rest of the name. If the name appears on your Item list after you're finished, QuickBooks Pro fills in the description and cost for you. (If the name doesn't appear on your list, you have the opportunity to add it to your list or cancel out the line.)

Enter the quantity that you anticipate using in the Qty column. QuickBooks Pro automatically calculates the amount, markup, and total for you. QuickBooks Pro also places a T in the Tax column if the item is taxable and figures out the tax if you indicated that you're responsible for charging sales tax when you created the company file. If the customer isn't charged tax, remove the check mark from the Customer Is Taxable check box at the bottom of the window by clicking the check box.

If you need to delete a line, no problem. Click the line that you need to delete and then choose Edit➪Delete Line. QuickBooks Pro takes the line out. No muss, no fuss, no dust.

At this point, you may be asking where QuickBooks Pro is getting all the information for its calculations. Well, if you choose Lists➪Items and double-click one of the items, you see an Edit Item window similar to Figure C-2. (I've chosen blue mugs as an example.) You use this same window to set up each item. Because the estimate is a document that you'll want to show the customer, QuickBooks Pro uses the Description on Sales Transactions in the Description column, the Cost in the Cost column, and so on. The Markup percentage (which, by the way, doesn't show up on the printed estimate) is calculated by comparing the Cost (in the Purchase Information box) to the Sales Price (in the Sales Information box).

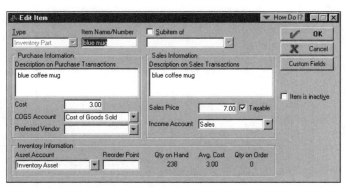

Figure C-2:
An Edit
Item
window.

Any part of the information on the estimate form can be changed. If you want to charge a higher markup for an item, for example, change the Markup column on the form, and QuickBooks Pro will adjust the Total column accordingly. You won't affect the settings in the Item list by doing this.

4. **Add any optional information.**

   If you want to, click the Customer Message drop-down list box (shown in Figure C-1) and write a friendly message, or use one from the drop-down list. Try to avoid a tone like, "Pleeeease! I neeeeed this job!" It's not becoming.

   Then click the Memo line and write a note to yourself regarding the project, if you'd like. Or maybe some notes for the screenplay that you've been thinking about pitching to the studios. Whatever suits your fancy.

Figure C-3 shows an example of a completed Create Estimates window. See the totals underneath the Tax list box, near the bottom of the window? The totals represent your cost ($30.00), the markup percentage you're charging (40%) and the final total, after tax ($75.53). I don't know about you, but I think this information is pretty cool.

If you want to include other items in the Create Estimates window, you can customize that window. Choose Customize from the Template drop-down list box in the upper-right corner of the Create Estimates window. QuickBooks gives you a list of your estimate forms. Choose the one you want to edit (only one estimate form may be on the list if you've never created a new one). Click either the New or Edit button. If you click New, QuickBooks displays the Customize Estimate dialog box shown in Figure C-4.

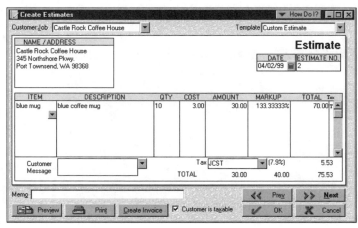

Figure C-3:
A completed Create Estimates window.

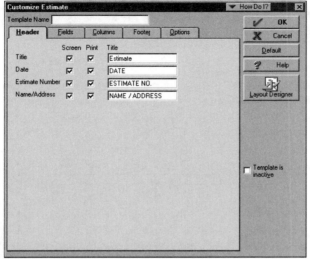

Figure C-4:
The
Customize
Estimate
dialog box.

The Customize Estimate dialog box lets you customize the on-screen and printed versions of the estimate form. The first column lists the items you can include in the estimate. The Screen and Print check boxes determine whether the items appear. The grayed-out boxes can be changed only by the system, if at all. (For example, if you click the Print check box for the Markup item on the Columns tab, then the Print check box for the Amount item is automatically checked, too.)

On the Header tab, for example, you may want to call your estimates Bids or Proposals. Or John Jacob Jingleheimer Schmidt, for that matter. (Hey, that's my name, too!) Whatever your little heart desires. When you've made all your changes, click OK. If you experiment just a little too much and want to go back to the way the form was in the beginning, click the Default button. If you give up completely and don't want to save your changes or see this window ever again, click the Cancel button.

The Create Estimates window returns. Before you print that estimate, remember that the Create Estimates window isn't the same information that appears on the written estimate. To see how the printed version looks, click the Preview button at the bottom of the window. The result is a full-page image, shrunk to fit on the screen (see Figure C-5).

To examine the estimate more closely, either click the Zoom In button at the top of the screen or move the mouse cursor over the image. When the cursor looks like a magnifying glass with a plus sign in it, click the left mouse button. Because you can see only part of the preview at a time this way, use the scroll bars at the bottom and right of the window to move around to the

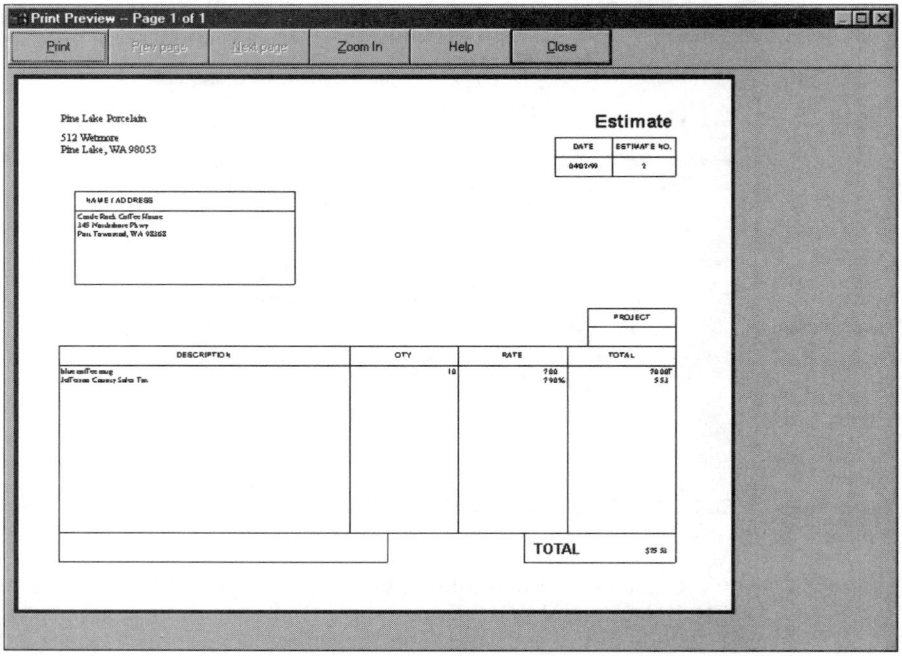

Figure C-5:
A preview
of coming
attractions.

different areas. Note that the magnifying glass now has a minus sign in it, and the Zoom In button has changed to Zoom Out. If you complete more than one estimate, you can use the Prev Page and Next Page buttons to look at other estimates. After you're finished, click the Close button.

Now you're back to the Create Estimates window. You're the extremely confident type — I can tell — and you can just feel in your bones that the estimate couldn't possibly be improved. Click the Print button, and QuickBooks Pro displays the Print One Estimate dialog box. Click Print to print the estimate without any further ado.

Note: If you haven't used QuickBooks to print estimates before, you may first need to set up your printer to do so. To do this, choose File⇨Printer Setup and select Estimate from the Form Name drop-down list box. Then specify the printer settings you want for printing estimates. (This works the same way it does for printing other forms, such as invoices, as described in Chapter 4.) Click OK when you're done. The Print One Estimate dialog box QuickBooks displays after you click Print in the Create Estimates window also works the same way as the Print One Invoice dialog box does. Turn back to Chapter 4 if you need help with this dialog box.

Revising an Estimate

Say, however, that after consulting with your client, you decide that it probably won't take you four hours to repair the seagull teakettle set. There are only a few small cracks, so three hours should do. Click the Sales and Customers tab of the QuickBooks Navigator and click the Customers icon to open the Customer:Job list. Then highlight the appropriate customer and job by clicking it. Click the Activities button at the bottom of the window and choose View Estimate.

QuickBooks Pro brings the estimate right back up. Make your changes, and QuickBooks Pro recalculates all the totals. Smile. Imagine doing this by hand — the recalculations, the looking up of the prices, the retyping, the inordinate amount of time. Making these changes automatically with QuickBooks Pro doesn't quite beat a hot dog with sauerkraut in the park on a sunny day, but it's pretty close.

Remember, though: You can only keep one estimate per job. After you click OK, any changes you make automatically take the place of the old estimate.

Turning an Estimate into an Invoice

Okay, you've fine-tuned the estimate, and it reflects exactly what you think it should. If your customer is paying a fixed amount, based on the estimate, you can easily turn the estimate into an invoice by following these steps:

1. **Display the estimate.**

   Click the Sales and Customers tab of the QuickBooks Navigator and click the Estimates icon to open the Create Estimates window. Then use the Prev and Next buttons at the bottom of the window to move to the estimate that you want to use.

2. **Click the Create Invoice button at the bottom of the window.**

   Go ahead. Live on the edge. Click that puppy with everything you've got. You see a dialog box that asks whether you want to create an invoice based on the estimate. You can choose to create an invoice for the entire amount of the estimate or for a percentage of the estimate if you want to invoice the job in installments. (To specify a percentage of the estimate, type the percentage into the text box provided.) Click OK to continue.

3. **(Optional) Make any necessary changes to the resulting invoice.**

   The invoice that you see is a regular QuickBooks Pro invoice, and you can edit it the same way that you edit any invoice. Until you click OK, the invoice isn't recorded in your records.

4. **After you make all your changes, click OK to record the invoice.**

   That's right. Show them what you're made of. Click that thing. Yeah!

   Whew! What a workout!

Charging for Actual Time and Costs

If you're going to charge the customer for actual costs, you need to track the costs and time as you incur the charges for them. For example, Figure C-6 shows the Enter Bills window. Under the Items tab, I recorded a purchase of glue for a project at Coastal Collectibles. (See how the customer is indicated in the Customer:Job column?) Here's how to charge Coastal Collectibles for those costs:

1. **Open the Create Invoices window.**

   Click the Sales and Customers tab of the QuickBooks Navigator and click the Invoices icon to open the window. (I can only hope that you don't get too drafty.)

2. **Change the name in the Customer:Job drop-down list box to the proper customer.**

   This step is easy: Activate the drop-down list and choose Coastal Collectibles. You've done this a million times by now. (Note that, depending on how you've set up QuickBooks, you may see a message box that asks whether you want to create an invoice based on the estimate. If you do, click the Yes button, and QuickBooks grabs the data from that estimate.)

Figure C-6:
The Enter Bills window, showing costs incurred.

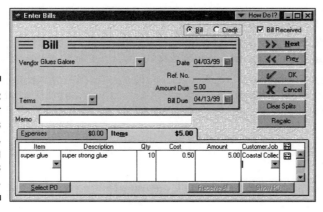

3. **Click the Time/Costs button on the right side of the window.**

   Figure C-7 shows what you get after clicking the Time/Costs button — the Choose Billable Time and Costs dialog box. You probably haven't seen this dialog box before. (Didn't know there were any left, did you?) Note that the dialog box already shows the expenses from the bill that I entered at the beginning of this section.

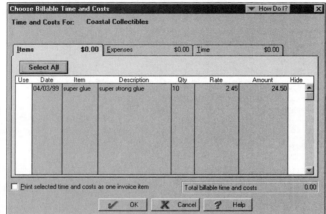

Figure C-7:
The Choose
Billable
Time and
Costs
dialog box.

4. **Choose the proper tab for the kind of expense you're charging.**

   The Items tab lists, well, items that you've bought specifically for the project. Parts, subcontracted services — that type of thing. The Expenses tab is sort of a catchall for anything that doesn't fit into the other two categories. The Time tab lists billable time spent on the project.

5. **Choose the expenses you want to charge the customer on this invoice.**

   If you want to charge the customer for everything that appears on this tab, just click the Select All button. Otherwise, click the Use column next to the charge that you'd like to pass on. By the way, if you know for sure that you're going to accept a particular expense without charging the customer, just click the Hide column next to that expense so that it doesn't show up on subsequent lists.

6. **(Optional, Expenses only) Indicate the markup.**

   The Expenses tab has a couple of extra fields at the top of the tab to indicate the Markup Amount or % and the Markup Account. If this is applicable, go ahead and fill in the fields with the appropriate information.

7. (Optional) Indicate whether you want the charges to appear as a single item on the invoice.

If you want to avoid detailing the gory details of the charges to your customer, click the Print Selected Time and Costs As One Invoice Item check box to place a check mark in it.

At this point, the Choose Billable Time and Costs window looks something like Figure C-8.

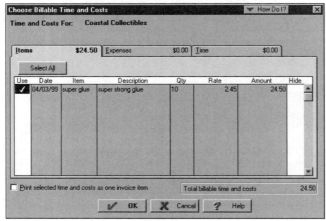

Figure C-8:
A completed Choose Billable Time and Costs dialog box.

8. (Optional) Repeat Steps 4 to 7 for the other tabs.

I'm not even going to mention this. It's too obvious. Mmmmmmm, no, not me.

9. Click OK.

After you have everything the way you want, click OK. As if by magic (even if it was your hard work and the sweat of your own brow), the invoice appears (see Figure C-9).

10. (Optional) Add anything else you want to include on the invoice.

This invoice is a regular QuickBooks Pro invoice, remember? Bend the invoice or shake it — any way you want it. Intuit suggests that, at this point, you may want to click the Preview button to make sure that only the job costs that you want appear.

11. Click OK.

Yes, again. That's how you record the invoice.

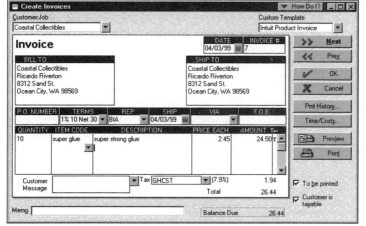

Figure C-9:
As if by
magic.
Yeah, right.

After you record the invoice, the job costs that have been billed are re-moved from the Choose Billable Time and Costs window. You're finished. Breathe easier.

You've got to admit, QuickBooks Pro makes this whole process a lot less time-consuming. And, along the way, you have less chance for error — trying to juggle all those different files and items and bills and invoices could get slightly nerve wracking and drive anyone a little buggy.

But then, you don't have to worry about all that juggling anymore, do you?

Appendix D
Timing Yourself

● ●

*T*he Pro version of QuickBooks includes a separate Timer program that you can install and use to accurately track the time you and your employees spend with different customers or on different jobs. For instance, if one of your customers or clients is constantly calling you on the phone, you can track how long each conversation lasts so that you can bill the person for your time. You can also track how long you spend drafting a report on your computer or how long your assistant spends word-processing a memo. The Timer program is a great tool for tracking all sorts of office activities, especially those spent at the computer.

Note: Timer is only available in QuickBooks Pro. If you have the standard version of QuickBooks, you can skip this appendix. Or if you're considering upgrading to QuickBooks Pro, you may want to read on to learn about Timer's features.

Installing Timer

The QuickBooks Pro Timer is a separate program from QuickBooks, so you need to install it separately if you want to use it. To install Timer, first exit all programs you have running (including QuickBooks Pro). Then insert the QuickBooks Pro CD in your CD-ROM drive. In the QuickBooks Pro 6.0 CD window, click the Install button next to Install Timer. Then follow these steps:

1. **Click Next to begin the installation.**

2. **Accept the default storage location for the Timer program by clicking Next.**

3. **Accept the default location for the Timer item on your Programs menu by clicking Next.**

   The setup program copies the Timer files to your computer. After you install Timer, it appears with QuickBooks in the QuickBooks Pro folder on the Programs menu.

   When the setup program finishes, it tells you that it needs to restart your computer.

4. **Remove the QuickBooks Pro CD and any floppy disks from their respective drives and click Finish.**

   The setup program restarts your computer.

A Brief Word about the Timer Program

Although the Timer program comes on your QuickBooks Pro CD, it's a completely independent program and functions as such, which means that Timer and QuickBooks unfortunately aren't very smart about the way they talk to each other — they basically don't talk to each other at all, translating to a lot more work for you. You can't simply record some data in Timer and then use it when you go to do payroll in QuickBooks. No, the process is much more complicated than that. First, you need to set up Timer so that it can use the data you've already entered in QuickBooks (the names of your employees and customers, for example). This, my friend, is a two-step process. (It also needs repeating whenever you update your lists in QuickBooks.) Then, after you've recorded data in Timer, you need to get that information back to QuickBooks so that you can use it for your payroll, again a two-step process. So using Timer isn't all quick-and-easy. As a matter of fact, it may not even be worth it to you. In any case, it probably makes sense to minimize the number of times you have to move information back and forth between Timer and QuickBooks. First, make sure your lists are up-to-date before you set them up in Timer. And second, only move Timer information to QuickBooks when you have to, like at the end of the pay period, and not every day. I talk about how you do both of these tasks later on.

Exporting Your QuickBooks Lists to Timer

Before you begin using Timer, you must first export customer, employee, service item, and class names from your QuickBooks file to the Timer program. You do this so that QuickBooks can later make sense of the Timer data you've collected when you move it back to QuickBooks. You can then use the data to do payroll and to bill your customers for the time spent on projects.

The process of moving your lists into Timer is quite a time-consuming chore, so if you're like me, you don't want to do it any more than you have to. This being the case, before you export your QuickBooks lists, do make sure they're up to date. Timer can only record data for the employees and customers you have included on your employee and customer lists. This means that if you don't count yourself as an employee (say, because you're the owner of the business and you don't pay yourself a salary), you need to add yourself to the employee list if you want to track your time using Timer. See Chapter 2 for more information about adding list items.

To export your lists to Timer, follow these steps:

1. **Click the Payroll and Time tab of the QuickBooks Navigator and then click the Timer Import/Export icon.**

2. **Click the Export Timer Lists option button and click OK.**

   QuickBooks displays the Export dialog box shown in Figure D-1.

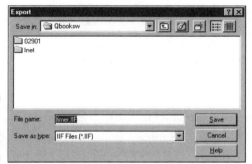

Figure D-1:
The Export
dialog box.

3. **Enter a name for the Timer List file and specify a location for the file.**

   Use the Save In drop-down list box and the list box beneath it to specify a file location. It doesn't really matter where you save the file; you just need to remember where you save it because in a couple of minutes, you'll need to import the file into Timer.

4. **Click Save.**

   QuickBooks saves the file to the location you specified. It waits there patiently, in limbo land on your computer, until you import it into Timer (as described a little later).

5. **Click OK in the message box QuickBooks displays.**

Starting Timer

To open the Timer application, click the Start button and choose Programs⇨ QuickBooks Pro⇨QuickBooks Pro Timer. If this is the first time you've started Timer, click the Create New Timer button and click OK. Timer displays the New Timer File dialog box and asks you to choose a name and storage location for your first Timer file. If you're the only person using

Timer on your computer and you only have one QuickBooks company, it doesn't matter what you name the file or where you store it. If more than one person will use Timer on the computer or if you have more than one company for which you're recording time with Timer, you'll want to set up a separate Timer data file for each person or each company. You can create additional Timer data files by choosing File➪New Timer File. Save the additional files wherever Timer suggests.

Importing Your QuickBooks Lists

After you create a Timer data file (described in the preceding section), Timer warns you via a message box that it can't create a new file without a QuickBooks list. Click Yes in this message box. You now need to import the lists you exported from QuickBooks (see the section "Exporting Your QuickBooks Lists to Timer," earlier in this chapter). To import the lists, follow these steps:

1. **Choose File➪Import QuickBooks Lists, and click Continue.**

   Timer displays the Open File For Import dialog box shown in Figure D-2.

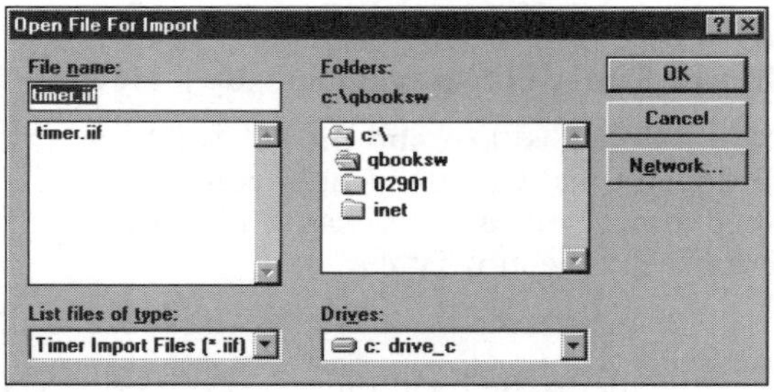

Figure D-2:
The Open
File For
Import
dialog box.

2. **Select the file you just exported and click OK.**

   Do you remember where you stored the file you created in the previous set of steps? I hope so. Locate this file using the Folders list box and the Drives drop-down list box. When you find the file, select it and click OK. Timer imports the file.

3. **Click OK in the message box Timer displays after it imports the file.**

If you're the only one using Timer on your computer, you can save yourself a little time by telling Timer that you're the default user. When you do this, Timer enters your name automatically on the activities you record. To specify yourself as the default user, choose File➪Preferences➪Default Name. Then select your name from the drop-down list box. You also can select the Time Defaults to Billable check box to tell Timer that you want the activities you create to be marked as billable by default.

Timing Activities

Timer records the things you do in records called Activities. You use separate activities to describe what each person does on each day. To create a Timer activity, click the New Activity button in the Timer window. Timer displays the New Activity dialog box shown in Figure D-3.

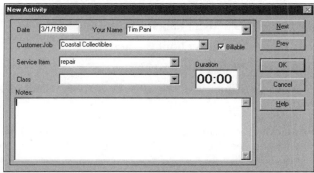

Figure D-3:
The New
Activity
dialog box.

To describe the new activity, follow these steps:

1. **Enter the Date in the Date text box.**

   You can use the same date entry tricks that you use in QuickBooks. See Chapter 4 or the Cheat Sheet at the front of this book for a list of these tricks.

2. **Enter your name in the Your Name text box.**

   If you set yourself as the default Timer user as described earlier, Timer automatically enters your name.

3. **Select the Billable check box if you're going to bill a customer for the time recorded for the activity.**

4. **If the activity is billable, enter the customer or job to whom you're billing the activity.**

   Select a customer or a job from the Customer:Job drop-down list box.

5. **If the activity is billable, enter a Service Item.**

If you're billing a customer for the activity, you need to have a service item set up in your QuickBooks file. If you want to make the activity billable and you haven't yet set up a service item, open QuickBooks and do so. (Setting up items is described in Chapter 2.) Then re-export your updated QuickBooks lists from QuickBooks and re-import them in Timer.

6. **(Optional) Enter a class for the activity.**

If you're using QuickBooks' class feature, you can enter a class for the activity.

7. **If you've already spent time on the activity, enter the time in the Duration box.**

Enter the time spent on the activity in hours and minutes. Timer then uses this time as a starting time and adds minutes to this time whenever you choose this activity and start the Timer.

8. **(Optional) Enter any notes about the activity.**

9. **Click OK to begin timing the activity.**

Timer displays the Timer window with the activity selected, as shown in Figure D-4.

For more information about timing activities, including how to start, stop, and resume the Timer, see the section, "Working with the Timer Window."

Figure D-4:
The Timer
window
ready to
record the
time on an
activity.

Working with the Timer Window

Select the Activity whose duration you want to record by using the Current Activity drop-down list box. To start timing, click the Start button. To stop timing, click the Stop button. (The Start button becomes the Stop button once you begin timing.) To resume timing after you've stopped, click the Resume button. To edit the activity you're timing, click the Edit Activity button.

You don't have to keep the Timer window active on your screen for it to record time — Timer continues to record time even if the window is hidden. Click anywhere outside of the Timer window to make another open application active. To view the Timer again, click its button on the Windows taskbar.

Moving Timer Data Back to QuickBooks

After you use Timer to record the time you spend on various activities, you want to move this information back to QuickBooks so that you can bill customers and pay employees for the time you recorded. To export all previously unexported Timer activities into a file that you can import in QuickBooks, follow these steps:

1. **Choose File⇨Export Time Activities and click Continue.**

2. **Enter the date through which you want to export activities and click OK.**

   Timer enters the current date by default. After you click OK, Timer displays the Create Export File dialog box (which bears a striking resemblance to Figure D-1).

3. **Specify a name and location for the Timer file and click OK.**

   Remember the file name and storage location you choose, because in a minute you'll need to find the file to import it in QuickBooks.

4. **Click OK again in the message box Timer displays.**

To export only specific activities from Timer, regardless of whether you've previously exported them, choose View⇨Time Activity Log. Then review and, if necessary, edit the date range for the activities you want to export. Select the activities you want to export, click the Export button, and click Continue. When Timer displays the Export Time Activities window, select the Selected Activities button and click OK.

To import the Timer data in QuickBooks, follow these steps:

1. **Click the Payroll and Time tab of the QuickBooks Navigator and click the Timer Import/Export icon.**

2. **Click the Import Timer Data option button and click OK.**

   QuickBooks displays the Import dialog box (which bears a striking resemblance to Figure D-2).

3. Locate the file you just exported from Timer and click Open.

If an employee for whom you recorded time in a Timer activity is not set up to use time data, QuickBooks displays a message alerting you to this. Go ahead and click OK. (To set up an employee to use time data, just open the employee from the Employees list and click the Payroll tab. Then check the Set Employee to Use Time Data in Paycheck Creation box.)

If you've never recorded Timer data for the employee before, QuickBooks displays the Enter Single Activity window (shown in Figure D-5) so that you can specify the payroll item (hourly wages, overtime wages, and so on).

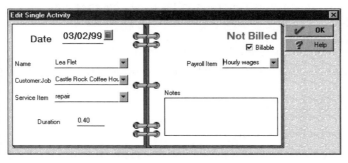

Figure D-5:
The Enter Single Activity window.

4. Enter any additional information about each activity in the Enter Single Activity window.

When you finish entering all activities, QuickBooks displays the window shown in Figure D-6.

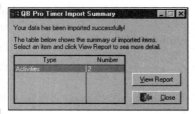

Figure D-6:
The QB Pro Timer Import Summary window.

5. Click Close.

You can also use the Timesheet feature in QuickBooks to record time spent on jobs. Click the Payroll and Time tab of the QuickBooks Navigator and click the Enter Single Activity icon to enter information for activities singly as you accomplish them during the day, or click the Use Weekly Timesheet icon to enter a whole week's activities at once.

Index

• •

(continued)

• O •

online banking
advantages of, 192–193
changing information, 198
definition of, 192
disadvantages of, 193
making payments, 195–196
sending e-mail message, 199–200
signing up for service, 194–195
transferring money, 197
transmitting instructions, 198–199
Online Banking Center window, 198
online bill payment feature
description of, 194
vendor-assigned account number and, 53
Online menu options, 191
Online Payroll Service, 208
Online⇨Internet Connection Setup command, 188
Online⇨Online Banking⇨Create Message⇨Online Banking Message command, 199
Online⇨Online Banking⇨Create Message⇨Online Payment Inquiry command, 200
Online⇨Online Banking⇨Getting Started command
banks with online banking services, obtaining list of, 192
signing up for online banking service, 194
Online⇨Payroll Service⇨Payroll Service Sign-Up command, 208
Open File for Import dialog box, 338
Open Purchase Orders dialog box, 125–126
Opening Bal Equity register, 25
opening balance, reconciling, 217, 218
ordering item using purchase order, 141–142
organizing lists, 56–57
Other Charge field (New Item window), 34, 36
Other Names list, 55
Other Reports category, 228
outstanding credit of customer, 106

owner's equity
credit card account balance and, 165
tracking
corporation, 296–297
partnership, 296
sole proprietorship, 295
owner's equity account
debit versus credit balance, 13
trial balance and, 11

• P •

Pacioli, Lucia, 313–314
page-oriented paper, 84
Palo Alto Software Web site, 258
paper type, designating for printer, 84
Partial Page tab (Printer Setup dialog box), 177
partnership, tracking owner's equity in, 296
password
case-sensitivity of, 64
selecting, 63
Pay Bills window, 130–132
Pay Liabilities window, 209
Pay Sales Tax dialog box, 133
paying bills. *See also* check writing
accounts payable method
deleting bills, 128–129
entering bills, 126–128
overview of, 115–116, 122–123
recording bills, 123–126
reminders to pay bills, 129–130
check writing method
"fast way," 121–122
"slow way," 116–121
Reminders message box, using to pay on time, 129–130
Payment field (New Item window), 35, 38
payment terms
description of, 48
specifying for customer, 46
vendor's, 53
payments
mistakes, correcting, 107

(continued)

YOUR ONLINE RESOURCE

WWW.DUMMIES.COM

Discover Dummies Online!

The Dummies Web Site is your fun and friendly online resource for the latest information about ...For Dummies® books and your favorite topics. The Web site is the place to communicate with us, exchange ideas with other ...For Dummies readers, chat with authors, and have fun!

Ten Fun and Useful Things You Can Do at www.dummies.com

1. Win free ...For Dummies books and more!
2. Register your book and be entered in a prize drawing.
3. Meet your favorite authors through the IDG Books Author Chat Series.
4. Exchange helpful information with other ...For Dummies readers.
5. Discover other great ...For Dummies books you must have!
6. Purchase Dummieswear™ exclusively from our Web site.
7. Buy ...For Dummies books online.
8. Talk to us. Make comments, ask questions, get answers!
9. Download free software.
10. Find additional useful resources from authors.

Link directly to these ten fun and useful things at
http://www.dummies.com/10useful

SURF THE NET

WWW.DUMMIES.COM

For other technology titles from IDG Books Worldwide, go to
www.idgbooks.com

Not on the Web yet? It's easy to get started with *Dummies 101*®: *The Internet For Windows*®*95* or *The Internet For Dummies*®, *5th Edition*, at local retailers everywhere.

IDG BOOKS WORLDWIDE™

Find other *...For Dummies* books on these topics:
Business • Career • Databases • Food & Beverage • Games • Gardening • Graphics • Hardware
Health & Fitness • Internet and the World Wide Web • Networking • Office Suites
Operating Systems • Personal Finance • Pets • Programming • Recreation • Sports
Spreadsheets • Teacher Resources • Test Prep • Word Processing

IDG BOOKS WORLDWIDE BOOK REGISTRATION

Register This Book and Win!

We want to hear from you!

Visit **http://my2cents.dummies.com** to register this book and tell us how you liked it!

- ✔ Get entered in our monthly prize giveaway.

- ✔ Give us feedback about this book — tell us what you like best, what you like least, or maybe what you'd like to ask the author and us to change!

- ✔ Let us know any other *...For Dummies*® topics that interest you.

Your feedback helps us determine what books to publish, tells us what coverage to add as we revise our books, and lets us know whether we're meeting your needs as a *...For Dummies* reader. You're our most valuable resource, and what you have to say is important to us!

Not on the Web yet? It's easy to get started with *Dummies 101*®: *The Internet For Windows*® *95* or *The Internet For Dummies*,® 5th Edition, at local retailers everywhere.

Or let us know what you think by sending us a letter at the following address:

...For Dummies Book Registration
Dummies Press
7260 Shadeland Station, Suite 100
Indianapolis, IN 46256-3945
Fax 317-596-5498

BUSINESS AND GENERAL REFERENCE BOOK SERIES FROM IDG

COMPUTER BOOK SERIES FROM IDG